Highlights of
100 YEARS
IN MOBILE

FOREWORD

This is a book of memories: Memories of an institution which for a century has been inseparably linked with the daily life of Mobile, sharing alike the city's victories and vicissitudes.

Just as an individual, in passing another milestone on his life journey, is prone to think back and relive certain events which are indelibly stamped on his memory, so does this bank, on reaching its Hundredth Anniversary, feel inclined to muse over the highlights of an eventful past.

On the bank's Diamond Anniversary in 1940, the first seventy-five years of its life were reviewed, and in the first 114 pages of this book some of the information is presented as of that date.

Such reminiscing calls old friends to mind, for they are the essence of pleasant memories. And so, in reviewing the memorable events of the past 100 years, the First National Bank cordially invites its friends to share in these recollections. No individual remembers all his yesterdays in detail; neither does this bank. This volume, therefore, is not an attempt to narrate a complete history of Mobile since the bank was born in 1865, but rather to recall as an individual remembers . . . "highlights".

ACKNOWLEDGMENTS

Realizing the virtual impossibility of preparing a volume of this kind without unknowingly committing errors of commission or omission, the First National Bank took the liberty of calling on certain of its good friends to act as assistant editors in determining which "highlights" should be included, and to make a critical review of the manuscript prior to publication. To them, the bank wishes to express its grateful appreciation for unselfish devotion to a tiring task. If errors appear herein, they should not be chargeable to the intentions either of these persons or of the bank.

MR. FRANCOIS LUDGERE DIARD

MR. FRANK CRAIGHEAD

MRS. JAMES W. JOYNER

MR. OLIVER P. DIX

MRS. W. S. PUGH

MRS. EMMA C. HARRIS

MISS LELIA AUNSPAUGH

and other members of the

HISTORIC MOBILE PRESERVATION SOCIETY

Detailed research and narrative by
C. E. MATHEWS AND ANDERSON BROWNE
of the editorial staff of the Mobile Press-Register,
who made a search of the files of that
newspaper beginning with 1865

Pen sketches by
MARIAN ACKER
of Mobile

Portraits of bank's presidents by
MALTBY SYKES
Professor of Art
Auburn University

Printed and bound under supervision of
POWERS COMPANY, Inc.
of Mobile

General design and supervision by
SPARROW ADVERTISING AGENCY, Inc.
of Birmingham

INDEX

The old Guard House Tower, viewed from St. Emanuel Street, looking southeast, as it appeared in the 1860's.

APRIL, 1865—MOBILE'S DARKEST HOUR

THE COMING of Spring, 1865, brought the end of The War Between the States —four years of terrible conflict which had sapped both the manpower and the resources of the South. The smoke that rose from Sherman's raid still hung like a cloud over the Southern scene, and want from war's waste still gnawed at the vitals of a defeated but unconquered Confederacy. Echoes from Appomatox had hardly died away when resolute Southerners—their spirit surmounting the shock of surrender —determinedly faced the grim reality of Reconstruction.

Theirs was a staggering task. Conditions everywhere were chaotic. Government was in the hands of Federal military authorities. "Carpetbag" adventurers were swarming southward to prey upon a prostrate people. Business was at a standstill. Banking was paralyzed. Confederate currency was worthless, and almost the only Southerners who had any money were those who had succeeded in secreting gold or cotton during the war.

Despite that dark outlook, the people of Mobile—then a town of approximately 41,000 population — courageously turned their backs on the tragic past and began immediately to plan and work toward a restoration of order and progress in their beloved city.

**The First National Bank's first home, located on the northwest corner of
Royal and St. Francis Streets, as it appeared in 1865.**

MAY, 1865—A NEW BANK IS BORN

ONE OF the first and most necessary steps in rehabilitating Mobile was the creation of additional banking facilities. Accordingly, on May 8, 1865, a group of prominent Mobile citizens gathered at the old Battle House for the purpose of organiz- ing a new bank in Mobile.* Those present at that meeting were: B. F. Fleming, M. S. Foote, Moses Waring, Wm. J. Ledyard, Wm. Flash, Jno. M. G. Parker, D. O. Grady, C. W. Gazzam and C. K. Foote.

It was felt that the purpose in mind

*Three banks were already in existence in Mobile in 1865—the Southern Bank of Alabama, located at the southeast corner of St. Francis and St. Joseph Streets; the Mobile Savings Bank, on the present location of Julius Goldstein & Son on Royal Street; and the Bank of Mobile on the northeast corner of Conti and Royal Streets.

could be best accomplished through the organization of a bank to be chartered under the National Banking Act. Various meetings followed the first, and formal application for a charter was made in August, 1865. The original subscribers to the stock of the bank were:

H. Chamberlain	D. O. Grady
J. C. Chamberlain	J. Kirkbride
F. H. Chamberlain	W. J. Ledyard
D. L. Campbell	E. W. McGinnis
B. F. Flanders	L. Merchant
A. Flash	C. G. Richards
W. Flash	J. M. G. Parker
C. K. Foote	A. H. Ryland
M. S. Foote	R. H. Slough
C. P. Gage	H. F. Stickney
C. W. Gazzam	G. W. Tarleton
D. W. Goodman	M. Waring
G. Woodward	

The first directors of the bank were: C. W. Gazzam, who served until April, 1868; J. C. Chamberlain, who served until 1866; Wm. Flash, who served until 1866; M. S. Foote, who served until 1866; D. O. Grady, who served until 1872; W. J. Ledyard, who served until 1868; C. G. Richards, who served until 1889; G. W. Tarleton[1], who served until 1875; and Moses Waring[2], who served until 1885. C. W. Gazzam was the first president of the bank, and served in that capacity until April 23, 1868. Lloyd Bowers was the bank's first cashier and held that office until he resigned in 1891.

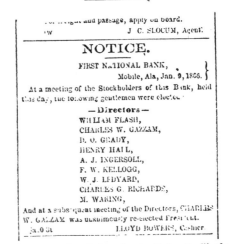

Another example of how banks "advertised" three-quarters of a century ago. Facsimile of a notice appearing in The Mobile Daily News in January, 1866.

The First National Bank's first newspaper "advertisement." Facsimile of a notice dated October 18, 1865, as it appeared in The Mobile Daily News of October 31, 1865.

It was originally contemplated that the bank start with $100,000 capital but the Federal authorities required that not less than $200,000 be subscribed. The required amount was raised and the charter was issued on October 18, 1865. So began the First National Bank of Mobile, which is now the oldest bank in Alabama, and whose charter also antedates those of all other National Banks in the Southern states of Arkansas, Florida, Louisiana, Mississippi, North Carolina and South Carolina.

---

(1)George W. Tarleton was the grandfather of D. P. Bestor, Jr., president of the bank from 1921 to 1938 and later chairman of its board of directors.

(2)Moses Waring was the great-grandfather of Richard Inge of Mobile, and his brother, Francis H. Inge, who was U. S. District Attorney in Mobile, and a director of the bank from 1940 until 1959.

C. W. GAZZAM
President of The First National Bank from 1865 to 1868.

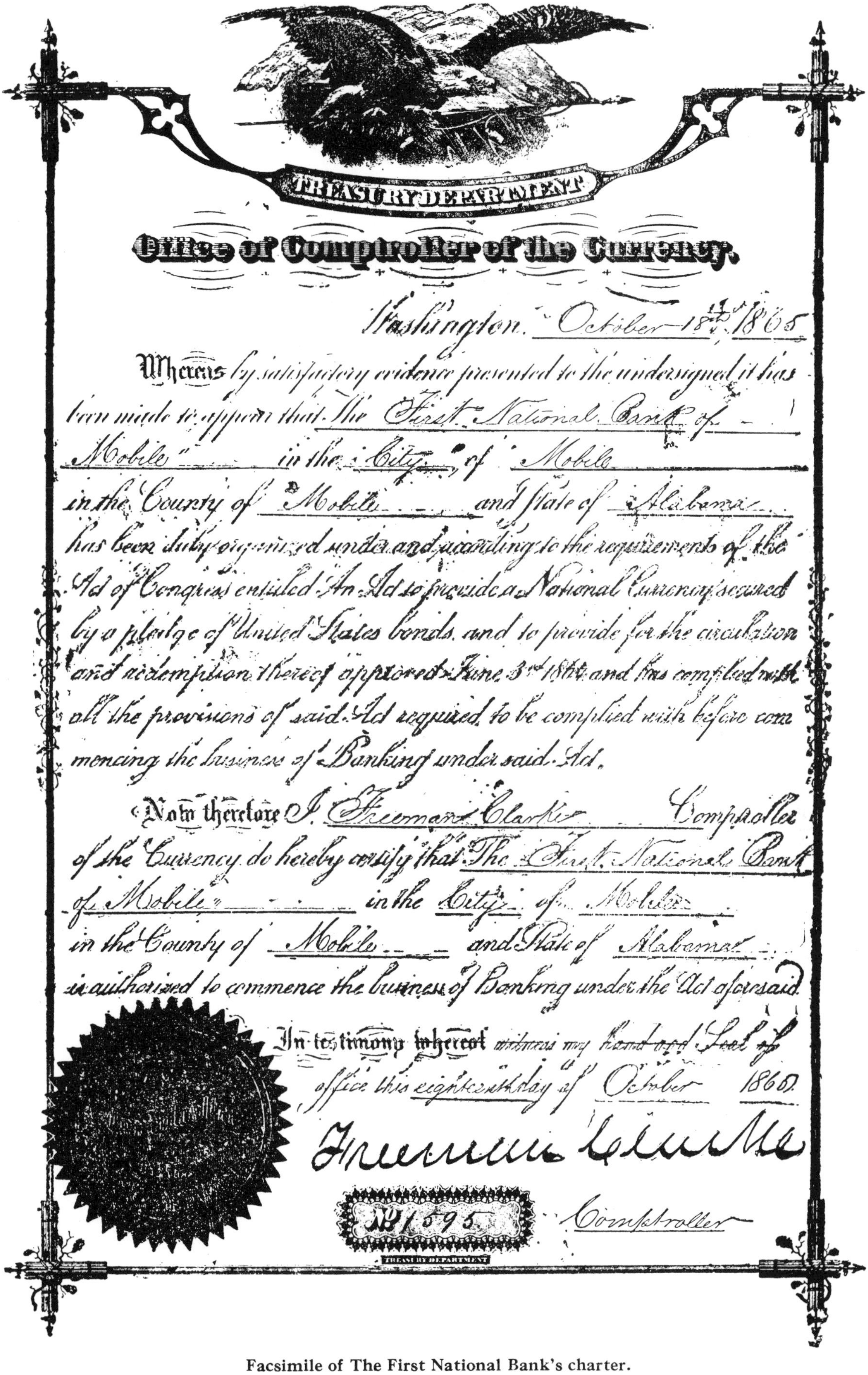

TREASURY DEPARTMENT

Office of Comptroller of the Currency.

Washington. October 18th 1865

Whereas by satisfactory evidence presented to the undersigned it has been made to appear that The First National Bank of Mobile in the City of Mobile in the County of Mobile and State of Alabama has been duly organized under and according to the requirements of the Act of Congress entitled "An Act to provide a National Currency secured by a pledge of United States bonds, and to provide for the circulation and redemption thereof" approved June 3rd 1864 and has complied with all the provisions of said Act required to be complied with before commencing the business of Banking under said Act.

Now therefore I Freeman Clarke Comptroller of the Currency do hereby certify that The First National Bank of Mobile in the City of Mobile in the County of Mobile and State of Alabama is authorized to commence the business of Banking under the Act aforesaid.

In testimony whereof witness my hand and Seal of office this eighteenth day of October 1865

Freeman Clarke

No 1595

Comptroller

Facsimile of The First National Bank's charter.

Artist's conception of a distant view of the great magazine explosion,
as it appeared in Harper's Weekly in 1865.

1865—THE GREAT MAGAZINE EXPLOSION

AS IF the shock of war and defeat were not enough, Fate dealt Mobile a terrific blow on May 26, 1865. It was the "great magazine explosion" which snuffed out the lives of hundreds of persons, wrecked countless business buildings and dwellings, and demolished merchandise and other property with a loss authoritatively estimated at $728,892.

The death-dealing blast took place in the main Ordnance Depot—located at Commerce and Lipscomb Streets—of the United States Army force who were charged with enforcement of martial law under which Mobile was placed immediately after the close of The War Between the States. Ranking as a major holocaust, it was featured as the leading news of the day in Northern newspapers, which declared that the explosion was deliberately set by certain ex-Confederate officers — "unreconstructed Rebels"—bent on revenge. It is hardly believable, however, that ex-Confederates, no matter how "unreconstructed" or vengeful they were, would have visited such a rain of death on their own people. The generally accepted version of the cause in Mobile and elsewhere in the South was that the explosion was caused by some laborers who were careless in handling explosives at the dump.

Whatever the cause, it was a terrible catastrophe for Mobile. So terrific was the explosion that it destroyed or damaged all buildings in the area bounded on the north by Bloodgood Street, on the west by Conception Street, on the south by St. Anthony Street and on the east by the river. Windows in the Battle House, which suffered an estimated $15,000 damage, and in buildings as far south as Conti Street, were shattered. Force of the blast was so great that it caused carriages to capsize on Royal Street, and horses to collapse as if shot to death. A man was blown off the wharf into the river at the foot of Church Street, and a steamer and schooner were wrecked at their moorings in the river.

Accompanying illustrations show a newspaper artist's conception of the disaster as it was pictured for northern readers. A reporter for the *Mobile Morning News* who rushed to the scene of destruction described the explosion as "a writhing giant—gaunt and grim—poised in midair . . . bursting shells, flying timbers, bales of cotton, horses, men, women and children co-mingled and mangled into one immense mass. The heart stood still, and the stoutest cheek paled as this rain of death fell from the sky and crash after crash foretold a more fearful fate yet impending; the lurid flames began to leap farther from the wreckage. Old and young, soldier and citizen vied with each other in deeds of daring to rescue the crumbled and imprisoned . . .".

The detonation was heard as far distant as Fort Morgan, where soldiers, frightened by the sound, rushed to their parapets, thinking a monitor had set off its magazine. And after a thorough study of records, army officials estimated that 200 tons of munitions had gone up in the explosion.

AWFUL CALAMITY AT MOBILE, ALA.—SCENE AMONG THE RUINS AFTER THE EXPLOSION

THE ORDNANCE DEPOT AND MAGAZINE, MAY 25.—FROM A SKETCH BY A CORRESPONDENT.

1866—LAYING OFF OF NATIONAL CEMETERY

ON MAY 11, 1866, Mobile's Board of Aldermen, with Mayor J. M. Withers presiding, adopted a resolution donating three acres of land to the United States Government, to be used as a National Cemetery.

The resolution, published the following day in *The Mobile Daily News*, read as follows:

"Resolved, that the mayor, aldermen and council hereby donate to the United States Government three acres of land in the new burying ground as a place of burial for United States soldiers, to include the ground now occupied by the Federal dead, and that the committee is hereby required to set aside and designate the boundaries of the said three acres . . . ".

Action of the aldermen was in compliance with a request made by Col. W. D. Wickersham, chief of the quartermaster department of Alabama, and was the first step toward establishment of the now beautifully-kept burial ground for those who died in the military services of the United States.

Immediately after the parcel of land was laid off, the government started transferring bodies of those who died at Fort Gaines, Fort Powell, Spanish Fort, Fort Blakely, Fort Morgan, and from other points in Alabama to the Mobile cemetery.

In 1894, the city donated an additional strip of land to the National Cemetery, extending it to Virginia Street and enlarging it to 5.24 acres. In this addition the remains of soldiers who died at Fort Jackson (Bienville's old Fort Toulouse) are buried. In 1935, the U. S. Government purchased 2.41 acres of land on the south side of Virginia Street and immediately north of the Jewish Cemetery as another addition. In this latest addition, the United Daughters of the Confederacy placed a marker on the site of the old Confederate breastworks which were located there.

At present 4,704 persons, including victims of The War Between the States, the Indian Wars, Spanish-American War, Phil-

lippine Insurrection and both World Wars are interred in the area. One thousand four hundred and twenty-one of those are unknown.

Soldiers of The War Between the States buried in the plot came from the following states: Connecticut, Illinois, Indiana, Iowa, Kansas, Kentucky, Louisiana, M a i n e , Maryland, Massachusetts, Michigan, Minnesota, Missouri, New Jersey, New York, Ohio, Pennsylvania, Tennessee, Vermont and Wisconsin.

Adding to the beauty of the cemetery, which now comprises 7.65 acres, are two magnificent azalea beds planted there by the Francis Marion Inge Chapter of the American War Mothers.

Records of the National Cemetery also show that the bodies of 15 men were brought back from Europe and reinterred here.

¶*Within four months after receiving its charter as a National Bank on October 18, 1865, the business of the First National Bank had increased to a point where an addition to its original capital stock was deemed advisable. The directors of the bank therefore decided at their meeting on January 15, 1866, to increase the capital stock to the sum of $300,000.*

At this same meeting, the president and cashier of the bank were authorized to arrange for obtaining daily gold quotations from New York and New Orleans, and to select a London correspondent. That authorization evidences the fact that ever since its earliest days, the First National Bank has been actively engaged in furnishing complete banking service for its customers.

¶*At the annual meeting of the stockholders of the bank in 1866, three new directors were elected: A. J. Ingersoll, who served until 1868; Henry Hall, who served until 1890; and F. W. Kellogg, who served until 1867.*

"Lord Mayor's Barge."—A float in the O. O. M. Parade "Odd Crafts",
on February 26, 1884

1866—REVIVAL OF CARNIVAL CELEBRATION

THE War Between the States caused virtual suspension of Mobile's Carnival celebrations during the four years 1861-1865. The conflict drew most of the city's young manhood to military services of the Confederacy and dampened too the cheerful spirit necessary to such occasions.

But Mobile, proudly claiming the title, "*Mother of Mystics**," would not long be deprived of her parades, colorful tableaux and dances. On Shrove Tuesday of 1866, Joe Cain, a market clerk, revived the annual celebration by staging a one-man show. Cain, according to the late Erwin Craighead, in his book, "*Mobile: Fact and Tradition*," appeared on this occasion dressed as an Indian chief, calling himself *Slackabamirimico*. Another version, also taken into

account by Craighead, says that Cain arrived in a decorated charcoal wagon, and played music. On Shrove Tuesday of the following year (1867), Cain reappeared—this time leading a group of sixteen former Confederate soldiers, who called themselves "*The Lost Cause Minstrels*".

If newspaper accounts are to be taken as conclusive, revival of carnival celebrations in Mobile began in earnest in 1868. On the morning of February 25, 1868, *The Mobile Tribune* carried the following description of carnival events of the previous day:

"The society which turned out was the 'L. C.', which has recently sprung into existence. About four o'clock in the afternoon a covered wagon with a bale of hay in it, drawn by two horses, suddenly ap-

*Mobile's Mardi Gras celebrations began with the pranks perpetrated by soldiers under Lt. Marlos Langlois (the father of Fifise Langlois, who introduced the azalea in Mobile) at Fort Louis de la Mobile. The soldiers held their celebration yearly on St. Louis Day (August 25th) beginning in 1704 and continuing up to 1842. When Bienville moved the settlement to the present site of Mobile in 1711, Lt. Langlois instituted the Shrove Tuesday celebration of Boeuf Gras, which was continued intermittently until the outbreak of The War Between the States in 1861.

Also in Spanish times in Mobile, there was a Spanish Mystic Society, which paraded on Twelfth Night (January 6th). Those celebrations continued until January 5th, 1835, when the society gave its last demonstration on the night preceding Twelfth Night.

In 1830, Michael Krafft and others paraded on New Year's Eve, and three years later called their society *Cowbellion de Rakin*. Out of this society grew the *Strikers*, the *T. D. S.*, and other groups who also paraded on New Year's.

All those societies, however, were practically dormant during The War Between the States. The Joe Cain, mentioned in the foregoing story, enjoyed quite a reputation as a wit in Mobile.

peared on Royal Street, near Dauphin. The occupants of the curious looking vehicle numbered five and represented a strolling band of minstrels. Each individual had a musical instrument in his hand. This novel crowd stopped in front of *The Tribune* office and favored us with a 'delightful serenade' ".

In closing, the reporter stated: "The '*L. C's.*' deserve credit for having taken the initiatory step in celebration of Mardi Gras, and we have every reason to believe that the next Mardi Gras day will be celebrated in a most magnificent manner".

But Mobile did not have to wait until "next Mardi Gras Day" to witness a celebration in the "magnificent manner". On the very evening of the day on which the foregoing newspaper story appeared in *The Tribune*, the *Order of Myths* presented their first Mardi Gras parade, which was described by *The Tribune* on the morning of February 26, 1868, as follows:

"The first anniversary celebration of the *Order of Myths* society was a grand success, and the observance of Mardi Gras of 1868 will long be remembered by the community of Mobile.

"Shortly after eight o'clock Tuesday night, the *O. O. M's.* appeared at the corner of Government and Royal Streets and launched a parade through downtown streets to Temperance Hall, where the remainder of the evening was devoted to a grand ball.

"Prior to the ball, several tableaux from '*Lalla Rookh*' were presented. The celebration was a magnificent affair and far surpassed the expectations of all beholders. There are few of our readers who have not pored over the pages of '*Lalla Rookh*' and who are not acquainted with the history of this Eastern romance.

"The tableaux of last evening were excellent and elicited warm applause . . . The lateness of the hour and our little acquaintance with the history of the organization of the society, which is strictly secret, precludes our giving as extended a notice as we might desire. We can only say that as to the first anniversary turnout, the O. O.

"Mexican Gulf Privateer"—Another float in the O. O. M. Parade "Odd Crafts", on February 26, 1884.

M's. have every reason to be pleased with themselves".

¶The First National Bank during its first year of existence demonstrated its faith in and loyalty to the people it served. For instance, in 1866, when carpetbaggers had straddled the state, tax collections were at a low ebb and the State of Alabama was hard pressed for funds. Responding to the need of the times, the First National Bank lent the state $25,-000—a large sum in those hard times. It took a patriotic spirit to place faith in a state that was helpless beneath debt and the rule of those not interested in its future.

On many other occasions the First National has responded to Alabama's call for financial help, and has also many times helped local governments through the extension of credit.

¶In the early days of banks, there were no "Safe Deposit Boxes" as we know them today. If a customer wished to leave valuables with the bank, he would simply put them in a box of his own choosing, mark the box, and ask the bank to store the box in the bank's vault. No receipt was given at the time the box was left, and none was taken when the box was called for.

That practice is in striking contrast with modern Safe Deposit service now offered. For a trivial sum, any person can rent from the First National Bank a Safe Deposit Box to which he, and only he, has access. Those boxes are housed in concrete-and-steel vaults, providing the same protection afforded the bank's own cash and securities.

1867—THE SHOOTING OF JUDGE RICHARD BUSTEED

ABOUT 9:30 in the morning on December 28, 1867, the silence of placid old Royal Street, between Dauphin and St. Francis, was abruptly shattered by the sharp report of pistol fire. Employees of the First National Bank (then located on the northwest corner of Royal and St. Francis) looked up from their work, and, like scores of others in nearby buildings, rushed into the street.

To their amazement, they saw U. S. District Judge Richard Busteed—a northerner appointed by President Abraham Lincoln—collapse in the street, badly wounded.

Immediately after Judge Busteed fell, they saw U. S. District Attorney L. V. B. Martin advance from a point near the steps of the Customs Building (now headquarters of the Mobile Chamber of Commerce) and fire two more shots into Busteed's crumpled form.

Thus violently did personal differences between Judge Busteed and Attorney Martin flare into the open, drawing an expression of fear from The Register & Advertiser that the episode would result in reprisal action from the Northerners then ruling the city. Although the people of Mobile well knew that Judge Busteed was incompetent and probably guilty of corrupt practices which had caused bad blood between him and Attorney Martin, the entire city at that time was so intimidated by the abusive powers of carpetbag domination, that the blame was placed on Martin, while Busteed's virtues were extolled. In its story of the shooting, published on December 28, 1867, The Register & Advertiser said:

"The moral character of the Mobile public is not so bad that a murderous deed like this—shooting an unarmed and defenseless man down in the street in cold blood, without a word of warning—is looked upon with indifference; and we doubt whether the dastardly assassin could have safely passed through the excited crowds that thronged Royal Street for several hours after the affair. . . ."

" . . . The cause of this murderous assault naturally attracts inquiry, and will be fully investigated and made public. Judge Busteed is a sworn enemy to the monstrous corruptions in office with which this country is cursed. He has proved it, and was proceeding to prove it in the most

THE SHOOTING OF JUDGE RICHARD BUSTEED BY DISTRICT ATTORNEY L. V. B. MARTIN, DECEMBER 28TH, AT MOBILE, ALA.

**Artist's conception of the shooting of Judge Richard Busteed, as it appeared in
Frank Leslie's Illustrated Newspaper, January 18, 1868.**

emphatic manner; whatever may have been said or printed about his public history, nobody can deny that. . . ."

" . . . We charge our friends in the North to see to it that the odium of this wretched and cowardly deed is not cast upon the people of Mobile, nor attributed to any malevolent spirit prevailing among the Southern people. Its perpetration is not of us. Mr. Martin may be a Southern-born man, but he belongs to the class known here as 'Southern renegades'. He is a radical".

Judge Busteed recovered rapidly from his wounds, and subsequently—as carpetbag rule weakened—a movement was launched to have him impeached. Serious charges were brought against him, but he remained in office until his resignation from the bench in 1874, after which time he returned to the North. Attorney Martin, meanwhile, resigned his post as District Attorney and moved to Texas; prosecution

of charges against him in connection with the shooting were never pressed.

By the time Judge Busteed resigned in 1874, the people of Mobile had regained their rights. *The Register*, which had praised Judge Busteed in 1867, now pictured him in the true light. It was shown that on visits to the North prior to his resignation, he attempted to flank impeachment proceedings against him by "suddenly turning radical and heaping the vilest abuse upon the Southern people". That change in the character of the newspaper's remarks about Judge Busteed indicates the end of carpetbag rule in Mobile.

¶*In the year 1867, at the annual meeting of the stockholders, Jas. Robb was elected a director of the bank. He served until 1868. The records of the year 1867 also show that J. H. Masson was elected a director of the bank during the latter part of the year. He served until 1904.*

— 11 —

The old Southern Market, constructed in the early 1850's. Originally this building was used as a market place and militia armory. After The War Between The States, several of Mobile's municipal offices were removed to the upper floors of this building. Today only a few shops remain on the ground floor, and the building is generally known as the City Hall.

1868—MOBILE'S FIRST SEWER LAID

MOBILE'S first sewer was laid down Conti Street in 1868, at the time the famous old Gulf City Hotel, later known as the Southern Hotel, was erected at the southeast corner of Conti and Water Streets.

The *Mobile Weekly Register* of November 21, 1868, told of the construction of the sewer and hotel as follows: "The hotel being constructed by Mr. D. O. Grady, at the southeast corner of Conti and Water Streets, is rapidly approaching completion, and when finished, will present a very creditable appearance. The workmen were busily engaged yesterday in building a large sewer from the hotel to the river, and the Board of County Commissioners, by continuing it to the courthouse just a short distance above, would abate the nuisance in that building, which has been the subject of frequent complaint by persons living in the vicinity and especially

by those whose business brings them hither".

The next major development of sewer facilities on Conti Street came in 1889, when the City granted a franchise for construction of a line by the Conti Street Sewer Company, a private company This line, with laterals into several side streets, extended as far west as the Lavretta home on Government Street and served the Jacob Pollock[3] home, opposite Barton Academy, the E. L. Russell place, and the Minge and Goldsby homes. It served homes and business places in the Cathedral Conti St. block, the Bishop's residence on Government, the section occupied by the Lyric Theatre; stores on Dauphin between Joachim and Jackson; Conception Street from Conti St. to Grant's, then east on Dauphin to where Gayfer now has a store; on St. Emanuel Street, Conti to Gov't St. and numerous other places on Royal, Water,

---

[3] Jacob Pollock, who later became a director of the bank, was the grandfather of Jay P. Altmayer, a large realty holder in Mobile.

Commerce and lower Conti Street.

In May 1899, almost 10 years after the sewer was installed, the city council voted to acquire it and make it a part of its general sewer system.

Fortunately for persons owning property which was served by the old Conti Street Sewer Company, they were exempt from sewerage taxes levied by the city. The Conti Street Sewer Company's contract provided that "It is also further mutually agreed that the City of Mobile, acting through its proper authorities, shall have the privilege of substituting for connections now existing, a connection with any other line or branch of the general sewerage system of Mobile; provided, however, that when such substitution is required or made, the property and person thus required to make a connection with any other portion of the city's general sewerage shall be exempt from the payment of any charge, tax or fee as fully and to all intents and purposes as if his original connection remained intact".

For years each user of Mobile's sanitary sewer system was required by law to pay a fixed charge of 30 cents a month where the amount of water used did not exceed 3,750 gallons a month, plus a monthly charge of 10 cents for every 1,000 gallons used in excess of 1,750 gallons and not exceeding 3,750 gallons. Where the use was in excess of 3,750 gallons a month, a schedule of fixed monthly charges ranging from 30 cents up to $7.50 applied, and in addition the user paid a charge based on the quantity of water used. Considerable savings therefore resulted to owners of properties which were exempt from charges due to a former connection to the old Conti Street Sewer Company lines.

Old Custom House and Post Office, built in 1856. On this corner the new 33 floor building of the First National Bank is being erected at this time.

Mr. Origen Sibley who owned the Sawmill that cut the timbers used in the foundation of the Old Custom House has a grandson, G. Eager Barnes and a great granddaughter, Mrs. Barton Greer, Sr., living in Mobile.

Validity of the old agreement was tested in the Alabama Supreme Court in 1937, in a case which attacked the legality of sewer taxes in general. The court upheld the legality of the sewer tax in general, and likewise held that the old agreement was still in force, although opposing counsel pointed out that the effect of the decision was to declare the agreement operative in perpetuity.

¶*On April 23, 1868, C. W. Gazzam resigned the office of president of the bank, after having rendered two and one-half years of service to the institution. Moses Waring, one of the bank's founders and original directors, was elected to succeed Mr. Gazzam.*

On the following day, the board of directors met and elected James H. Masson, prominent Mobile business man and private banker, to be vice-president of the First National Bank.

¶*In 1868, The First National Bank, then only three years old, had deposits totaling $447,872.72.*

¶*During the First National's early years, the South was flooded with counterfeit money, some of which was exceptionally well done. It therefore became important for a bank to have personnel who easily and quickly recognized counterfeit money. The First National sent to Charleston, S. C., and obtained the services of a Mr. Horace E. Walpole as bank teller. Mr. Walpole had a reputation for counting money quickly and detecting counterfeit very readily.*

¶*In the early days of the bank, the propriety of smoking in the banking rooms was seriously questioned. When the bank's board of directors met on March 12, 1868, they adopted the following resolution: "During business hours, no smoking will be allowed in the public banking room, and no visitors can be permitted to come behind the counter".*

¶*At the annual meeting of the stockholders in January, 1869, Charles Lanier was elected a director of the bank. He served until 1875.*

View on Front Street, in the 1870's.

MOSES WARING
President of The First National Bank from 1868 to 1870.

View of the City and Harbor of Mobile about 1870.
(From an old print.)

1870—FEDERAL SURVEY OF MOBILE HARBOR

IN A LETTER from the United States Chief of Engineers, dated July 20, 1870, Major C. B. Reese, Corps of Engineers, in charge of the Mobile district office, was directed to submit a project for improvement of Mobile's harbor and the ship channel through the bay.

The order came on the heels of appropriation by Congress of $50,000 for the work. This project was the first since 1857, when work on the harbor was stopped owing to the threat of civil war. Prior to 1857, the government had undertaken several Mobile harbor projects at various times since 1826, and in those days the depth of the channel at Dog River bar was about 7½ feet. Moving swiftly, Major Reese, in a letter dated August 5, 1870, outlined the following proposals on the project:

"1. To dredge out Choctaw Pass, Dog River bar, and the channel above and below Dog River bar so as to give a channel which shall be 300 feet wide and 13 feet deep at mean low tide; the location of said channel through the bay."

2. To remove the upper and lower lines of obstructions consisting of rows of piles, driven close to each other, and of sunken hulks, filled with bricks or rather heavy material, so as to make the openings where the channel will pass through the obstructions 600 feet at the upper and 1,200 feet at the lower line.

3. To prosecute the survey of the harbor, especially in reference to determining more definitely what are the obstructions which will require removal, and their exact positions; and also to determine, by soundings, the present depth of water down the proposed channel, until 13 feet of water at mean tide is reached.

4. Leave in abeyance and for future study the question of the propriety of closing any of the outlets of Mobile River, above Choctaw Pass, or of confining the current of the river in any way, with a view of producing a useful effect from scouring".

Major Reese's project was given formal approval of the Chief of Engineers in a letter dated August 18, 1870. Bids were invited for dredging the proposed channel, and the contract was awarded to John Grant, who bid 50 cents a cubic yard for dredging—although original estimates had been based on anticipated price of 40 cents a cubic yard.

Grant started work on September 20, 1870, but progress on the undertaking was impeded by yellow fever which during those days took many lives in Mobile, including that of Major Reese. Before the project was completed, it became necessary for Col. J. H. Simpson, who then was in charge of the engineers here, to obtain an additional appropriation of $200,000.

Following is an outline of the amount of dredging required under the project:

"For dredging Choctaw Pass, to give a channel 300 feet wide and 11 feet of water at low tide—110,000 cubic yards.

For dredging Dog River bar, to give 11 feet of water, and a channel 300 feet wide—129,000 cubic yards.

For dredging below Dog River to give 13 feet of water through the lower bay, 300 feet wide—887,000 cubic yards".

¶*Toward the close of 1869, Moses Waring notified the bank's board of directors of his desire to resign from the office of president of the bank, and at the meeting of the bank's directors on January 11, 1870, James H. Masson was elected president to succeed Mr. Waring.*

While serving as vice president of the First National Bank in 1869, Mr. Masson also carried on a private banking business, according to the City Directory of that year.

The directory listed him as a "money broker" and as vice president of the First National. At that time, his private bank was conducted at 32 St. Francis Street.

Directories do not give evidence of his having continued his private banking concern following his election to the presidency of the First National in 1870.

¶*The year 1870 was characterized by severe business depression, which culminated in the financial panic of 1873. The First National Bank's deposits were $289,721.58. Despite the depressed conditions and shrinkage in deposits, however, the bank continued to be a tower of strength during those hard times in Mobile.*

St. Francis Street Slip, in the 1880's.

JAMES H. MASSON
President of The First National Bank from 1870 to 1904.

Facsimile of a check drawn in 1867 on the private banking house of James H. Masson, who later became president of The First National Bank. Note the expression "Second of Exchange (first unpaid)" on the check. In those days people buying goods out of Mobile paid for them with checks like the above, and every check was drawn in duplicate. The original check would first be mailed, and then the duplicate would be sent by a later mail! The reason for this practice of mailing duplicate checks was that the mail service was irregular and undependable.

1871—EXPLOSION OF THE "OCEAN WAVE"

WHILE hundreds of excursionists clambered aboard the 27-ton ferry boat *Ocean Wave*, as she prepared to sail from the Point Clear pier on the afternoon of August 27, 1871, a terrific explosion wrecked the boat, killed more than a score of her passengers and injured many others.

The following is part of an eye-witness account of the tragedy as given *The Mobile Register* by Ben Lane, who happened to be sitting on the porch of the Point Clear Hotel at the time of the explosion.

"It was my ill fortune yesterday to witness the saddest scenes I ever beheld. I have seen many battle fields strewn with hecatombs of gory dead and wounded, but there the victims were strong men, and such scenes were normal, usual and anticipated. But yesterday I witnessed a catastrophe in which helpless women and children were the chief victims. I saw bodies frightfully mutilated, torn, scalded; some struggling in a last vain effort to escape from the overwhelming waters; some rescued only to prolong their sufferings for a few hours. The boat gave out a queer hissing sound before the explosion. Then came the report, followed by a rumbling, hissing sound. Fragments of timber and metals flew in all directions. The fore part of the boat and cabin was completely carried away. . . . The guests of the hotel and the residents turned out in a body and rendered every possible assistance. Large numbers of boats were hurried to the scene, but they arrived too late to save the drowning. All was over with them in less than five minutes. But many of these were so badly wounded that they would have died, if rescued.

The number of passengers on the *Wave* is only conjectural, and so is the number of the lost. But the boat was certainly crowded, and it is safe to estimate the number aboard at over two hundred. Very many of these were children, and many little hats and bonnets came ashore to tell the tale of the little victims beneath the waves. How many were lost, it is impossible to know. The number will probably never be accurately known. . . . The boiler was torn open, with a long seam. It was so rotten as literally to tear open. If it had been stronger, so as to explode with greater violence, the destruction would probably have been greater."

— 19 —

The ill-fated bay ferry boat "Ocean Wave"

"The *Ocean Wave* has for some time been considered an unsafe boat. A criminal responsibility rests somewhere, and it ought to be visited upon those to whom the recklessness and incapacity are attributable. The system of inspections everywhere is loose, careless and reckless, and officers who give an official safety certificate to such old shells of boilers ought to lose their official heads, if not their necks".

Weighing cotton for shipment from Mobile in the 1870's.

Old Mobile Cotton Exchange and Chamber of Commerce Building, formerly located at St. Francis and Commerce Streets.

1871—FOUNDING OF THE MOBILE COTTON EXCHANGE

ON DECEMBER 4, 1871, a group of Mobile business men, who thought that the cotton business should be concentrated in the South instead of in New York, met in the offices of Mobile's Board of Trade to inaugurate a movement which shortly thereafter resulted in the establishment of the *Mobile Cotton Exchange.*

Reporting that development, *The Register* on the following morning stated:

"According to notice, a meeting was held last night at the rooms of the Board of Trade for the organization of a Cotton Exchange in this city. Col. D. E. Huger was called to the chair, and Mr. E. C. Dorgan requested to act as secretary. Col. Huger, on taking the chair, explained the object of the meeting and stated that there were already 50 merchants who had authorized their names to be used as subscribers to the enterprise."

In a follow-up story on a subsequent meeting, *The Register* on December 8, stated:

"A meeting of the *Mobile Cotton Exchange* took place yesterday evening at 7 o'clock, Col. D. E. Huger, president pro tem, presiding.

The committee on organization submitted the constitution and by-laws, which were adopted.

The committe of seven, appointed at the previous meeting, was continued for the purpose of obtaining signatures to the constitution, with instructions to file a copy of the constitution with the Judge of Probate for the purpose of incorporation. The committee was requested to urge the signing of the constitution, and suggest a meeting for final organization and election of officers".

Discussing establishment of the exchange, *The Register* said editorially:

"As we understand, this is a part of a general policy to be adopted throughout the cotton states, and has as its object concentration of the cotton business in the South instead of having it controlled almost entirely in New York, as has been the case since the war. New Orleans inaugurated the move last year, and its exchange has grown to large and important dimensions, and she is now using her influence to build up similar institutions in all southern ports".

The Exchange first occupied what was known in those days as the *Old Arcade*, between St. Michael Street and Planter's Alley. In 1886 it joined with the Chamber of Commerce and built its own quarters at St. Francis and Commerce Streets. This building subsequently burned, destroying most of the records of the Exchange.

¶*At the annual meeting of the stockholders in 1872, Rittenhouse Moore was elected a director of the bank, and served in that capacity until 1885.*

1873—"BLACK FRIDAY" AND THE NATIONAL PANIC

"Mobile will ever be true to her past, and even those who bitterly complain that she is slow, never dared deny she is safe".

Thus editorialized *The Mobile Register* in a time when the city faced one of its greatest economic crises—the panic of 1873. This proud boast, representing a spirit which has brought Mobile to its present enviable place under the industrial sun, came just a few days after "Black Friday" (September 19, 1873).

Actually, Mobile's business on "Black Friday" failed to show any effects of the crash which subsequently was to bring so much woe to her economic life, and which on that very day precipitated pandemonium on Wall Street.

A special article dispatched by reporter DeLeon from New York to *The Register* described the economic upheaval as follows:

"Since the shaking of infamous Black Friday (1869), New York finance has never been so racked in the very marrow of its bones as it was yesterday. The ague that set its teeth chattering early in the day, culminated later in a terrible congestive chill, which shook and shattered it like a feather in the whirlwind. And the end is not yet; for today's symptoms—up to this hour of mailing—have not been hopeful for the ultimate recovery of the shaken patient.

"The Stock Market opened yesterday with a furious hubbub, known only within the mystic confines of the Board. Since the days of Black Friday (1869) no such pandemonium—made up of howls, hat-smashings, 'yahoos!' of the stronger, and bitter oaths of the crushed—has been known in New York; and the curious interest of the gallery audience composed of many well-dressed women, culminated in contagious excitement that was almost as fierce, and far more uncontrollable, than that below".

DeLeon's story, after listing names of prominent Eastern firms which were swept out of existence on the day of the crash, went on to charge that several New York financiers "entered into a combination to bear the market".

News from New York shocked Mobile business circles, made its leaders apprehensive, but generally the community assumed a calm attitude and methodically started getting its house in order for the worst.

Editorially, *The Mobile Register* issued daily pleas for sane action on the part of the public in the crisis. An example of its admonitions follows:

"It is now for our business community of all classes to act with great caution in making their choice as to the course to be pursued—whether to bring down the crops and slowly move them by degrees, or allow them to accumulate in the hands of the farmer until the imperative demands of trade and manufacturers burst open the

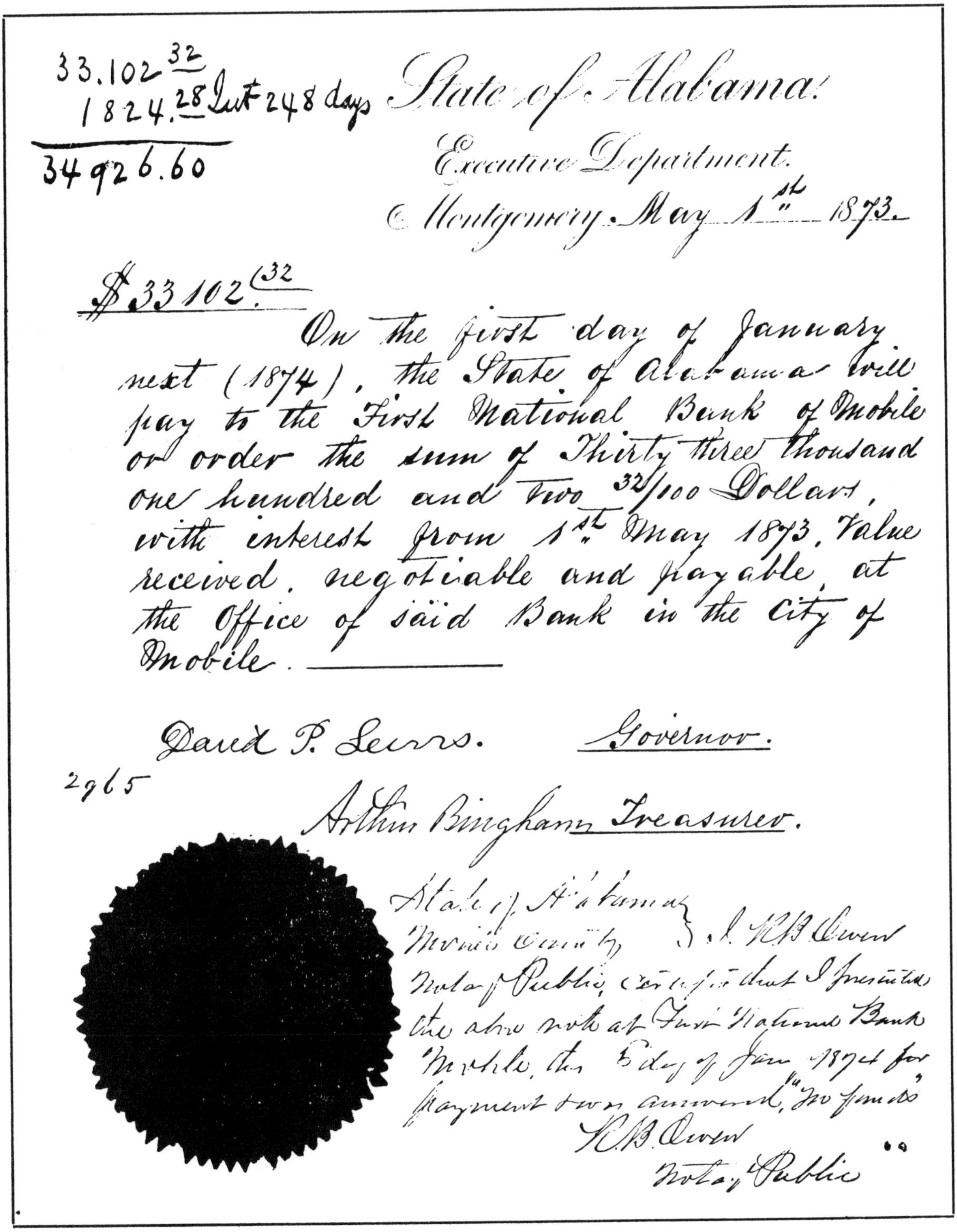

33.102 32
1824.28 Int 248 days

34926.60

State of Alabama.
Executive Department.
Montgomery. May 1st 1873.

$33.102 32

On the first day of January next (1874), the State of Alabama will pay to the First National Bank of Mobile or order the sum of Thirty three thousand one hundred and two 32/100 Dollars, with interest from 1st May 1873. Value received, negotiable and payable, at the Office of said Bank in the City of Mobile.

David P. Lewis. Governor.

2965

Arthur Bingham Treasurer.

State of Alabama
Mobile County

I, R.B. Owen
Notary Public, certify that I presented the above note at First National Bank Mobile, this 5 day of Jan 1874 for payment & was answered, "No funds"

R.B. Owen
Notary Public

The credit of the State of Alabama was not always as good as it is today. Above is facsimile of a note given by the State to the First National Bank of Mobile in 1873. The note, for what would be a negligible amount in State transactions today, was not paid at its maturity, presumably because the State was without funds to meet it. Collateral had been deposited to secure the debt and the note was liquidated from the proceeds of sale of the collateral, and the excess amount received from the sale was paid over to the State.

barriers retaining them captive. The skill, prudence and integrity of our banks and bankers will, doubtless, carry them through the present crisis, and although by wise and proper restraint in their dealings with the North they may lose some of their immediate profits, they will be ultimately amply compensated when these dealings may be resumed with more security".

Files of *The Register* trace the harrowing developments of the remainder of the panic era, reporting that scarcity of currency led to use of deposit certificates. The newspapers called upon the banks to issue daily statements on their condition, a request which was promptly granted by the First National Bank of Mobile.

¶*The First National's early cashiers lived in rooms over the banking room, and there was a large trap door in the ceiling of the banking room so that the cashier living above could raise it and see the whole bank at one time. There was also a big bell over the bank door outside, which the cashier could ring if he needed help.*

1875—ORGANIZATION OF FIRST REGIMENT, ALABAMA STATE TROOPS

THE GRAND REVIEW.—Drawn by Schell and Hogan

Sketch of Alabama State Troops drilling at Mobile during their annual encampment in 1885, as it appeared in Harper's Weekly.

AFTER the close of The War Between the States, the Federal Government took steps to discourage control of military activities by individual States. As a result, Mobile's several militia organizations of long standing were forced to curtail their training.

However, the early 1870's brought a demand for state militia, and on September 9, 1875, the *First Regiment, Alabama State Troops*, was formed here. The organization meeting was held in the old armory, which was then a part of the City Hall property, the armory being located on the north side of Church Street, between Royal and Water Streets.

Organizations making up the regiment were the *Mobile Cadets, Mobile Rifles, Washington Light Infantry, Gulf City Guards, Alabama State Artillery, Baldwin Rifles, Cleburne Guards* and the *Demopolis Rifles.*

With its individual members and companies engaging vigorously in all its activities, the *First Alabama* soon earned a fine reputation. During its encampments, held on the Bay just south of the city, governors of Alabama paid official calls, and reviewed its maneuvers and drills. Many present-day Mobile business men are descendants of the original officers of this regiment. Among them are two members of the present First National Bank organization: James T. Overbey, Senior Vice President, who is the grand-nephew of Maj. W. H. Sheffield; Wythe L. Whiting, Jr., vice president, who is the grandson of Lt. Col. J. W. Whiting.

¶In 1875, Mobile was still feeling the effects of the panic of 1873. The First National Bank, however, was working shoulder to shoulder with the people of Mobile toward business and financial recovery. In that year the bank showed deposits of $285,765.55—practically the same as the deposits of 1870, although the five-year period was one of the most trying Mobile ever encountered.

The First National Bank's second home, as it appeared in 1875. The bank's third home (now occupied by the Bidgood Stationery Co.), was erected on this site.

1877—DEATH OF JOHN FORSYTH, FAMOUS EDITOR

ON MAY 2, 1877, death ended the career of one of Mobile's most famous newspaper editors—John Forsyth.

A Princeton graduate and son of a congressman from his native Georgia, John Forsyth first came to Mobile in 1835 and established a law practice. Two years later, he purchased *The Mobile Register*—a step which led to such success that he became known as one of the South's most able journalists.

President Pierce, recognizing Forsyth's contributions to the prestige of the Democratic party, appointed him Minister to Mexico—a post he held for a brief period.

Coming back to his desk at *The Register* office, Forsyth vigorously championed Stephen A. Douglas and his doctrine of local sovereignty.

The following excerpts from *The Register's* story on the morning after his death attest to the esteem with which Forsyth was held by his colleagues and his readers:

"Last evening at 10 minutes past 6 o'clock, passed away that spirit which for nearly 40 years has been felt through these columns; which by its straight, unswerving course toward the right, has made Southern journalism a power and a name; that spirit which, in every more intimate relation of life, as husband, as father, friend and associate, blended the tenderness and gentle truth of woman with all the higher attributes of man.

" . . . In 1859, he went to the Legislature. Steadily he labored; ever quick to detect and to resent a wrong to his beloved South; ever a faithful watchman through that long and black political night that followed the bloody course of the Southern sun and settled down upon our land with its Lost Cause.

" . . . And as we write these words, with a sadness deeper than their cold formula can tell, the busy brain is still, the honest hand is cold and the true heart is quiet forevermore. But, even as we realize not wholly the power of the blow that has fallen, so will the public who sorrow with us gauge only gradually the full measure of the loss to them and their best interests in the death of John Forsyth".

1878—YELLOW FEVER EPIDEMIC

IN 1878, Mobile, along with Memphis, New Orleans and other cities of the South, was visited by a terrible epidemic of yellow fever. Eighty-three persons died of the disease in Mobile and 297 were made ill by it. Most of the deaths occurred in the southern part of town.

The infection in Mobile supposedly came from Biloxi, Miss., the first case having been reported here in August of 1878. Invasion of the "yellow scourge" struck terror into the hearts of local residents. In a serious state of panic, hundreds sought to flee the city, but their hopes of escape in most cases were crushed by strict quarantines adopted by other towns and cities against infected areas.

From day to day the number of afflicted increased to alarming proportions. Doctors, nurses and able-bodied individuals worked day and night to alleviate suffering of the unfortunate victims. As evidenced by the toll, their efforts on individual cases were often nullified.

Taking foremost parts in relief activities in the epidemic-gripped city were Father Abram J. Ryan, poet-priest of the Confederacy, and those brave and charitable members of the *Can't-Get-Away Club*. Many are the stories detailing the charities of Father Ryan and the club members. The priest stood ready at any hour of the day or night to administer to the sick and dying, while throughout the city nurses and doctors toiled with patients who had been found by club members. The *Can't-Get-Away* men, aside from raising funds for nurses' hire, pitched in themselves and nursed the sick.

Out of the tragic period arose bitter disputes between Mobile and other cities—principally New Orleans. Authorities of both cities accused each other of withholding from the public the extent of the disease in their respective communities. Harsh words were exchanged between cities over the question of the quarantine.

Actually, the Mobile Board of Health did clamp down on its bulletins to the press on the disease. *The Daily Register* of October 5, 1878, published an apology to the public over its failure to carry details on the number of cases and deaths. The newspaper explained that the Board of Health had adopted a policy of not giving out such reports.

It was not until October 30 that the disease lifted its hold on Mobile. On that date the last death was reported.

"Barrett Lightning Matinee Train" which ran between Mobile and New Orleans, as it appeared in the 1870's. Ober Anderson & Co., later became the Alabama Corn Mills Co., whose officers were L. Le Baron Lyons, president, Herbert Lyons, vice-president, and S. O. Starke, Sr., secretary-treasurer.

1879—INSTALLATION OF FIRST TELEPHONE IN MOBILE

AN amazed group of Mobilians gathered in the coal yard of A. C. Danner[4], in 1879 and witnessed for their first time a demonstration of telephonic communication.

They were accorded this privilege because of the interest Mr. Danner took in the invention of the telephone by Alexander Graham Bell in 1876. Mr. Danner, who at that time was engaged in the coal business, bought two phones, connected them with 100 feet of wire, and for some time made use of the hookup in the conduct of his business.

Subsequently, a movement was launched by Mr. Danner and C. G. Merriweather, to

[4]A. C. Danner was the father of Paul Danner of Mobile. His grandson, Robert S. Bacon, is now executive vice-president of the bank.

establish a telephone exchange in Mobile. Successful in their efforts, the first exchange phone was installed at Danner's Coal Yard on Friday, November 13, 1879, and the exchange was formally opened November 16. At the time of its opening, the fledgling exchange had only 32 subscribers.

On the 50th anniversary of the invention of the telephone (November 30, 1926) the Mobile office of the Southern Bell Telephone Co. held an anniversary banquet at the Scottish Rite Cathedral. To this banquet were invited all the surviving subscribers to Mobile's pioneer telephone exchange. Among those attending the banquet were: F. C. Bromberg, Mr. and Mrs. Neander Crane, Sen. John Craft, Major and Mrs. James K. Glennon, Mr. and Mrs. E. T. Toomer, Mr. and Mrs. Harry Pillans[6], George B. Toulmin, Col. Fred S. Cox, and Gregory L. Smith[7]. Also among the guests at the banquet were representatives of the following present Mobile business firms who were pioneer subscribers to the service: First National Bank, Battle House, Bidgood Stationery Co., Adam Glass & Co., L. Hammel Dry Goods Co., The Mobile Register, Stonewall Insurance Co., Western Union Telegraph and the Mobile Cotton Exchange. J. L. Bedsole[†], who was president of the Chamber of Commerce, was principal speaker at the dinner.

Facsimile of a check drawn on the First National Bank in 1879. The black square in the upper left-hand corner of the check marks the place where the Internal Revenue Stamp was affixed to the check, as was required in those days. The dotted-line cross in the lower right-hand corner shows where the check was "cancelled" with a tin paper-cutter. Even as late as 1879, banks did not furnish checks for their depositors; each depositor had to pay for his own.

1879—MOBILE ADOPTS "PORT GOVERNMENT"

COMING to the aid of Mobile's financially distressed municipal government, the Alabama Legislature on February 11, 1879, passed bills placing the city under jurisdiction of a new governmental agency known as *The Port of Mobile*. The city's old charter was repealed, and new governing bodies established, including three Port Commissioners, and a Board of Police Commissioners. Appointed by the governor to serve as Port Commissioners were L. M. Wilson[*], W. J. Hearin,[5] and James A. McCaa. Subsequently, as provided by the new legislation, the people of Mobile elected eight citizens to serve as a Board of Police Commissioners; members of that original

---

(5) W. J. Hearin was the grandfather of W. J. Hearin now co-publisher, general manager and executive vice-president of The Mobile Press-Register.

(6) Mr. and Mrs. Harry Pillans were the parents of Palmer Pillans of the law firm of Pillans, Reams, Tappan, Wood & Roberts, and Harry T. Pillans of Mobile.

(7) Gregory L. Smith was the father of Harry Hardy Smith and the grandfather of Gregory L. Smith of Mobile.

†Mr. Bedsole was at this time and still is a director of the bank.

*Mr. Wilson later became a director of the bank.

Board were: Richard B. Owen, Price Williams, Sr., Joseph Cahill, Jonathan Kirkbride, John Callaghan, James McDonnell, Frank P. Andrews and Palmer J. Pillans.

Principal reasons for repeal of the city's charter and adoption of the new form of government were financial. The municipality owed debts totaling approximately $3,000,000—a comparatively large indebtedness, mostly inherited from days of carpetbag misrule. It was openly charged that more than $1,000,000 of the city's bonds had been given two railroads which had no existence except on paper.

Explaining the necessity for the Port Government legislation, *The Register*

pointed out that "Mobile simply asked the State to throw around the city the same protection which she assumed herself. The State, after repealing the law under which she could have been sued for her debts, offered a compromise with her creditors, whereby she discarded a large amount of interest due on her old debt of $6,000,000, for a new direct and contingent debt."

Passage of the Port Government legislation was a great relief to the people of Mobile. It substantially reduced the expenses of municipal government, which in turn was accompanied by a reduction of city licenses and the re-establishment of the city's credit.

1882—INTRODUCTION OF JERSEY CATTLE IN MOBILE

ONE of the most significant developments in the history of Mobile's dairving industry occurred December 8, 1882, when the late George G. Duffee, onetime mayor of the city, brought the first shipment of Jersey cattle into Mobile County. The shipment comprised 20-odd head of cows, all of which had been selected by Mr. Duffee during an extended visit to the Isle of Jersey.

While not the first Jerseys to be brought here, Mr. Duffee's herd was the first group of mentionable size to be imported. Records of the American Jersey Cattle Club show that the first purebred Jersey cow brought to Mobile county was *Rose of Isle*, transferred from J. E. Phillips, of Baltimore, Md., to F. S. Cox, of Mobile on October 15, 1874.

Files of *The Mobile Weekly Register* of December 2, 1882, tell of the arrival of Mr. Duffee's cattle at New Orleans, and of how a quarantine law in force at the time prevented his landing them there. After an exchange of telegrams with the Secretary of the Treasury at Washington, in which the Mobilian was told the quarantine law could not be modified to allow entrance of his cattle, it was agreed that Mr. Duffee could bring his stock to Mobile by ship provided he isolated them upon

arrival. It was explained that the quarantine actually was designed as protection of the country from importation of Mexican cattle.

Following is a story carried in *The Weekly Register* of December 9, 1882, describing the arrival of Mr. Duffee's shipment:

"The twenty-six head of cattle purchased to order in the Isle of Jersey by George G. Duffee, of this city, reached here on Monday at 1 o'clock on the steamer *Georgia Muncey*, from New Orleans. Notice of the arrival of the little butter cows in that port was only made in these columns, as was also the discussion that then arose as to the quarantine. Of the transfer of the cattle from the steamship *City of Lincoln* to the *Muncey*, *The Times-Picayune* gives the following description:

" 'The transfers were attended with several amusing incidents. Five of the sailors of the *City of Lincoln* were engaged to lead the cattle, but more help being necessary, Mr. Duffee employed a boy about 14 years of age to hire the services of seven others, allowing him $4 to pay himself and them. When the time came for the transfer of the cattle, the five sailors and eight boys were promptly on hand, but the Jerseys were rather difficult to

Mobile as it appeared in 1884 (from a drawing in Harper's Weekly, Feb. 2, 1884).

handle. The calves, which were too small to walk, were placed upon the shoulders of the sailors, which treatment of their off-spring the mothers did not think was the proper thing, so they pulled at the ropes by which they were led, and behaved in such an obstreperous manner that persons along the route from the river to Magnolia Bridge were under the impression that another menagerie circus had arrived, the procession of animals and men being such a lengthy and lively one.'

"On arrival here, the cattle were taken at once to Mr. Duffee's farm at the head of Conti Street. A few days rest will greatly freshen the animals, and they will then be exhibited to all who care to inspect them. In the meantime, they are in retirement."

On his second cow-buying trip to the Isle of Jersey in 1884, Mr. Duffee brought 125 head of stock, described by *The Register* as being "the largest shipment that had been sent from the island, and the largest which has been sent for such a distance."

1884—FIRST PARADE OF THE "COMIC COWBOYS"

BILLED as *Dr. Cutter's "Wildest Westest Show,"* the *Comic Cowboys*, who annually bring laughter to Mobile's Mardi Gras throngs, made their first appearance in the annual carnival celebration on February 26, 1884.

The organization, founded by Dave Levi, drew praise from *The Mobile Register* following its initial parade.

This is what the newspaper had to say on the following day:

"In all the years of day parades, devoted to absurdity pure and simple, nothing funnier has ever been seen than the burlesque pageant of *Dr. Cutter's Wildest Westest Show*, originated and carried out to exemplify the untamable and unquenchable vim of Mobile flat marksmanship. First rode forth on a fiery steed, *Dr. Cutter*, *'The Devil Spirit of the Flats'*; prompt to the second, for the doctor's watch always knocks the block out of standard time. With him rode the famous *'Eagle Eye,'* *White-brown Chief of the Chick-aha-saws*, a brave famed on many a street corner; and *Major Lillie* of the flaxen locks, *Whiter-browner Chief of the Papoosa Mamas*, a hero noted in more word-battles than Hector, the Greek of old.

"First following, the crowds read the emblem of—

'The New Society, First Anniversary—We Never Speak as We Pass By!'

"With its guard of 10 Indians in wildest western war paint, each mounted on his model mustang, the procession moved along. Then rolled on the world-renowned *'overland coach'*, mud-splashed from tire to hub, and covered with skins of slaughtered deer. The coach was driven by a bearded border ruffian, who handled six marvelous mules, freshly lassoed on the flats of Whistler; and inside rode eight of the blood-drenched chiefs who had assisted at the massacre of many a free-lunch and danced in the sand, which dance is celebrative of victory. Standing on top of the coach was the antlered stag, *'Pet of the Petticoats'* in the *wildest westest show*. Conspicuous on the front of the coach was read, *Dr. Cutter's copyright sign: 'We Show, Rain or Shine'.*"

"Then followed mounted Indians and cowboys by the score, guarding the float on which shone and glittered Dr. Cutter's prizes, won in many a close contest. It was evident the doctor shot not only for glory, but for tin. Many rich plates proved this; while cups, medals and spoons showed his peerless prowess. A huge swinging coffee pot, with cup on spout, was trophy of his 90-hour test match with the famous *Capt. Bombardus;* while in a glittering sauce pan with cake broiler was told the story wherein he beat *Frank Carmelich*, who beats the drum. There glittered, also, the huge razor to tell how close was the shave by which he 'shot out' *Laurine Williams*, at Coney Island last summer. In that match, Dr. Cutter shot 10,000 pins out of paper without tearing it, driving the pins through a four-inch plank, in the form of his monogram.

"Yesterday, in riding through the streets, Dr. Cutter showed equal proofs of his great skill. A cowboy would throw up a bottle of Mum's 'Extra Dry'. Loading his repeating rifle, the doctor would cut the six wires with as many bullets; shoot off the foam as the cork flew, and then right the bottle with another shot. With the last two he would straighten the cork and drive it home in the mouth of the bottle, before a drop spilled.

Cutter's reception by the G. C. G. C. which next followed, should not be taken *au pied de a lettre*, as a bore. A huge and magnificent specimen of the wildest western paternal swine, garnished with carrots and other highly-colored vegetables, surmounted this float. It was a splendid specimen of papier-mache work, and typified the solid side of the feast. An empty bucket, bottom upwards and labeled 'Punch' and two ditto nursing bottles told of the fluid 'Joys We Have Tasted'.

Then came more cowboys, and finally a squaw, hauling, in Indian cradle, 'Mrs. Eagle-Eye's Baby'—a red and feathered chief in miniature, strapped in its sling. Between its feet rested 'the little brown jug'; six feet of rubber hose leading to its painted lips. Then came more cradle slings, more infantile charges, and more novel nursing bottles. They included '*Major Lillie's Baby*,' '*Mamma's Baby*,' and last, a '*Mobile Baby*,' black as the 10 of spades, which is nine times blacker than the '*Burro*' ridden by '*Peanuts*,' a colored boy.

The clever burlesque wound up with placards repeating the familiar formula— 'We Show, Rain or Shine.'

All along the line, laughter greeted Dr. Cutter's Wildest Westest Show.''

¶*Recognizing the fact that Mobile's annual Carnival celebrations play an important part in the social and recreational life of the city—as well as being a powerful tourist attraction—the First National Bank has always been a subscriber to the Mobile Carnival Association.*

¶*At the annual meeting of the stockholders in 1885 two new directors were elected: Lorenzo M. Wilson, who served until 1891, and Henry A. Schroeder, who served until 1892.*

¶*By 1885, Mobile had recovered from the financial troubles of the 1870's and deposits in The First National Bank had climbed to $726,187.94.*

View on Dauphin Street, looking east from Royal Street, in the 1880's.

— 32 —

IN 1886, S. R. Bullock & Co., of New York, organized the Bienville Water Supply Co., a firm which subsequently furnished Mobile the purest water it had used up until that time.

Papers of incorporation, filed with the Judge of Probate, set forth that the firm was organized under authority of a legislative act approved in 1885.

Named as incorporators of the new concern were Dr. George A. Ketchum, O. Hamilton, D. R. Dunlap, W. J. Hearin and D. P. Bestor (father of D. P. Bestor, Jr., later chairman of the bank's board of directors). Stock subscription was opened on April 9, 1886, and more than $50,000 was immediately subscribed. The stockholders elected a board of seven directors as follows: George A. Ketchum, president; A. Pope St. John, secretary; Emil Waltman, treasurer; P. Hamilton, D. R. Dunlap, W. J. Hearin and D. Bestor.

But despite its wonderful source of water —Clear Creek—and its capital resources, the fledgling water supply company ran into many obstacles.

Its first disappointment came when the city, through its Board of Police Commissioners, turned a cold shoulder to its offer to supply the municipality fire protection and water for other public use for $21,000 per year. Shortly thereafter, the company substantially reduced its offer, which the city accepted. Operating under this agreement, the company installed several hundred fire plugs and furnished water for public and private use during a period of 20 years. During that time, however, the company confined its service to the more thickly settled sections of the city—a policy which led to public dissatisfaction with the service and which finally resulted in the building of a municipal water works system in 1899. One year earlier, the city had purchased the privately-owned Stein Water Works. Faced with competition from this city-owned system, the Bienville Company finally sold out to the city in 1907, as described later on in this volume.

Of the company's early proposals to furnish the city with water, *The Item* of May 15, 1886, said:

"A special meeting of the Police Board was held on Tuesday evening to hear the proposal of the Bienville Water Supply Co., in relation to a supply of water for our city. The report was quite lengthy, and it proposed to supply fully the long-needed amount of water necessary in the case of fire. The ordinance was received and referred to the board. Quite a number of insurance men and other citizens were present. At the request of the recorder, they took part in the discussion. The following is the account of their remarks:

"Hon. D. P. Bestor was the first to speak, and his remarks were mainly addressed to consideration of the fact that there is no adequate supply of water here for the extinguishment of fires. He said that loss by fire is not always to be measured by money. The dread of fire was something and the loss of a feeling of security is to be added to the money consideration. In addition, there are many things in one's house which money cannot replace, and there are times when a fire finds one's family in sickness and trouble.

Dr. George A. Ketchum, president of the Bienville Co., was called upon for remarks. He addressed himself to a consideration of the hygienic value of a plentiful supply of water. The abolition of wells and pumps would reduce the rate of sickness in this city fully 25 per cent. A scientific fact ascertained by the experts of the national Board of Health, shows that there is but one well in the city free from matter injurious to health. Dr. Ketchum spoke long and interestingly on the subject.

Mr. A. P. Bush, president of the Planters and Merchants Insurance Co., stated that the plentiful supply of water for the extinguishment of fires would warrant the underwriters in reducing insurance 25 per cent. The rates run all the way from one to three and four per cent, but as for himself, speaking as an insurance man, he would rather have an all-round rate of one per cent than the present rates."

The Item says that in its offer to the Police Board, the water company offered to place 300 fire hydrants in various points, so as to cover "every part of the city." It also proposed to supply all public institutions such as jails, public schools, churches and hospitals with free water, and to erect a free drinking fountain for man and beast in each of the eight wards. The company further agreed to furnish water to the citizens for half the price they were paying at that time and to give twice the pressure for half the rate.

1886—RESTORATION OF ALDERMANIC FORM OF CITY GOVERNMENT

ON DECEMBER 10, 1886, the General Assembly of Alabama passed a law placing Mobile under a new charter which ended authority of the Port of Mobile government instituted in 1879 and returned the city to the aldermanic form. The change came after much opposition had arisen to the reign of the Police Board, which was the executive body under the Port of Mobile government.

Under the new charter, the municipal legislative body was composed of a mayor, board of aldermen and board of councilmen, which meeting together were styled "The Mayor and General Council". Councilmen and the mayor were elected for terms of three years, while aldermen, elected at large, were named for terms of one year.

City officials under the new aldermanic form of government, who took office upon its installation, were:

Hon. Richard B. Owen, Mayor.

Councilmen: Thomas T. Dorman, first ward; Winfield S. Lewis, second ward; Robert A. Savage, third ward; Abraham Baerman, fourth ward; John Callaghan, fifth ward; Steven A. Leonard, sixth ward; and Blount Sossaman, eighth ward*.

Aldermen: John J. McAfee, John G. Carlen, Garrett B. Shawhan, William Rankin, Frederic Pickhard, Michael Smith and Conrad Fischer.

The city operated under this aldermanic government until adoption of the commission form in 1911.

1886-87—REORGANIZATION OF THE FIDELIA SOCIETY

DURING THE WINTER of 1886-87, members of the *Fidelia Society*—membership of which at that time was composed chiefly of Jewish people—decided to reorganize the society as a social club and limit the membership exclusively to Jews. Older Jews of Mobile state that this reorganization was due to the desire of Jewish business men of Mobile to have a town club similar to other such clubs in Mobile.

Prior to 1887, the Fidelia Society's membership included both Gentiles and Jews. When originally organized in 1859, the purpose of the society was stated to be "the mental improvement of its members and friends through the medium of social reunions, soirees, musicals and *disantes* and dramatic productions in German and English." During the early years of the organization, many dramatic productions were staged, including an extensive series of charitable performances for relief of suffering during The War Between The States. Dramatic performances were continued at frequent intervals until February 23, 1887, when the society's last play was staged.

That last performance was a memorable one. The play selected was an old-time favorite *All That Glitters Is Not Gold* and its cast included Charles Brown[8], Joseph Metzger, Julius Goldstein[9], Edward Metzger, Henry Frolichstein, Minna Greenhood, Julia Soloman and Fanny Jacobson. S. H. Soloman was stage manager of the

---

*No councilman from the seventh ward was listed in the Mobile City Directory for 1887.

[8]Charles Brown was the father of Herbert C. Brown, now residing in Mobile, where he owns the Brown Bagging & Paper Co. and is a director of the bank.

[9]Julius Goldstein was the father of Mendel P. Goldstein, of Julius Goldstein & Son, Inc.

Old Fidelia Club, formerly located on the southeast corner of Government and Conception Streets.

production, and on the reception committee were the following: Major A. Proskauer, Prof. S. Schlesinger, I. Brisk, G. F. Werborn, S. Haas, Nat Strauss, J. H. Leinkauf, S. Hirshberg and Leopold Strauss[10]. Flowers in profusion were passed to the performers as tokens of admiration from their friends in the audience and after the play a grand ball was given.

For many years after the Fidelia Society's reorganization as a strictly Jewish society, it retained its club rooms on Dauphin Street, between Jackson and Joachim Streets. Later it built a handsome club and office building on the southeast corner of Government and Conception Streets (see accompanying sketch) and occupied those quarters for many years. From there it moved to newly-built rooms on the northeast corner of Government Street and Washington Avenue, which it occupied until the organization disbanded in 1936.

1888—VOLUNTEER FIRE-FIGHTING SYSTEM ENDED

ON SEPTEMBER 8, 1888, a special committee of the city formally organized a paid Fire Department for Mobile—thus ending the volunteer system that had been in effect since the community's earliest days.

The change came only after lengthy controversy, during which existing fire companies, through their parent organization—the Fire Department Association—carried out a threat to close their engine houses in protest of what they contended was the

---

[10]Leopold Strauss was the grandfather of John L. Strauss, executive vice-president of L. Hammel Dry Goods Co., and a director of the bank.

A Mobile fire engine, as it appeared in the old days.

city's failure to make proper payment for their services. Crowds gathered at the fire stations on the night of the closing, and records reveal violence was narrowly averted when a demonstration was staged at one of the headquarters.

Groundwork for the committee's action, however, already had been laid by Mayor J. C. Rich, who returned from Bladon Springs just in time to take full charge of the situation before the volunteer companies went on strike.

In face of failure of the city council and the fire companies to compromise their differences, Rich proceeded to assure the public of fire protection by purchase of whatever equipment was available to him at the time.

According to *The Register* of September 1, 1888: "The mayor told the special committee that knowing that the duty of providing a fire service in this emergency devolved upon him, by virtue of a resolution adopted by the General Council July 5, he had set to work early in the day, had seen the citizens' committee, and received

assurances that the committee would supply the city with all needed apparatus for the extinguishment of fires. The citizens' committee agreed with him that it would be better, if practicable, to purchase engines of the home companies than to buy from outside parties. Therefore, he had at once opened negotiations with *Merchants' Steam Fire Company, No. 4*, and later in the afternoon had purchased all the apparatus of that company, consisting of an engine, a hose truck and three horses, three extra wheels, and tools, etc., the price paid being $3,500. He would proceed today, he said, to purchase other engines, if they could be obtained. He would today organize a paid fire company to use the engine already purchased, and would take possession of the hook and ladder truck owned by the city. The citizens' committee has on hand a hose truck, and the city owns all the hose now used by the department and has, besides, a number of nozzles. This apparatus can be brought into service at once, the mayor added, and, with the aid of water pressure in plugs, a shift can be made to take care of the city when the volunteer companies close their doors at 12 o'clock tonight."

Creole Steam Fire Company No. 1 was enrolled as a paid company, in the service of the city, and to serve according to the rules and regulations governing the paid fire department. For this service, the city was to pay the lump sum of $160 per month, with the company owning and operating its apparatus and providing 20 men on its active rolls. The company surrendered all association with the volunteer department and became a paid servant of the city.

The payment of this Creole company, the maintenance of the other two steam engine companies organized and the hook and ladder company, together with salaries of those companies, cost the city a total of $9,890 per annum. First Fire Chief was Matthew Sloan, whose salary was fixed by the city at $1,200 a year. C.Walter Soost[11] was Assistant Chief at a salary of $400 a year. The grand total of annual payroll and expense was fixed at $11,990.

Sloan also played a rather important role in actual proceedings of changing over from the volunteer to the municipal basis. It fell his lot to walk into the various volunteer stations and take over in the name of the city. His presence, with that of Police Chief Slatter, at Fire House No. 3 was credited by *The Register* with avoiding violence at that place. *The Register* said a group of young men had gathered at the station at the closing deadline, for the purpose of taking the engine, owned by the city, from the fire house, which was owned by one of the private companies.

1888—23-FOOT SHIP CHANNEL PROJECT ADOPTED

AFTER much agitation on the part of Mobile civic leaders over a long period of time, a project designed "to afford a channel of entrance from the Gulf of Mexico to the City of Mobile of 280 feet in width on top of the cut, with a central depth of 23 feet at mean low water" was finally passed by Congress in August, 1888.

Originally the depth of the channel (at Choctaw Pass) was approximately 5½ to 7½ feet. Between 1827 and 1885, the Federal Government had expended more than a million dollars in increasing the depth of the channel at various times until in the 1880's it was 17 feet.

The following extract from records in the U. S. Engineer's office at Mobile picture conditions at the time the 23-foot channel was being agitated:

"The depth of 17 feet at mean low tide was practically demonstrated on January 21, 1886, by the safe and quiet passage down the dredged channel of the British steamship *Wandle*. The draught of the vessel at anchor was 16.3 feet, the reading of the tide gauges called for 15.8 feet in the channel, and the vessel with a full cargo of 4,137 bales of cotton (the largest cargo of cotton ever loaded at the wharves) passed down without delay of any kind. Again on May 29, 1886, the British bark *Pricilla*, partially loaded with cotton, drawing full 17 feet at anchor, passed down on an ebb tide, and when about half-way down the tide gauges read 1.1 foot below 17 feet."

That the 17-foot depth of the channel was inadequate for the rapidly growing Port of Mobile, was indicated in a report from A. N. Damrell, Major of Engineers at Mobile, to the Chief of Engineers, in 1885. Major Damrell strongly urged approval of the 23-foot channel project for the following reasons:

"1. The cost of the improvement probably will not exceed $1,500,000. The present commerce is large, as is shown in statements hereunto appended, which is greatly inconvenienced by the fact that the draught of the vessels seeking the port for cargoes is such that the present depth of water only allows them to take on part of their cargoes at the wharves, and compels them to finish loading in the lower bay, 28 miles distant, by lightering and rafting. The prospects for an extensive increase, in

(11)C. Walter Soost was the father of Thomas B. Soost, senior vice-president of McGowin-Lyons Hardware & Supply Co.

Hunter's Wharf as it appeared in the old days.   This location is now the site of the
Cold Storage Plant at the Alabama State Docks.

the near future, with improvement effected, are sure.

"2. The harbor is destined to be a very important one to the United States Government, as being the point on the Gulf where the cheapest coal and iron can be obtained, owing to the fact that it is connected by three short water routes—the Cahaba, Black Warrior and the Coosa rivers—with the coal and iron deposits of Alabama."

Following Congressional approval of the 23-foot channel in 1880, the *Rivers and Harbors Act* of September, 1890, extended the work up Mobile River to the mouth of Chickasabogue.

Mobile soon learned that a 23-foot channel was inadequate if she was to become one of the nation's outstanding ports. Continued efforts on the part of local leaders and their representatives in Congress, brought about an increase in the channel depth to 27 feet.

The channel was next enlarged to a depth of 30 feet in the bay and river, and to 33 feet at the bar, under authority of the Rivers and Harbors Act adopted March 8, 1917.

Under the project completed in 1939, the channel was dredged to depths of 36 feet across the bar and 32 feet in the bay and river. The channel now is 450 feet wide as it crosses the bar, 300 feet wide from deep water in the bay to a point at the north edge of the proposed quarantine anchorage basin, 350 feet wide from the north of the quarantine anchorage basin to the mouth of the river, and 500 feet wide from the mouth of the river to the highway bridge across Mobile river.

¶In 1889, at the annual meeting of the stockholders, A. M. Quigley became a director of the bank and served until 1894. Subsequently he was made vice-president in June, 1894, and held both offices until December of that year.

"Confederate Rest", in Magnolia Cemetery.

1890—ORGANIZATION OF RAPHAEL SEMMES CAMP, U.C.V.

IN THE EVENING of June 28, 1890, Mobile's Confederate Veterans turned out in full force to attend a meeting in response to a call for organization of a local Camp, under the constitution of the United Confederate Veterans—at that time headed by Gen. John B. Gordon.

It was a gathering which embraced every branch of the Confederate service, including representatives of all the Armies of the Confederacy. Among the assemblage were men who had seen service in the Army of Northern Virginia, the Army of Tennessee in Missouri, and in the Trans-Mississippi Department. Field officers, staff officers and line officers mingled with enlisted men as the Civil War spirit was revived—not in the sense of vain regrets and bitter memories, but in a feeling of comradeship and honor to the memory of past heroes and events.

The meeting was called to order by Col. Dick Roper, and Col. Joseph Hodgson was unanimously elected temporary chairman. Col. Hodgson explained that the object of the meeting was to organize a Camp of Confederate veterans, which would subsequently affiliate with the United Confederate Veterans' organization.

Capt. Harvey E. Jones was then elected temporary secretary and the group heard the reading of the U. C. V. constitution. Following the reading of the constitution, Col. Price Williams moved that the assemblage resolve itself into a Camp organization and the motion was promptly carried.

Many of Mobile's oldest and most prominent families were represented in the charter membership of the Camp, and a great many direct descendants of those charter members still live in Mobile.

Several names for the new Camp were suggested, but all were withdrawn when the name *Raphael Semmes* was proposed.

About a week later, another meeting was held for the purpose of formally approving a constitution and by-laws and electing permanent officers.

At this meeting, Col. Sands was chosen Commander by the casting of one ballot by the Adjutant. Other officers were then unanimously eiected as follows: Dr. W. G. Little, first lieutenant commander; Col. Dick Roper, second lieutenant commander; Col. Daniel E. Huger, third lieutenant commander; Capt. Harvey E. Jones, adjutant; Wm. E. Mickle, sergeant major; Capt. E. B. Vaughn, treasurer; Dr. J. Gray Thomas, surgeon; Dr. Caleb Toxey, assistant surgeon; Col. Stark Oliver, quartermaster; James Pendergast, officer of the day; Wm. H. Monk, color bearer; Felix H. Aubert, first color guard; Hiram L. Griffling, second color guard; Major Wm. H. Sheffield, vidette.

Following the election, Col. Wiliams offered the use of the Armory to the Camp, saying that he knew his action would receive the endorsement of every man and officer of his regiment (First Alabama). A resolution of acceptance and thanks was promptly adopted.

Thus did Raphael Semmes Camp, U. C. V., come into being. It has now passed out of existence—its last surviving member having died in 1937.

¶*In 1890, two Mobile boys joined the staff of the bank—M. O. Discher, who was then 15 years old, and Joseph D. Beroujon, who was then 16 years old. Both served the bank continuously for 50 years, and in commemoration and appreciation of that long period of service, each was presented with an appropriately engraved watch by the bank in 1940.*

¶*In 1890, Louis Lowenstein was elected a director of the bank, and served until 1895.*

¶*By 1890, Mobile had entered upon an era of population growth and business expansion which characterized the period 1890-1915. The bank's Report of Condition as of February 28, 1890, showed deposits totaling $1,065,063.47.*

¶*In 1891, A. C. Jones was elected by the board of directors as assistant cashier of the bank and served until he resigned later on that year.*

¶*In March, 1891, Chas. D. Willoughby was made assistant cashier of the bank. In 1895 he became cashier; in 1911 he became a director, and was made vice-president and cashier in 1915. He held those positions until July, 1918.*

¶*At the annual meeting of the stockholders in January, 1891, Arthur T. McGill was elected a director of the bank, and served until 1894.*

¶*Gilliat Schroeder was elected a director of the bank in 1892, and served in that capacity until June, 1893.*

1893—MOBILE'S FIRST ELECTRIC STREET CAR LINE BEGINS OPERATION

THE FIRST electrically-powered street car to operate in Mobile rolled through the streets of this city on January 8, 1893, with Charles James, a Milwaukee, Wis., resident, who was visiting here at the time, as its first passenger.

The five-cent coin with which James paid his fare was preserved many years by the late J. Howard Wilson, president of The Mobile Light and Railroad Co. until shortly before his death in 1939. (Mr. Wilson was a director of the First National Bank from 1905 to 1907). A tiny wooden box, containing the five-cent piece and a newspaper clipping chronicling initial operation of electric street cars here, was found among Mr. Wilson's effects after his

Mobile's last horse-drawn street car.

death. Mr. Wilson had written on the outside of the box, the names of W. F. Ross, conductor, and Jack Diamond, motorman, on that first electric car.

The Register of January 9, 1893, described the event as follows:

"The Electric Railway Company started for the carriage of passengers yesterday morning at half past ten o'clock. The car made trips all day from the termini, Dauphin and Jackson, and Virginia and Marine, and was crowded every trip. Mr. Charles James, of Milwaukee, Wis., a visitor in the city, paid the first fare received by the new enterprise."

On January 11, 1893, *The Register* quoted *The Memphis Commercial* as stating that Raphael Semmes, Jr., was coming to Mobile to manage the electric railway system: "The Memphis Commercial of the seventh instant says: 'Raphael Semmes and his family left yesterday for Mobile, Ala., where they will reside. Mr. Semmes goes to Alabama's seaport to take charge of the

street railway system of that city. Semmes, son of the famous Admiral Semmes, went to Memphis at the close of the war and became affiliated with the street railway business there'." On returning to Mobile, Mr. Semmes managed the old "White Line" street railway for many years, which was later acquired by the Mobile Light & Railway Company.

With Mobile's continued growth, the city's street railway facilities were extended from time to time and in 1939 the city was being served by 50 route miles of street car lines. Before his death in 1939, the late J. Howard Wilson had reached an agreement with the City of Mobile whereby motor buses would be gradually substituted for the street cars, and a few buses were actually being operated in 1939. After Mr. Wilson's death, however, the National City Lines acquired a controlling interest in the Mobile Light & Railway Co. Buses were then substituted for street cars throughout the entire system, which now consists of approximately 420 route miles of motor buses.

View of Mobile, looking northwest from the Courthouse Tower, in the 1890's.

1893—REVIVAL OF EMPEROR FELIX PARADE

FOR A NUMBER of years, Emperor Felix, ruler of Mobile's Mardi Gras, failed to appear for his annual carnival reign.

The custom, however, was revived in 1893 by Thomas Cooper DeLeon, with S. T. Prince as Chief Marshal of the Royal Pageant.

Wearing the crown as Empress, according to files of *The Mobile Register*, was pretty Miss Hallie Triplett, whose court name was "*Felicia*".

On the afternoon of February 13, 1893, Felix, Emperor of Joy, arrived in his capital city of Mobile and was received by the people with every manifestation of pleasure. Steamboats and railroad trains had brought great crowds of people to the city and the populace turned out *en masse*, so that when the emperor arrived, the streets were crowded and all the galleries along the line of march were filled.

His Majesty arrived at 4 o'clock from the *Ruby Isle*. He was brought up Mobile River by the U. S. revenue cutter *Walter Foward*, which was decorated from bow to stern with bunting. Due to her deep draught,

the emperor and his staff were transferred in midstream by boat to the cutter *Seward* and by that vessel was taken to the wharf. The *Walter Foward*, meanwhile, fired an imperial salute of 19 guns, which was echoed by the whistling of all the steam tugs in the vicinity.

The *Seward* was also gaily dressed with flags and Emperor Felix's orchestra (consisting of five men of the *Seward's* crew) played lively music as the vessel approached the wharf. On landing, His Majesty was welcomed by Mayor Joseph C. Rich and members of the General Council and by a host of his loyal subjects.

Mayor Rich addressed the Emperor in becoming words, relating the joy the people felt in having him visit his capital, and stating that the city was at his disposal. In token thereof, he presented a massive key which had up to that moment reposed upon a cushion in the hands of City Clerk Summersell—said key being a new one, having just been turned out at the gold foundry of E. J. Pine & Son. This was, the mayor said, the token of the city's submission to Felix's imperial power. The emperor was graciously pleased to accept the key which he turned over to his Imperial Chamberlain, and then signified his intention of viewing his capital and noting the improvements which had taken place since his last visit.

Following the ceremony at the wharf, pandemonium broke loose along the pageant's route as Felix's float passed. Later in the day, the Knights of Revelry honored the Emperor and Empress at a reception, where they were seated on their royal thrones and received vows of fealty from their subjects.

¶Elder Mobilians will recall the year 1893 as the year in which there was an acute national financial crisis which emphasized the strength and soundness of the First National Bank. In that year, money was being hoarded and currency was at a premium. Banks in most of the principal cities of the nation were compelled to curtail cash payments. The First National Bank was one of the very few banks that not only furnished cash for the people and for Mobile business houses, but also provided large sums to the railroads entering Mobile so that they might meet their payrolls and provide for their workmen. At that time, the First National was a comparatively young bank—only 28 years old—and its conduct during that period of stress was early evidence of the good management which has always been characteristic of the institution.

1893—MOBILE'S SEVEREST STORM

ON OCTOBER 2, 1893, Mobile was swept by the severest storm ever recorded in her history. A southeast gale, rising at its height to 72 miles an hour, drove the bay waters into the rivers—causing them to overflow into the city—inundated and destroyed the east end of the Old Shell Road, wrecked numerous vessels, leveled innumerable trees and scores of structures. While only a few lives were lost in Mobile proper, an estimated 25 persons were drowned or killed in outlying areas, and the death toll along the Mississippi coast was staggering.

Preceded by record-breaking rainfall during the daylight hours of October 2nd, the

Boats beached by the storm of 1893.

storm rapidly increased in force until at 8 o'clock in the evening the waters in the rivers backed up even with the top stringers of the wharves. Within a short time thereafter Front Street was under water, and soon the flood covered the wharves and Commerce Street—rising so rapidly that merchants had to abandon efforts to save their goods on lower floors.

At 10 p. m., the high-water line of previous floods was reached, but still the water continued to rise, covering all of Water Street and reaching to Royal Street and beyond at State Street, and to Royal at St. Louis Street. On St. Michael Street the water came up to within 50 feet of Royal, and on Dauphin Street it approached within 100 feet of Royal. In the southern part of town, the low-lying land was deeply flooded and houses badly damaged.

By 11 o'clock the storm was said to have reached its greatest intensity, and trees began falling everywhere in the city. Some of the most magnificent trees in Bienville Square toppled.

Conditions along the river front were chaotic. Ships, barks, schooners, steamers and other craft broke loose from the moorings and were dashed about at the mercy of the angry waves. Mobile River was filled with craft of every description, all the way to the head of Twelve-Mile Island. The tugboat *Louise* broke loose from her moorings at Elmira Street, ran several miles up the river and knocked a hole in her side. The schooner *Emma B.* broke loose from her moorings at the foot of Government Street, headed for mid-stream, collided with the schooner *Villa y Hermano* and was badly damaged. A flatboat and oyster sloop were left stranded in Commerce Street. The Eastern Shore boat *Crescent City* was wrecked on the beach between Frascati and Arlington. The tug *Dixie* was driven into a lumber yard on Palmetto Street. The largest yacht on the bay—M. J. Marshall's *Annie M.*—sank bottom-up near the mouth of Chickasabogue. Other vessels reported missing were the *Olive, Siren, Carrie G,* and *Seadrift.*

Extensive wreckage was reported at Daphne, Montrose, Battles Wharf, Zundell's and Point Clear. The schooner *Alice Graham* was wrecked two miles out from Cedar Point and all aboard her—including Capt. Louis Graham, Miss Susie Herron, and the mate—lost their lives. Heavy losses of life were likewise reported at

South End Cottage, Old Shell Road (Frederic's) in the 1890's.

Grand Isle, Bayou Andre, Chinese Camp, Grand Lake, Rigolets, Biloxi, Chandeleur Island, in the Grande Bource, Chiniere, and on vessels along the Mississippi and Louisiana coasts.

Street car, telephone and power facilities were disrupted, shutting Mobile off from communication with the outside world. Railway service was discontinued for a long period because of damage to lines leading into Mobile and elsewhere along the coast.

Several days were required to reckon the full extent of the storm's havoc. Then it was discovered that the property damage most generally felt throughout Mobile was the destruction of the east end of the Old Shell Road. All that part from Frascati to the highlands below the bend was ruined.

The bluffs were undermined and extensive sections of the roadway were completely washed out.

In those days, the Old Shell Road was a private thoroughfare, owned and operated by the Shell Road Company. It had been constructed by private capital, and although a toll road, it had never been a paying proposition. For years it had been a center of social activities in Mobile, and one of the city's most prominent tourist attractions. At the time of the storm it was said to have been "in as nearly a perfect condition as can be imagined".

Within a few days after the storm, *The Register* expressed the hope that the citizens of Mobile would cooperate with the Shell Road Company in restoring the ruined portions, or constructing a new road.

1894—FAMOUS EVANGELIST T. DeWITT TALMADGE PREACHES TO RECORD CROWD

TOWARD the close of the 19th century, one of the world's greatest religious figures was Dr. T. DeWitt Talmadge, a Baptist minister of Brooklyn, N. Y. Possessed of remarkable personal magnetism and stirring eloquence, his weekly sermons made him probably the most famous evangelist of his time. Newspapers throughout the world, including those in Mobile, frequently printed his sermons in full.

On March 11th and 12th, 1894, Dr. Talmadge came to Mobile and delivered two sermons to huge assemblages. On Saturday night, March 11th, a crowd of 1,500 persons gathered to hear his sermon *A School For Scandal;* on the following night his text was *Unappreciated Services.* His audience numbered more than 2,000 persons —the largest crowd ever assembled in Mobile's old Princess Theater, then located on West Royal Street between St. Louis and St. Michael, just north of Geo. Coumanis' restaurant on southwest Royal and St. Michael.

Newspaper accounts of Talmadge's visit indicate the evangelist's tremendous appeal

to the public. Reporting the sermon of Sunday, May 12th, *The Register* said:

"Before dark the crowd began to rush in and by 7 o'clock people were being turned away by the hundreds. Every seat and all the standing room in the immense building was occupied and not less than 2,000 people were present. The heat was intense, but this did not affect or lessen their determination to hear the great divine".

Rev. Mr. Shell, of the Palmetto Street Baptist Church*, opened the services and Dr. Taylor of the St. Francis Street Baptist Church assisted with the program.

The evangelist, displaying the same eloquence and fervor which brought him fame as a minister of the Gospel at his home town of Brooklyn, N. Y., kept the crowd spell-bound with his lecture.

In its story covering the Saturday night sermon *The School for Scandal, The Register* said:

"Dr. Talmadge treated exhaustively the ways of the scandal monger, the slanderer and the liar, and of the immense and irremediable injury such an evil-hearted per-

---

*This building is now St. Peter Clavers Catholic Church.

View on Dauphin Street, looking west from Water Street, in the 1890's.

son does to his fellow men. He showed that the liar and the slanderer were one and the same person. He next spoke of the slanderer's victims, often victims of misfortune who should not be measured by ordinary standards. This led him to treat of the heredity of crime and of virtue. His conclusion was that it is one's duty to be charitable and to show every mercy to the erring; in short, to stop back-slashing, lying and slandering one's neighbor's failing strength. The lecture as a whole was an amplification of the injunction taught by the Golden Rule."

¶*The year 1894 found three new directors' names appearing in the records: A. M. Hall, who served until 1895; Felix McGill, who served until 1906; and Winston Jones, who served until 1901. Felix McGill was made vice-president of the bank in January, 1905, but resigned that office shortly thereafter.*

1894—U. S. CRUISER *MONTGOMERY* VISITS MOBILE

IN NOVEMBER, 1894, the U. S. Cruiser *Montgomery*, then a new craft, visited Mobile, and in formal ceremonies received the handsome gift of a silver service from a large delegation representing the citizens of Montgomery, Ala., the city for which the cruiser was named. At the same time, Mobile was highly honored by having as its guest, the Hon. H. A. Herbert, then Secretary of the Navy.

The Montgomery delegation, including Gov. and Mrs. Thomas G. Jones, State Auditor Purifoy, Montgomery's Mayor John G. Crommelin, Representatives Rogers and Robinson and a party of young ladies and prominent citizens, came here aboard a special train on the night before the ceremony. The latter train's passengers included members of the *Montgomery True Blues*, a military company.

Upon arrival here, Lt. Col. Peyton Bibb, member of the governor's staff, took a skiff and rowed out to the cruiser, which was anchored in the river at the foot of Conti Street. Boarding the vessel, Col. Bibb presented the governor's compliments to Commander C. H. Davis and Lieut. Knapp. These officers, in full dress uniform, returned ashore with him and were escorted to the Battle House, where the ladies of the silver service committee and gentlemen of the party were presented.

PUBLIC RECOGNITION
OF
GOOD MANAGEMENT

It has been frequently and truthfully stated that the caliber of a bank's management is most clearly revealed during times of stress. In that connection the following editorial reproduced from *The Mobile Register* of March 11, 1894, speaks volumes:

"In response to the call of the comptroller for a report of the condition of all National Banks at the close of business on February 28, 1894, the First National Bank of Mobile has made its statement, which was published in this paper last Wednesday morning. It is a statement of which the officers of the bank may well be proud. . . .

The past year has not been favorable to the banking business. For several months of last summer, very little business was transacted in any part of the country because of the panic, and very many banks were forced to suspend in order to weather the financial storm then raging. The First National Bank was one, however, that needed no assistance from any source, and was prepared, even in the midst of the panic, to supply as usual the funds for moving of the cotton crop. All the banks here united in a precautionary agreement relative to payments on deposit accounts, but experience proved that there was no panic in Mobile and the banks enjoyed the confidence of the people. The statement of the First National shows this. The bank's handsome line of deposits is the measure of this confidence, while the declaration as to the disposal of the bank's funds, and the amount of the bank's earnings, is proof that the confidence is well placed. The bank is an institution skillfully managed and is in the enjoyment of a phenomenally successful career."

Management of The First National Bank in those days was under the direction of James H. Masson, who had been president of the bank since 1870. The bank statement to which the editorial refers, showed the bank's deposits to be $1,181,324.77.

During the afternoon, the governor's party, members of the Montgomery delegation, and others, were taken aboard the cruiser for the ceremonies attendant to presentation of the silver. After a brief talk, M. B. Houghton, a Montgomery business man, introduced Governor Jones, who in his talk recalled that 30 years before that time, Secretary Herbert, like himself, was fighting in the Confederate Army. The state's chief executive expressed the pride which the City of Montgomery felt in having the cruiser adopt its name, and re-emphasized the loyalty of all Alabama citizens to the U. S. Government. Secretary Herbert and Commander Davis returned the governor's compliments, and expressed their appreciation for the magnificent gift. Then the party went ashore to receive an official welcome from Mobile's Mayor J. L. Lavretta at the City Hall and to enjoy a banquet in honor of Secretary Herbert and the cruiser's officers.

Though Mobile's part in that important naval and civic ceremony was secondary, the event gave the Port of Mobile widespread publicity, and *The Register* especially commended Mayor Lavretta in an editorial which said, in part: "By the circumstances of the case, Mobile being but the means by which the City of Montgomery accomplished her act of tribute-paying to the cruiser named in her honor, the field of hospitable demonstration was necessarily limited, but within the prescribed limits, the mayor did all in his power to show that Mobile appreciated and was worthy of the honor".

1895—SIX-INCH SNOWFALL IN MOBILE

ON FEBRUARY 15, 1895, Mobilians were treated to a sight very rare in this latitude—a six-inch snowfall.

Beginning at 1 o'clock in the morning of February 14, a light snow began to fall and by daylight the streets were covered to a depth of half an inch. By 10 o'clock in the morning, however, the half-inch blanket had well-nigh disappeared. About 2:30 that afternoon light snow flurries again appeared, rapidly increasing until by 6 o'clock the snow was so deep as to impede traffic. The fall continued until almost 9 o'clock that night, when the official Weather Bureau measurement showed that snow had fallen to the record depth of six inches.

The unprecedented snow turned Mobile topsy-turvy. Schools were dismissed, and children joined their elders in the streets to engage in snowball battles. Many residents took the wheels off their buggies, attached boards for runners, and went sleighing. Crowds gathered at prominent street corners and every avenue was lined with merrymakers whose gay shouts could be heard above the whistling north wind whirling the flakes over the city.

Mobile under its white blanket was a strange and beautiful sight—especially at Bienville Square, where the overhanging boughs of snow-laden trees, and long icicles hanging from the fountain, composed a scene of rare splendor.

The snow-storm had its serious side, however. Lacking the necessary equipment to keep tracks clear, street cars practically suspended operations within four hours after the heavy snowfall began, and not until nearly midnight had all cars been worked into the car-barn.

The only casualty reported was James W. Gray, of the firm of Overall, Bestor & Gray, who fell and sprained his elbow.

¶In 1895, Leopold Lowenstein was elected a director of the bank, and in June of that year he became a vice-president, serving in both capacities until July, 1898. Henry Hall was also elected a director in 1895, becoming president of the bank on May 25, 1904, and serving in both capacities until February 10, 1921.

Snow-covered Bienville Square as it appeared in January, 1881.

1896—BUILDING OF THE GRAIN ELEVATOR

MOBILE'S most important business development of the year 1896 was the building of the city's grain elevator. It not only exerted considerable influence on business through the Port of Mobile, but also it constituted an early example of aggressive promotion on the part of Mobile citizens to attract new business firms and industries to the city.

The idea of promoting a grain elevator for Mobile is said to have originated with Henry Fonde who, in 1891, advanced his suggestion in the form of an open letter which was printed by the Mobile Commercial Club. It was generally agreed at that time that provision of facilities for handling grain at the Port to serve as stiffening for cotton vessels, was essential to continued success of Mobile as a cotton port.

Minutes of the Commercial Club show that the elevator idea came before the Club several times during the next three years, but not until March 2, 1894, was organized action taken. On that date the Club appointed a special committee composed of Henry Fonde, Murray Wheeler, E. L. Russell, J. W. Black and W. H. Fitzpatrick, to look into the proposed project. That committee arranged a joint meeting between the Chamber of Commerce and Cotton Exchange, and it was decided to launch an organized effort to interest some private firm or individual in building the elevator, by offering a bonus of $10,000 to $15,000—the bonus to be raised by subscription among Mobile business men. L. C. Dorgan and John E. Mitchell were likewise added to the special committee at that meeting.

Monroe Park, as it appeared in the old days.

During the following year and a half, various outside firms and individuals considered taking advantage of Mobile's bonus offer, but it was not until October, 1895, that arrangements were finally completed. Then it was C. W. Stanton, a Mobile business man, who became interested in the project after a talk with Capt. J. G. Mann, general manager of the M. & O. Railroad. Mr. Stanton posted a check for $5,000 and within a short time the Commercial Club's committee had raised the $15,000 bonus which assured the building of the elevator.

Construction began immediately and the new structure was ready within 100 days. Designed by the A. Maritzen Company, of Chicago, and built under the supervision of the Heidenreich Construction Co. of the same city, it was strictly modern in every respect, with a 250,000-bushel capacity and the very latest machinery and equipment.

A conveyor 600 feet long connected the elevator with the then new M. & O. Railroad slip, permitting the delivery of grain into vessels at a rate of 10,000 bushels an hour. Unloading capacity was 150 railroad cars in 24 hours.

Busiest years, so far as the elevator was concerned, were those in which Argentine and other foreign grain crops failed. Then, in 1937, when our own grain belt suffered from drought conditions, millions of bushels of grain poured through the elevator from foreign countries for shipment to interior United States. In 1937, more than 9,000,-000 bushels of grain were handled by the elevator within five months. During that period it was operated by the Continental Grain Co., which had leased it from its owners, the M. & O. Railroad.

The structure was rebuilt in 1918, and operated until 1943 when it was dismantled.

1897—YELLOW FEVER MAKES ITS LAST VISIT TO MOBILE

YELLOW FEVER struck its last serious blow to Mobile and vicinity in the fall of 1897.

Fully aware of death-dealing effects of the "yellow scourge", as it was called, appearance of the disease here precipitated one of the greatest panics in Mobile's history.

During the early stages of the epidemic, the City Health Office was besieged by the curious public. Many sought information as to the extent of the disease here, while hundreds of others sought vainly to obtain health certificates which would permit them to flee the city.

Files of *The Register* reveal that the first case in the epidemic (a man by the name of A. Hagan) was reported on September 18th by Dr. Rhett Goode. Immediately upon receipt of Dr. Goode's report, the Health Board rushed telegrams to other health units throughout the Mobile area, announcing invasion of the disease.

Authorities quarantined City Hospital, where Hagan was treated, burned the bed clothing in his Government Street boarding house, and took other unsuccessful steps to isolate the disease. Investigation showed Hagan had not been out of Mobile since he took up residence here four years prior to the time he became ill, and that it was believed the infection came from Ocean Springs.

Day in and day out, Mobile's railroad stations were crowded with panic-stricken residents, trying desperately to escape the dreaded fever. Dr. Gardiner C. Tucker, rector of St. John's Episcopal Church, who was a leading member of the *Can't-Get-Away Club*, says that each train leaving Mobile was forced to stop at intervals of about 10 miles to allow inspection of their passengers. Those who were allowed to pass were required to walk for some distance to board other trains which had not passed through infected areas.

The exodus from Mobile included the entire personnel of the M. & O. Railroad Company's auditing and passenger agent's department, which was transferred to St. Louis, Mo.

Streets of Mobile during the epidemic were practically deserted. Dr. Tucker, writing in his diary, says that on several

Water Street, looking north from Dauphin, in the 1890's.

occasions he encountered only five or six persons while walking from Royal to Ann Street, on Government.

Principal news item of each of the dark days of the epidemic were official bulletins issued by the Board of Health showing trend of the disease. A typical bulletin follows:

"November 1:

Cases previously reported	255
New cases	9
Total cases to date	264
Deaths to date	35"

Shortly after the epidemic got under way, Mobile newspapers published a list of symptoms, to aid the public in detecting the fever:

"Chilly sensations, pains in the bones, headache, pains in the back and knee joints; *sometimes sickness of the stomach . . . When fever shows itself, the skin becomes dry and hot, the pulse quick and full; if not attended to immediately, the fever goes to the brain and the patient becomes delirious."*

Day and night during the three-month epidemic, members of the *Can't-Get-Away Club*, doctors, nurses and others labored indefatigably to relieve suffering and to care for the dead. Receipts and disbursements of the *Can't-Get-Away Club* (which raised funds with which to furnish medical care for the unfortunates) ran into the thousands of dollars, as the organization pressed intensive campaigns for relief funds.

¶*On September 20, 1897, E. H. Shaffer was elected assistant cashier of the bank and served in that capacity until February, 1924.*

1897-1918—ADMINISTRATION OF MAYOR PAT J. LYONS

IF ANY individual could be singled out as having exerted greatest influence on the growth and progress of Mobile during the past 75 years, that individual would be Capt. Pat J. Lyons, who for 21 years served continuously as a city official during the period 1897-1918. During those years of the Lyons administration, more municipal improvements were effected than during any other similar period in Mobile's history.

Capt. Lyons was the son of Thomas and and Johanna Lyons, who emigrated from Waterford County, Ireland, and settled in Mobile in 1849. He was born in Mobile on January 16, 1855, and during his boyhood was a deck boy on river steamers. His native abilities and capacity for leadership early earned for him the position of boat captain—hence the title "Captain Pat" by which he was familiarly known even after he had left the river.

Following his years on the river, Capt. Lyons entered the business world and became a member of the wholesale grocery firm of Michael & Lyons. He was an immediate success as a business man, and soon was a director of many Mobile firms, later becoming vice-president of the City Bank & Trust Co. His keen interest in civic affairs led him to enter politics, and in 1897 he was elected to the City Council. As a city official, his thoroughness, business capacity and conscientious discharge of duty so distinguished him that in 1904 he was elected Mayor of Mobile. Seven years later, when the city changed from the aldermanic to the commission form of government in 1911, Capt. Lyons was elected by his fellow commissioners to serve another term as Mayor. He was again elected Mayor in 1915, and served until 1918.

Certain events which occurred during his long career in the public service, illustrate Capt. Lyons' abilities as a municipal official. In 1904, when he first became Mayor, the city had a floating debt of $150,000; within a few months, Mayor Lyons had paid off the debt and the city had a surplus on hand.

During the early part of Mayor Lyons' administration, Mobile's program of street paving and other expensive municipal improvements got under way. By 1907, the city's debt was approximately $2,000,000. Despite many difficulties, Mayor Lyons succeeded in refunding that debt, saving the people of Mobile approximately $125,-000 a year in interest charges and expenses, redeeming the city's wharf property which had been mortgaged, and reducing the city tax rate from $1.50 to $1.10. (In the tax year 1931-32, the 35-cent tax used to retire the old "carpetbag debt" was removed, reducing the city tax to 75 cents, the present rate).

Capt. Lyons was the central figure in the city's drive for a municipal water works system. He led the fight to purchase the privately-owned Stein and Bienville Water Works. In a newspaper advertisement published just prior to his re-election as Mayor in September, 1915, Capt. Lyons' supporters contended that he had induced the Bienville Water Supply Co. to reduce the price of their plant from $600,000 to $350,000—the price which the city finally paid for it.

In addition to his managerial abilities, Capt. Lyons was also alert to the civic benefits of city beautification. He was an ardent advocate of municipal park improvements. It was he who started the planting of azaleas in Bienville Square, and the purple azalea now growing there was purchased and planted by him. He likewise directed extensive improvements in Washington Square and was responsible for the establishment of a playground in the west end of Old Church Street Cemetery. During his administration, the city transformed the old Stein Water Works reservoir into a playground with a swimming pool, and employed Miss Margaret Austill as the city's first paid playground supervisor. In recognition of his pioneer work in beautifying Mobile, the city named Lyons Park— at Springhill Avenue and Catherine Street —after him.

1898—SPANISH-AMERICAN WAR *CAMP COPPINGER* ESTABLISHED

A T CRICHTON, on the site now occupied by a number of industries, thousands of regular army and volunteer troops were encamped for several months during the Spanish-American War. The camp was called *Camp Coppinger*, after its commanding officer, Brig.-Gen. John J. Coppinger, U. S. Army.

Site for the camp was chosen on April 19, 1898, and consisted of a tract comprising between 400 and 600 acres bounded on the north and east by Three-Mile Creek, on the south by Stein's Creek, and on the west by Moffatt Road.

Shortly after selection of the site, the camp was prepared for arrival of the troops. From Omaha, Neb., came Brig.-Gen. Coppinger and his staff, consisting of Maj. Enoch H. Crowden, Maj. George Andrews, Lieut. G. Hutcheson, Lieut. A.W. Perry and Clerk Frank W. Carpenter. Maj. James K. Glennon, of Mobile, gave up his offices in the *Bank of Mobile* building for use as camp quartermaster's headquarters.

First units to occupy Camp Coppinger were the Third, Eleventh, Nineteenth and Twentieth U. S. Infantry, and the Second and Fifth U. S. Cavalry; all of those were units of the regular army. Following transfer of the regulars to Tampa, Fla., the First and Second Alabama, First and Second Louisiana, and First and Second Texas volunteer units were stationed at the camp.

Newspaper accounts of those war days indicate that patriotic feeling ran high in Mobile. Crowds of civilians regularly visited the camp to welcome and bid adieu to the various units arriving and departing. Mobile ladies prepared box lunches and other gifts for the troops, many of whom were Mobilians.

After the close of the war, the camp was evacuated and the property returned to civilian control. In 1936, *Fitzhugh Lee Camp*, Mobile Department of Alabama, United Spanish War Veterans, erected a marker on the lawn of the Mobile Cotton Mills, designating the old Camp Coppinger site.

View of Mobile, looking northwest from the Courthouse Tower, in the 1890's.

1898—CITY PURCHASES STEIN WATER WORKS

ONE of the most amusing incidents in the history of Mobile's municipal affairs occured on May 15, 1898, when the city purchased the privately-owned Stein Water Works. On that day, various city officials indulged in a hot chase through city streets, seeking Walter Wood, a Philadelphia investor who was dodging them in an effort to avoid receiving payment for his interest in the Stein plant. The charter of the Stein Water Works required that should the city ever reach an agreement with the private owners to purchase the works, the purchase price would have to be paid on that same day, or the agreement would be void. An agreement had been reached through a Board of Arbiters, who had decided that the city should pay a total of $45,000 for the plant. The heirs of Albert Stein (founder of the water works) readily agreed to the decision of the arbitration board, but Mr. Wood did not wish to sell his interest; hence his game of hide-and-seek.

How Mobile's city officials finally caught the elusive Mr. Wood and forced him to accept payment—thus carrying out the legal requirements which made Mobile owner of the water works—was graphically described in *The Register* on May 16, 1898, as follows:

"The Stein Water Works passed into the possession of the City of Mobile yesterday afternoon, and Mayor J. C. Bush, City Attorney Boone, and Mr. J. B. Davis of the Water Works & Sewerage Commission, Mr. F. O. Hoffman, clerk to the mayor, Aldermen Delchamps and Hale, and Chief Matthew Sloan of the Fire Department, had a hot chase after Mr. Walter Wood in order to tender him the amount due him under the award as part owner of the Stein Water Works. . . . The first tender was made to Mr. Wood about 1:25 o'clock in the office of his attorneys, Bestor & Gray. When Mayor Bush, Mr. Davis and Mr. Boone, laden with bags of gold coin, tendered to him the sum of $12,298.27, Mr. Wood refused to accept the tender.

Later, city officials discovered they had made a mistake in their figuring and had made a tender to Mr. Wood which was $5,000 less than it should have been.

Then began a second hunt for Mr. Wood so that a correct tender might be made to him. About 6 o'clock, he was located at the office of the Bienville Water Supply Co., on St. Joseph Street, but when Attorney Faith, City Attorney Boone and Alderman Hale went there, they found the office closed.

While Mayor Bush and Mr. Davis were in a Mobile bank, counting out the money, they had dispatched a Mr. Hoffman to locate Mr. Wood, who seemed to be giving them the dodge. Mr. Hoffman went to the office of the president of Bienville Water Supply Co., Dr. George A. Ketchum, where he learned that Mr. Wood had left there some time ago, and that he was possibly at the office of Bestor & Gray. Chief Matthew Sloan, of the Fire Department, was also put onto the chase, and he later engaged Mr. Wood in conversation on St. Joseph Street, near the office of the Bienville Water Supply Co. But the oratorical powers of the suave Matthew were not sufficient to hold the attention of Mr. Wood for more than three seconds, for Mr. Wood looked as though he smelled a large-sized mouse. So, he left Chief Sloan; but Mr. Hoffman, who was an unknown quantity in Wood's reckoning, had spied the Philadelphian, and kept his eye on him. Mr. Wood sprinted down St. Joseph Street to St. Michael, turned east on the latter street and headed for the river.

He passed *The Register* under a full head of steam, but Mr. Hoffman was a close second. When Mr. Wood reached the corner of Water Street, he turned south and hurried along Water; Hoffman got there just in time to see him disappear around the corner, going west on St. Francis. By the time Hoffman got to the corner of St. Francis and Water, Mr. Wood had vanished from the face of the earth, so far as Hoffman was concerned, and the latter concluded that he must have disappeared up the stairs of the office of his attorneys, Bestor & Gray.

This conclusion was telephoned to the bank, where the assembled hosts of the city were waiting with the bags of gold. They promptly proceeded to the offices of Bestor & Gray a second time and tendered him more gold. So, likewise, on this occasion Mr. Wood refused again. But the mistake in amount had been rectified and the law had been observed, so as good citizens and officials, the mayor, city attorney and Mr. Davis were satisfied with the conclusion of their day's work in behalf of the citizens of Mobile".

¶*On July 23, 1898, Louis Lowenstein was elected to the bank's board of directors. On January 2, 1906, he was made vice-president of the bank and served in both capacities until 1912. He is survived by his son, H. C. Lowenstein, a large realty holder, who now resides in Mobile.*

1899—SUB-ZERO WEATHER MARS MARDI GRAS CELEBRATION

MOBILIANS needed sled runners instead of wheels, on which to send their Mardi Gras floats through the city on February 13, 1899. On that day, the mercury dove to "one degree below" and ice covered the streets to such an extent that all carnival festivities were postponed until Tuesday, Mardi Gras Day. So tight was the grip of Jack Frost that telegraphic communications were disrupted and the shores of the bay were bordered by thick ice.

The Carnival Association, realizing that it would be unwise to attempt to carry out the day's gay program, issued the following statement for publication in *The Mobile Item:* "Owing to the extraordinary degree of cold and the ice covering the streets, it is impossible for the reception of Felix III to be held. Therefore, by full vote of the executive committee, the exercises of today have been postponed until tomorrow, when, weather permitting, the reception and parade will take place, with fireworks at night". Although the weather the next day was also bitterly cold, Mobilians by the thousands turned out and outdid themselves in the annual celebration."

In striking contrast to the gaiety in the city, was the experience of the bay steamer *James A. Carney*, which lost a grim struggle with ice in the bay. On February 15, 1899, *The Item* described the beaching and sinking of the boat after it had ploughed through "a field of ice". W. B. Curran, the boat's purser, told of an unsuccessful attempt to reach the wharf at Daphne, then of a dash for Battles, and finally of the beaching of the vessel near the Fairhope landing. All passengers and crew of the *Carney* were rescued without injury, and they reported that the bay was frozen over with ice more than an inch thick, for a distance as far as three miles out from the eastern shore.

1899—CITY FORBIDS FURTHER BURIALS IN OLD CHURCH STREET CEMETERY

SELECTION of cemetery sites, so located as not to be overrun by the growing city, has been a problem confronting Mobile city officials since the earliest times.

In 1819, when Mobile's expansion threatened to obliterate the old Spanish Burial Ground, located in the area of the Cathedral of the Immaculate Conception, the city

Gates of Old Church Street Cemetery.

fathers purchased for $140 an area south of Government Street and west of what is now Washington Avenue. At that time, the land was designated the "new burying ground"; it later became known as the "Old Church Street Cemetery", the name it now bears.

Six years after purchase of the new site—an area covered by pine forest and gallberry bushes—bodies in the old Spanish Burial Ground were disinterred and removed to Church Street Cemetery. Hamilton, in *"Mobile Under Five Flags"*, points out that exhumation of the bodies was followed by a visitation of yellow fever. But transfer of the bodies opened the way for the city's growth, and Conti and Claiborne Streets were allowed to run through the erstwhile burial ground.

At the time of the purchase of new cemetery land, city authorities felt confident that the site was ample for a town of 2,000 population; but they were soon to learn differently. Hamilton states that in the early 1840's interments at the Church Street Cemetery became fewer—due chiefly to the fact that the city had subsequently authorized burials in Magnolia Cemetery.

Finally, the Old Church Street Cemetery was completely surrounded by buildings, and the city in 1899 passed an ordinance prohibiting further burials there. Some protests were voiced by families whose members occupied graves in the area, but space was completely taken up and there was definitely no chance to continue using the cemetery without blocking residential building in that section.

The ordinance (Section 59 of the Municipal Code) reads: "The bodies of deceased persons shall not be buried at any other place except Magnolia Cemetery within the limits of the city, under penalty not exceeding $50."

Today, Old Church Street Cemetery, with its graves and surface tombs of prominent individuals of Mobile's past, is hardly noticed by visitors to the city because of the fact that it is shut off from view by the imposing Mobile Public Library Building, on Government Street, and by high walls and dwellings along its other boundaries.

Old Church Street Cemetery was divided up for use by Catholics, Protestants and paupers. The larger or east division was set aside for Catholics, while the Protestants occupied the northern section. Paupers were buried in the south end.

The oldest headstone—that of a Judson child—is dated 1813, while an iron cross in the cemetery is dated 1812. Both markers were brought with the bodies from the old Spanish Burial Ground.

¶*Dawn of the Twentieth Century found The First National Bank growing steadily with Mobile. The bank's Report of Condition as of December 13, 1900, showed $2,026,081.48 in deposits.*

1900—MONUMENT TO ADMIRAL SEMMES DEDICATED

MOBILE paid tribute to one of her most illustrious sons on January 27, 1900. On that date, thousands of local residents and visitors gathered at the intersection of Government and Royal Streets for ceremonies marking the unveiling of a monument to Admiral Raphael Semmes—the hero whose triumphs as commander of the Confederate warship *Alabama* electrified the world during The War Between the States. The monument—a massive structure of stone and metal executed by the famous sculptor Casper Buberl—was financed with funds raised by members of

C. S. S. "Alabama", (from an old print).

Scene at dedication of monument to Admiral Semmes.
(From a newspaper photograph).

the Ann T. Hunter Auxiliary of Raphael Semmes Camp No. 11, U. C. V.

On a huge speaker's stand erected in front of the then veiled statue were ladies of the Auxiliary, Col. William J. Samford, of Opelika, candidate for governor and chief speaker of the day; Mayor J. C. Bush and members of the city council; members of the Semmes family; members of Confederate veterans units and their guests, including Major Paul Sanguinetti, aide de camp on the staff of General Harrison and Lieut. Col. John B. Fuller, adjutant general of the first brigade, U. C. V., both from Montgomery; Major Gantt, of Evergreen; Capt. Hooks of Washington county and Messrs. Chambers and Riley of Camp Lomax, Montgomery; Col. Harvey E. Jones, adjutant general of the Alabama division;

Dr. James T. Thomas, surgeon general; Major Thomas E. Roche, aide on General Harrison's staff, and General James Hagan.

With R. H. Clark as master of ceremonies, the program opened with invocation by The Rt. Rev. Edward P. Allen, Catholic bishop of the Mobile diocese.

Mrs. Electra Semmes Colston, daughter of Admiral Semmes, drew the cord which held the canvas about the bronze statue. As the covering fell away, the band struck up *Dixie* and a battery of artillery stationed at the foot of Government Street began firing the admiral's salute of 17 guns.

The monument was presented to Mayor Bush by Mrs. E. B. Vaughan, president of the Ann T. Hunter Auxiliary. In accepting the statue on behalf of the city, Mayor Bush eulogized Admiral Semmes, saying, in part: "Almost alone, upon the seas of the

world, the single name of Semmes made our Confederacy respected and feared. Mild of manner, brave of heart, he waged war as effective as it was daring, upon the Union navy and merchant marine".

Colonel Samford, in the principal address of the day, told his hearers that Mobile and Alabama "should be and is" proud of the record established by the famous admiral. The speaker outlined causes and effects of The War Between the States, stressing the fact that the South waged war not over slavery, but over the question of States' Rights.

In the midst of Colonel Samford's talk, rain began to fall, forcing the crowd to move into the Y. M. C. A. Building, where Samford continued his address. As the thousands fled indoors to escape the rain, a bugler sounded taps at the monument, the base of which by that time was draped with flags and flowers.

For the past 65 years, the statue has been a landmark of Mobile. During 1939 it was temporarily dismantled to make way for the Bankhead Tunnel.

Mobile-built steamboat in the early 1900's.

1901—SUMMER HEAT RISES TO 102.2 DEGREES

ON JULY 12, 1901, temperature in Mobile rose to 102.2 degrees, the highest ever recorded in the local U. S. Weather Bureau office up to that time. Although only one case of prostration was reported, Mobilians suffered severely from the blistering heat.

At 7 o'clock in the morning, the thermometer registered 80 degrees. But within three hours the mercury climbed 20 degrees to reach 100.3 degrees at 10 o'clock. By 3 o'clock in the afternoon the official reading was 101.7 degrees, and just before sundown at 5:30 o'clock it stood at 102.2—an all-time record. Unofficial readings placed the figure even higher. A thermometer on the shady side of Van Antwerp's store at the corner of Dauphin and Royal Streets, registered 105 degrees during the afternoon, while another thermometer on the sunny side of the same doorway was graded for 115 degrees and the mercury filled the tube to the top.

Lacking modern ventilation and air-conditioning systems, Mobilians of that day could do little about the heat except complain. The air was so dry that breezes from electric fans are said to have been "as hot as air coming out of a stove". In those days, whenever the weather was unusually hot, a favorite means of escape from the heat was riding the street cars. But on that record-breaking day of 102.2 degrees, even street car riding gave little relief. The scorching air burned the faces of street car motormen a fiery red.

Although business indoors was carried on as usual, Mobilians working out of doors found it difficult to stay on the job. Several switchmen and flagmen in the L. & N. Railroad yards were forced to quit work at 2 o'clock in the afternoon, and in other instances outdoor work was organized in short shifts for the purpose of avoiding heat prostration.

How effective are modern ventilating and air conditioning systems in relieving the discomfort of extreme temperatures, is illustrated by the comparatively small mention made in the newspapers on two occasions since 1901 when the temperature rose even higher than 102.2 degrees in Mobile. On September 5, 1925, and again on July 11, 1930, the mercury reached the all-time top of 103 degrees in the city . . . and while of course the newspapers and everybody else freely admitted it was "hot enough for them", the public apparently did not suffer nearly so much as on that blistering day in 1901.

1902—MOBILE'S FIRST MODERN STREET PAVEMENT LAID

ACTUAL LAYING of the first modern street pavement in Mobile took place shortly before noon on April 18, 1902, when Mayor Walter F. Walsh shoveled the first asphalt into the intersection of Water and Conti Streets and voiced the hope that "the work now begun will continue until Mobile takes her rank among the progressive cities of the United States".

Launching of the asphalt paving program marked the beginning of Mobile's modern system of paved streets. Prior to that time, a few streets had been paved with wooden blocks and by other early paving methods, but none of those had proved entirely satisfactory. After the development of asphalt paving laid on concrete foundation, Mobile's Board of Public Works unanimously decided to try that new paving method in the city. The Board—consisting of Lawrence Lavretta, president; Mayor T. S. Fry and Stewart Brooks—favorably reported to the City Council on July 30, 1901, a project calling for the pavement and improvement of Water Street from the south line of State Street to the north line of Government; Planter's Alley and Exchange Alley, from the east line of Water Street to the west line of Commerce; also, St. Michael, St. Francis, Dauphin and Conti Streets from the east line of Royal to the west line of Front Street, excepting the Commerce

Street intersection. Estimates prepared by J. N. Hazlehurst, chief engineer for the Board, placed the cost at approximately $56,000, to be shared among property holders, the city, and railways using the streets to be improved. The report was promptly adopted and Mayor Fry was authorized to sell $65,000 worth of 6% paving bonds to the People's Bank in $500 units maturing on December 1, 1916.

Begun in April, that initial paving project was delayed by bad weather and other obstacles, and was not completed until the late spring. It was so successful, however, that the City Council approved a second project on June 24, 1902, and since that time Mobile's paving program has steadily progressed until today the city has approximately 112 miles of paved streets.

¶In 1902, at the annual meeting of the stockholders, Robert W. Ennis was made a director of the bank, and served until 1908.

1902—BICENTENNIAL OF ESTABLISHMENT OF FORT LOUIS DE LA MOBILE

JANUARY 22nd of the year 1902 marked the 200th anniversary of the establishment of Fort Louis de la Mobile at 27-Mile Bluff, and the founding of the City of Mobile. To celebrate those important anniversaries, the people of Mobile held a double celebration—the one marked by a parade through the city streets, ending with ceremonies at the courthouse, and the other consisting of a trip to the site of old Fort Louis de la Mobile at 27-Mile Bluff, where a permanent granite marker was erected.

Both celebrations were well attended and highly successful. The weather was fine and

Klosky's famous restaurant as it appeared in the early 1900's.

mild, and thousands of Mobilians lined the principal streets of the city for several hours, awaiting the parade which began to move at 1:30 o'clock under direction of Col. James W. Cox, assisted by George A. Robinson. Behind the grand marshal came a detachment of mounted police, who were followed by Martin Drey's Band. Next marched cadets from Wright's Military Academy, under command of Commandant Caseman. And bringing up the rear was a body of United Confederate Veterans commanded by Col. Irwin. The colorful column proceeded to the court house, where commemorative exercises took place.

The trip to 27-Mile Bluff was made in a revenue cutter, gaily decorated for the occasion. The group on the cutter consisted largely of members of the Iberville Historical Society, who were credited with being the guiding spirit behind the celebrations. Along with them they took some friends, a brass band and luncheon, and proceeded up the river to the monument site, which had previously been selected by a committee from the Society consisting of Messrs. C. W. Butt, Erwin Craighead, Peter J. Hamilton and Paul deV. Chaudron.

Arriving at the location of the old Fort, the party climbed the bluff to conduct ceremonies consisting of an oration and the un-

veiling of the marker. Grace King, writing in *The Outlook*, described the occasion as follows: "The orator of the day was the young Mobile historian, Peter J. Hamilton. He narrated the story of Fort Louis to a group perhaps as picturesque as any ever gathered on the spot—ladies and gentlemen in the costume of the day, cadets in grey with buff leggings and Rough-Rider hats, officers from the revenue cutter in their brilliant blue and gold, sailors in uniform, a Catholic priest, an Episcopal rector, a Jewish rabbi, and others . . . As the orator brought his address to a close, the cannon of the cutter fired a salute; all stood, and the white cloth was withdrawn from the granite block which bears the inscription: *'Erected by the People of Mobile, January 23, A.D., 1902, to commemorate the founding here of Fort Louis de la Mobile, by Pierre Lemoyne, Sieur d'Iberville, and Jean Baptiste Lemoyne, Sieur de Bienville'* ".

¶On May 18th, 1904, James H. Masson, who had ably served the bank as its president for 34 years, resigned on account of ill health. His resignation and retirement from active business life was accepted with deep regret by the bank's board of directors, and Henry Hall, who had been a director of the bank for many years, was elected president.

1905—FIRE DESTROYS OLD BATTLE HOUSE

ON THE NIGHT of February 12, 1905, fire destroyed Mobile's famous old *Battle House** and severely damaged adjacent buildings, causing a loss estimated at $450,000.

The fire was discovered about 10:45 in the evening, by one of the hotel cooks. It had originated in several unoccupied rooms used for storage purposes over the kitchen in the north wing of the hotel, and apparently it had been burning for a considerable time, as it had gained much headway before being discovered.

Prompt alarm through the hotel annunciator system brought every one of the 147

guests out of the hotel safely, and a general alarm brought all of Mobile's firefighting apparatus to the scene. Notwithstanding the Fire Department's promptness in getting 10 leads of hose into the building, the fire defied all efforts to subdue it. Shortly after midnight the north portion of the roof fell in, cutting off power and communications in the city's downtown section. Within another hour it was apparent that the entire building was doomed; interior floors began falling in, one after another, sending up mountainous showers of sparks and embers. Accordingly, the Fire Department turned its efforts toward protecting

---

*Steward of the Battle House at the time of the fire was A. E. Reynolds, who was the father of Albert Reynolds, now vice-president of the bank.

HENRY HALL
President of The First National Bank from 1904 to 1921.

View of Royal Street in the early 1900's, showing the old Battle House as it
appeared before the fire.

adjacent property. Fortunately, a heavy rain helped extinguish sparks falling on nearby rooftops.

At 2 o'clock in the morning, a crowd estimated at 10,000 persons was watching the spectacular blaze, and Mobile's police force had its hands full in managing the surging throng. Their work, under active direction of Chief E. T. Rondeau and Lieut. Davis, was highly praised. Hundreds of volunteer firefighters were stationed in nearby buildings to help prevent spread of the fire.

Although Mobile's firemen stood at their posts in a biting north wind and poured water steadily into the burning building for approximately 20 hours, it was not until the close of the following day that the fire was finally pronounced fully extinguished. Then all that remained of the renowned old hostelry was "a mass of bricks and mortar and twisted iron rods, with the front wall still standing, outlined against the sky like a sentinel, as though keeping ward and watch over the ruins of a stately old pile about which clustered recollections of half a century".

Checkup of the fire toll revealed a loss of approximately $250,000 in the hotel proper and $200,000 in other business firms, some of which were located on the lower floor of the hotel and others in adjacent buildings. The following businesses and offices on the lower floor of the hotel were destroyed: Sutton Bros., druggists; Arthur C. Hall, news dealer and tobacconist; Battle House Bar; Mobile Transfer Co.; John W. Scheible, insurance agent; W. E. Gordon, real estate broker; J. C. Hensch, merchant tailor; J. W. Dolle, shoemaker; E. C. Cahall, fraternal insurance agent; Johnston-Gaillard Coal Co.; W. M. Provost, coal and wood dealer; Fitzhugh & William, grain brokers.

Businesses and offices in adjacent buildings which were destroyed or badly damaged included: L. S. Graham Printing Co., Commercial Hotel, Rosenfield Tailoring Co., Commercial Shaving Saloon, Mobile Coal Co., Central Trades Council Hall (including all the Council's records), Bidgood Stationery Co., Charles Hess, and George Winters.

Three years later the present *Battle House* was erected on the site of the old building.

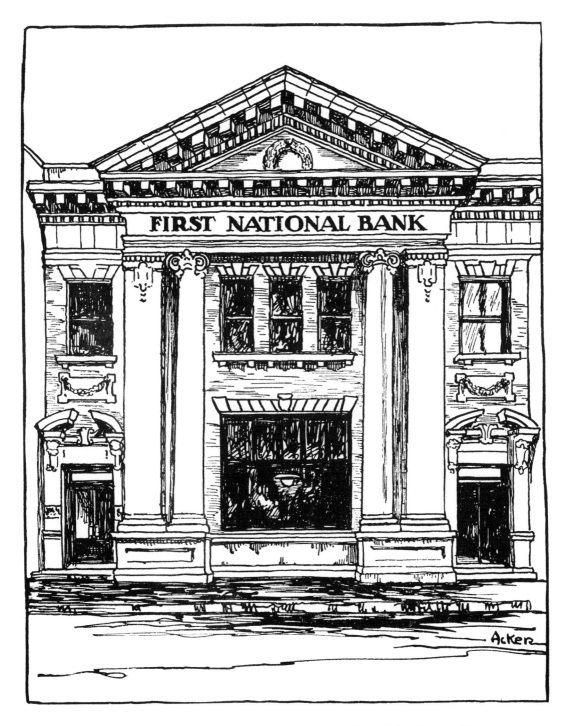

The First National Bank's third home, located at No. 68 St. Francis Street, as it appeared in 1906. These premises are now occupied by the Bidgood Stationery Co.

Scene at the dedication of the Wayside Cross, Bienville Square.

1906—"WAYSIDE CROSS" ERECTED IN BIENVILLE SQUARE

IN SOFT, clear tones, an army bugler sounded taps over Bienville Square, packed to capacity on the afternoon of February 25, 1906, by a large throng gathered to witness the unveiling of the *Wayside Cross* erected in memory of Mobile's founder—Jean Baptiste LeMoyne, Sieur de Bienville. As the bugle's last note faded away, the assemblage appeared to have been deeply affected by the touching tribute to the great French-Canadian whose name is inseparably identified with Mobile.

Erection of the Wayside Cross, and the commemorative exercises incident thereto, were sponsored by the *Colonial Dames* of Alabama. Following an invocation by The Rt. Rev. Edward P. Allen, then Catholic Bishop of Mobile, the late Joel W. Goldsby, then a member of the Alabama Senate, presented the Cross to Mayor Pat Lyons, who expressed the gratitude of municipal authorities and the people of Mobile for the monument. Then followed a brief talk by Prof. Alcree Fortier, of Louisiana, who pointed out the fact that Bienville's first colony was established at Mobile, antedating the founding of New Orleans. Principal speaker of the afternoon was Fr. E. D. de le Moriniere, Spring Hill College priest, who painted a vivid word picture of Bienville's career—sketching his life during the time he was a midshipman during the terrific struggle between the French and British in Hudson Bay, and later when he and his brother, Iberville, removed to France where they were commissioned by Louis XIV to discover and take possession of the mouth of the Mississippi River. Fr. Moriniere described in detail the arrival of the LeMoyne brothers in Mobile Bay in January, 1699, their subsequent founding of the colony at Fort Louis de la Mobile, and Bienville's administration as governor of Louisiana. Turning to the Wayside Cross he said: "In this cross Bienville has a monument which will do him as much honor as the colony he planted . . . Let me close with the hope that the Cross erected here today to the honor of their father and founder by a loyal and grateful people, may carry to all generations of future Mobilians the name and fame of Jean Baptiste Le-Moyne, Sieur de Bienville".

The Cross was hewn from granite and rests upon a gigantic base of the same material, each corner of which is capped with a polished ball. Located in the southwest corner of Bienville Square, it is one of Mobile's most familiar landmarks and daily attracts attention of tourists.

¶The year 1905 saw three new directors added to the bank's roster: J. H. Wilson, who served until 1907; Jacob Pollock, who served as director until January, 1915—in January, 1910, he was also made vice-president of the bank and served in that capacity until January, 1913; and L. Hammel, who served as director until May, 1914—he was also made vice-president of the bank in February, 1913, and served in that capacity until May, 1914.

¶The early 1900's, which were characterized by so many municipal improvements in Mobile, were likewise prosperous years for Mobile business—as reflected in the steady growth of deposits in The First National Bank. The bank's Report of Condition as of November 9, 1905, showed $2,316,181.71 in deposits.

¶In 1906, the stockholders at their annual meeting elected Jas. E. McDonnell a director of the bank. He served until March, 1925.

1906—HURRICANE DOES $15,000,000 DAMAGE

STRIKING FURIOUSLY, a West India hurricane roared into the Gulf Coast area on September 27, 1906, and destroyed millions of dollars worth of property in Mobile County. Although only two or three deaths occurred in the city itself, the storm sent more than 150 persons to a watery grave in the nearby vicinity, principally at Sans Souci Beach, Coden, Herron Bay and Navy Cove.

The storm began on Wednesday, September 25th with a driving rain borne on a strong northeast wind. By the evening of the 26th it was impossible to walk on the streets with umbrellas. The barometer continued to drop until it reached a record low of 28.84, fulfilling the Weather Bureau's prediction that the storm would be centered at Mobile.

All during Wednesday the force of the wind increased. By midnight Wednesday it was a northeast gale, and just before dawn Thursday morning it reached hurricane proportions. Daylight found the air filled with flying objects—shutters, signs, awnings, roofs, trees, timbers, and finally bricks from walls and chimneys. Communication and electrical transmission wires were leveled throughout the city.

During the early morning hours on Thursday, the wind veered to the east, and finally to the southeast, backing up water from the bay into the river until it overflowed the wharves and flooded city streets. By 8 o'clock Thursday morning, the yellow flood had reached Royal Street on St. Michael and was running into Royal Street gutters. It came within 25 feet of Royal on St. Francis—or approximately 30 feet farther up the street than the great flood of 1893. Upper Royal Street, from St. Louis to Beauregard, was also flooded, the water backing on St. Anthony nearly to Conception, and almost as far on State and

Mobile County Courthouse as it appeared in 1906, before the clock and steeple were damaged by the hurricane of that year. This building was razed and a modern county courthouse erected on this site in 1959.

Congress streets. Water Street at that point was a surging maelstrom, with the wind driving up St. Francis Street and rousing the water in great waves at the street intersection.

From 7:30 Thursday morning until about 10 o'clock Thursday the storm was at its height. Then the wind abated and the waters receded, allowing many persons to descend from trees which they had climbed to save their lives. By Friday morning, the storm was over and reckoning of lives lost and property damage began.

It was found that all the lower coast had been badly washed, with fully 150 lives lost, including many fishermen of the Herron Bay oyster and fishing fleet, where only three men and one vessel of the fleet were saved. Eleven steamboats and 22 sailing vessels were wrecked, and many others damaged, in the river. The quarantine station at Fort Morgan was washed away when the waves cut a great channel entirely across the land from the bay to the gulf. Scores of vessels were wrecked in the lower bay and just outside.

In Mobile itself, the destruction was not nearly so severe. Chief damage was caused by the flood waters, although the wind tore away parts of many buildings. Nearly every church edifice in the city was damaged to some extent: the steeple of Christ Church was blown away and the interior wrecked by falling debris; the Methodist and Baptist Churches on St. Francis Street lost their spires. The courthouse clock and tower were badly damaged, as were the Cawthon, Bienville, St. Andrew, Windsor and Southern hotels. The Old Shell Road and Garrow's Bend were washed worse than in the storm of 1893, and great sections of other roads and streets throughout the city were scoured away. Gross damage in Mobile County was estimated at more than $15,000,000.

The Mobile area was not the only one to be ravaged by the storm. The entire Mississippi-Louisiana coast suffered severely. Many persons lost their lives at Biloxi, and some 20 schooners and hundreds of small craft were lost at Pascagoula. The death toll at Pensacola was estimated at 50 persons, with $5,000,000 in property damage. At least 100 Malayans in a settlement on Lake Bourgne, La., were said to have been killed.

After normal conditions had been restored, the populace within the city counted itself fortunate in having withstood the hurricane so well. It was pointed out that in both the storm of 1893 and the most recent one, the city proper had proved to be relatively secure against such hurricane disaster—a fact which was later re-emphasized when an 85-mile-an-hour wind swept the city in 1916.

¶The severe storm of 1906 had hardly abated when a group of leading Mobilians began solicitations for a "Storm Sufferers' Fund" to help relieve distress in and around Mobile. Always among the first to support such worthy causes, the First National Bank made a substantial contribution to that fund.

¶In December, 1906, the bank's board of directors established a policy which is impressive evidence of the continuing good management which has always been an outstanding characteristic of the First National Bank. At their final meeting of that year, they voted to set aside a portion of the year's profits as the beginning of a secondary reserve or "emergency" fund.

1907—CITY PURCHASES BIENVILLE WATER WORKS

MOBILE'S last private water company passed under municipal ownership when, on January 8, 1907, the City of Mobile purchased the Bienville water works. For the sum of $350,000, the city gained possession of the private company's pump house and other buildings, its supply source on Clear Creek, its reservoir and the entire distribution system. Only nine years earlier, the city had purchased the Stein Water Works, and by 1900 had completed its own water works at a cost of $750,000. Purchase of the Bienville system completed municipal ownership of local water facilities.

The Bienville Water Supply Company had been operating in Mobile since 1886, and at the time of the sale of the property to the city, its officers were D. P. Bestor, Jr., president, A. W. McCallum, secretary, and H. S. Hopper, treasurer. Those three men met with the city's representatives in the office of Mayor Pat J. Lyons on the afternoon of January 8th. In the presence of the mayor, city councilmen H. T. Inge, Dennis Cashin and John A. Hughes, and C. W. Soost, the mayor's secretary, and J. J. McMahon, the company's entire property was transferred to the city. In return, the Bienville company received the city's bonds to the value of $350,000, at 3 per cent interest, to be redeemed within 20 years by annual reductions. The deed to the city of the property was signed by Messrs. Bestor and McCallum and was witnessed by Ernest F. Ladd, notary public. The mortgage supporting the bond issue was signed by Mayor Lyons, city clerk Adolph C. Danner, and the representatives of the Fidelity Trust Co., of Philadelphia. After details of the transfer had been completed, the Fidelity Trust Co. representatives congratulated the Mobile officials on the excellent bargain they had obtained for the city—pointing out

that the price paid for the system and the bond interest rate were exceptionally low.

For several months the then existing municipal system and the newly-acquired Bienville system were operated as separate units while the necessary connecting work was being completed. By 1908 all systems were being operated as a single unit, and today Mobile is served by approximately 350 miles of mains and has a water plant of 15,000,000 gallons daily capacity.

¶*Ferdinand Forcheimer and D. P. Bestor, Jr., were elected to the bank's board of directors in 1907. Mr. Forcheimer served until January, 1931.*

¶*On March 4, 1907, the Alabama state legislature passed an act authorizing the establishment of depositories for state funds. Five weeks later, on April 10, 1907, the First National Bank was appointed a state depository and for the past 58 years has continued in that capacity.*

1909—DEATH OF AUGUSTA EVANS WILSON

EARLY on Sunday morning, May 9, 1909, there died in Mobile a woman whose charm, influence and attainments made her name widely known throughout the literary world and a household word in Mobile—*Augusta Evans Wilson*. Her almost instant death following a heart attack shocked the entire city, for although 74 years old, she had been very active and apparently was in good health.

Mrs. Wilson was one of the most famous personages ever to be identified with Mobile. She was born in Columbus, Ga., but came with her family to Mobile in 1849 and lived here until her death. In 1868, she married Col. L. M. Wilson, prominent Mobile business man, and their typical southern mansion on Springhill Avenue

was for many years one of the city's showplaces. After Col. Wilson's death in 1891, she disposed of her Springhill Avenue home, and went to live with her brother, Howard Evans, on Government Street. It was there that she died.

Her literary career began early in life with the publication of her first book *Inez, a Tale of the Alamo* in 1856. Then followed such notable works as *Beulah, Macaria, Vashti, Inflici, At the Mercy of Tiberius,* and *The Speckled Bird.* Her most widely read work, on which her fame as authoress largely rests, was *St. Elmo,* which created a sensation. Her last book was *Devota,* published when she was 72 years old.

Aside from her artistic achievements, Mrs. Wilson was a leading Mobile citizen

Augusta Evans Wilson's home, destroyed by fire on March 15, 1926.

and an ardent civic worker. During The War Between the States she turned her energies toward relieving distress among Confederate soldiery, earning the name *Guardian Angel* at military establishments in and around Mobile. After the war, she was identified with many worthy projects, such as the Mobile Infirmary. One of her chief characteristics was liberality of views; it is said that she was among the first to signify her protests against the Prohibition movement by signing an opposition petition to the Alabama legislature; and when Woman's Suffrage was being agitated, Mrs. Wilson is said to have exclaimed: "If women attended to their privileges, they would not need to be keen about their rights."

One of the largest crowds ever to attend a funeral in Mobile, gathered to see Augusta Evans Wilson laid to rest. Honorary pallbearers were: T. C. DeLeon, O. F. Cawthon, A. C. Danner, L. Hammel, J. W. Whiting, Z. M. P. Inge, Robert Middleton and Howard Heustis. Active pallbearers were: Henry Chamberlain, Winston Jones, Peter J. Hamilton, S. T. Prince, C. D. Willoughby, Joe Hermann[18], John Quill and Samuel St. John. All Mobile newspapers published lengthy articles and editorials commenting on her career, the keynote of which was expressed by *The Mobile Item*, which said: "The life of Augusta Evans Wilson is worthy of emulation by any girl or woman."

---

[18] Among Joe Hermann's descendants now living in Mobile is Benito J. Hermann, who operates the real estate firm of Hermann & Hynde.

1910—CORNERSTONE FOR MOBILE INFIRMARY LAID

LONG-CHERISHED AMBITION of Bishop R.H.Wilmer[19], Augusta Evans Wilson, Mrs. C. J. Torrey, and a host of other Mobilians identified with the Mobile Infirmary Association were realized on June 9, 1910, when the cornerstone for the Mobile Infirmary was laid. At 5 o'clock that afternoon a large crowd gathered on the Infirmary site to attend exercises marking that important event.

The program, with Jacob D. Bloch as master of ceremonies, was conducted by high Masonic leaders from a large platform on which were seated the ladies of the Infirmary Association and the officers of the Grand Lodge of A. F. & A. M. of Alabama. After an invocation by Rabbi Alfred G. Moses, the assembly heard Mayor Pat J. Lyons, W. C. Fitts, and Lawrence H. Lee, Worshipful Grand Master of Alabama Masons, praise those responsible for the project and point out that "this building is worth 40 factories." Following the speechmaking, numerous items, including lists of officers of the Infirmary Association and of the various Masonic organizations, were placed in a compartment in the cornerstone, which was then set in place.

The list of officers of the Infirmary Association, sealed in the cornerstone, included: Mrs. C. J. Torrey, president; Mrs. Lee H. Marx, vice president; Mrs. F. S. Parker, treasurer; Mrs. J. St. G. Tucker, secretary; Mrs. R. G. Richard, former secretary, and Jacob D. Bloch, J. C. Bush, Godfrey Mertz, Ralph G. Richards, Ashbel Hubbard, William H. Monk, Jr., Henry A. Forcheimer, Murray Wheeler

and J. W. Phillips, directors. The following were listed as past presidents: Mrs. L. Hammel, Mrs. H. A. Forcheimer, Mrs. W. D. Stratton. In Memoriam: Bishop R. H. Wilmer, Mrs. Augusta Evans Wilson, originators of the infirmary association, and Mrs. George A. Ketchum, first president.

¶In 1909, J. W. Woolf was made assistant cashier of the bank. In July, 1918, he was made cashier and in 1921 was made a director and was given the title of vice-president and cashier, in which capacity he served until January, 1938.

¶In December, 1909, the First National Bank opened a Savings Department. During the 56 years this department has been in operation, it has enjoyed remarkable growth which has earned for it the descriptive title "Where Most Mobile Savers Bank." On June 30, 1940, it had Savings deposits of $9,785,488.02, and at the regular semi-annual interest payment period, it credited $89,218.83 in interest to its Savings depositors.

¶In 1910, J. C. Bush, Jr., was made a director of the bank and served on the board until 1912. L. LeBaron Lyons was also made a director in 1910; in July, 1921, he was made vice-president, and became president of the bank in 1938.

¶On November 10, 1910, approximately six years after Henry Hall became president of the First National Bank, the bank's deposits had climbed to $2,531,128.00.

1911—CITY COMMISSION FORM OF GOVERNMENT ADOPTED

AFTER a long and bitter battle in the state legislature, and a heated campaign for support of local citizens, the old Aldermanic form of municipal government

under which Mobile had operated since 1886 was overthrown and the present City Commission form was approved at the polls on June 5, 1911.

---

[19]Among the descendants of Bishop Wilmer now living in Mobile are three great-grandsons, Harvey J. and James F., Jr., and Dr. Frank H. Maury.

The former Mobile Infirmary in 1910. (From an architect's drawing).

The fight in the state legislature centered around a proposed legislative act designed to authorize any Alabama city or town to adopt the commission form of government. It was strenuously opposed by politically powerful representatives of cities and towns both smaller and larger than Mobile, who foresaw that institution of city commission government would weaken the control of "machine politicians" over various Alabama municipalities. Advocates of the commission form won, however, when the legislature approved on April 8, 1911, an Act entitled: "An Act to provide and create a city commission form of government and to authorize the adoption of the same in all cities and towns in the State of Alabama, etc."

Immediately following legislative approval of the Act, a local campaign for city commission government began. It was led by Mayor Pat J. Lyons (then Mayor under the old aldermanic form) who had the backing of many prominent Mobile business men and *The Register*. In a pre-election statement Mayor Lyons expressed himself: "I desire to say that I am unreservedly opposed to the present aldermanic form of government. There are too many people

running the city's business. The system is too unwieldly and it is too difficult to get results and get them quickly."

After a spirited political battle, in which it was charged that the aldermen were "working every dodge known to politics" and that members of the police and fire departments and other office holders were fighting vigorously against the measure, the issue was brought to the polls on June 5, 1911. Mobile voters cast 2,227 votes in favor of the commission form, and 1,041 votes against—a majority of better than two to one.

Mayor Lyons continued as mayor on the new commission, and Lazarus Schwarz and Harry Pillans were elected as the other two commissioners. Reaction of prominent Mobile business men to the change in municipal government was typified by the post-election statement of R. V. Taylor, vice-president and general manager of the M. & O. Railroad, who said in an interview published in *The Register:* "I believe that the commission form of government reduces to the simplest possible basis the necessary supervision of the affairs of the city. Any business enterprise with too many managers is bound to suffer some, for the managers will at one time or another work at cross purposes. This is true in all business, whether ordinary or governmental. For these reasons, I believe that the commission form of government will be better."

¶*On August 20, 1912, an audit of the books and accounts of The First National Bank (as of the close of business on July 30, 1912) was completed by a Public Auditor. In his "General Remarks" ac-companying his report of the audit, the Public Auditor stated: "I found the affairs of the bank in excellent shape, evidencing good management, with your Discounts in exceptionally fine condition. In fact, your paper is clean and will compare favorably with any of the other banks which it has been my privilege to examine". At that time the deposits of The First National Bank were $3,300,000.*

1913—PRESIDENT WOODROW WILSON SPEAKS IN MOBILE

"I want to take this occasion to say that the United States will never again seek one additional foot of territory by conquest. She will devote herself to showing that she knows how to make honorable and fruitful use of the territory she has and she must regard it as one of the duties of friendship to see that from no quarter are material interests made superior to human liberty and national opportunity."

"This is not America because it is rich. This is not America because it has set up for a great population opportunities of material

Lyric Theatre, where President Woodrow Wilson spoke in 1913.

prosperity. I would rather belong to a poor nation that was free than to a rich nation that had ceased to be one with liberty. But we shall not be poor if we love liberty because the nation that loves liberty truly, lets every man do his best and be his best."

Author of that significant commitment of the nation to a policy of non-aggression was Woodrow Wilson, President of the United States, and the occasion for the utterance was his visit to Mobile on October 27, 1913, when he addressed representatives from Latin-American countries gathered here to attend the Southern Commercial Congress. The entire world turned an attentive ear to those words of the President. He spoke from the stage of Mobile's old Lyric Theater; it was the first time he had addressed a large body of citizens since becoming President.

Mobilians, thrilled at the experience of witnessing the first visit of a U. S. President to the city, cheered him from the time he appeared at the door of his sleeper at the L. & N. railroad station at 7:30 a. m. until he boarded his train at midnight. In that brief period, President Wilson was honored by the Chamber of Commerce at breakfast at the Battle House, moved through packed streets to the Lyric Theater where he delivered his historic address, paraded through the streets, then witnessed a pageant of civic and fraternal organizations from a reviewing stand on the St. Joseph Street side of Bienville Square.

President Wilson was scheduled, and was personally willing, to speak again to the admiring throng in Bienville Square, but his physician refused to let him speak in the open.

On October 27, 1924—the 11th anniversary of President Wilson's visit to Mobile —the Mobile Chapter, Daughters of the American Revolution, placed on the Lyric Theater building a memorial tablet bearing the heretofore quoted excerpt from his epochal address.

¶*In 1913, D. R. Burgess was elected to the board, and served until February, 1915. Among his descendants now living in Mobile is a grandson, A. P. Bush, Jr.*

1913—MONUMENT TO FATHER ABRAM JOSEPH RYAN DEDICATED

IN RYAN PARK, located at Springhill Avenue and St. Michael Street, stands the bronze figure of a Catholic priest, the one hand extended in a blessing, the other holding a prayer book. It is the monument to Fr. Abram Joseph Ryan, the South's beloved poet-priest, which was unveiled on Saturday afternoon, July 13, 1913.

Attending the unveiling were hundreds of Mobilians who gathered to take part in elaborate exercises arranged to pay homage to that humble religious man whose life and works touched and inspired thousands of Southerners and who was intimately identified with Mobile during the 13 years he was rector of St. Mary's church here.

Formal presentation of the monument to the City of Mobile was made by Dr. Erwin Craighead. The monument was financed with funds given by Southern children, ten cents at a time.

Following Dr. Craighead's remarks, the statue was unveiled, showing the bronze figure wrapped in the Stars and Stripes and the Stars and Bars. Cords holding the two flags around the statue were then released by Carolina Randolph Ruffin, a grandniece of Gen. George W. Randolph (one time Secretary of the Confederacy) and Margaret Calametti, a granddaughter of Sgt. John Calametti, C. S. A.

Commissioner Pat J. Lyons received the monument for the city, saying in part: "In behalf of the City of Mobile, I accept this memorial and pledge the municipality to preserve and care for it, and keep the grass around it green in tender and respectful recollection of one whom this city and nation may well be proud of."

Following acceptance by Commissioner Lyons, the Rev. Matthew Brewster, D. D., read two of Fr. Ryan's poems, and Judge Safford Berney delivered an address on Fr. Ryan's two-fold connection with the Confederacy—both as army chaplain and as a poet who "crowned the Southern arms with the immortal story of his verse."

Judge Berney was followed by Fr. E. C. de la Moriniere, the orator of the day, who traced Fr. Ryan's career as priest and poet —dealing particularly with his power as an orator and writer, recalling his matchless courage and patriotism as army chaplain and his heroic work during Mobile's yellow fever epidemic of 1878.

¶*On December 23, 1913, the Congress of the United States created by one of its most constructive and wise laws, the 12 Federal Reserve Banks of the United States. The First National Bank accepted the Federal Reserve requirements, made application for membership in the Federal Reserve System, and at once qualified. To its individual strength it thereby placed behind it the mighty strength of the strongest banking system in the world. During the 52 years that the Federal Reserve System has been in existence, the First National Bank has always maintained its membership.*

Monument to Father Ryan in Ryan Park.

Royal Street frontage of the present home of the First National Bank as it appeared about 1912.

¶On May 20, 1914, Julius Hammel was elected a director of the bank, and served in that capacity until June, 1926.

¶At the annual meeting of the stockholders in January, 1915, J. W. Phillips was elected a director of the bank, and served until January 4, 1922.

¶On July 7, 1915, W. Marshall Turner was elected a director of the bank, and served until March, 1929.

¶On October 18, 1915, the First National Bank celebrated its 50th Anniversary. The bank lobby was crowded with visitors calling by to extend greetings, and to renew friendships of long standing. Numerous letters and telegrams, and gifts of flowers to be placed in the bank lobby, were received from well-wishers in Mobile and in other cities throughout the nation.

¶On November 9, 1915, The First National Bank took over the business of the National City Bank of Mobile, whose deposits for several weeks previously had been declining, due to withdrawals by uneasy customers. During the evening of that day, The First National Bank moved from its old quarters at No. 68 St. Francis Street, and opened for business the following morning in the quarters formerly occupied by the National City Bank at No. 15 N. Royal Street— the present home of the bank.

The First National's decision to take over the National City Bank was made after several detailed examinations of the latter's affairs, including an examination by a representative sent from Washington by the Comptroller of the Currency for that purpose. Those examinations showed that the assets of the National

City Bank exceeded its liabilities, and the First National's agreement to absorb the National City was approved by the Comptroller of the Currency. By that agreement, the deposits of the First National Bank were increased from approximately $4,000,000 to about $6,000,000. Subsequently the liquidation of the assets of the National City Bank produced substantial equities for its stockholders.

¶On November 10, 1915, R. K. Bodden was made auditor of the bank, and served until 1919.

¶On December 1, 1915, M. O. Discher was made assistant cashier of the bank.

¶In December, 1915, when the First National Bank acquired the business of the National City Bank of Mobile, the latter was operating a Christmas Savings Club which was taken over along with the other assets of the bank. For 25 years, deposits in the First National Christmas Savings Club grew steadily year by year. In December, 1939, checks aggregating more than $487,000 were mailed to thousands of First National Christmas Club members.

That part of the First National Bank's present quarters, located at No. 15 North Royal Street, into which the bank moved in 1915 when it took over the business of the National City Bank of Mobile.

1916—MOBILE IS SWEPT BY 85-MILE-AN-HOUR WIND

ALTHOUGH no lives were lost within the city proper, the violent tropical hurricane which swept Mobile on July 5, 1916, caused property damage estimated at approximately $1,500,000. Newspapers in other cities—notably the New Orleans *Times-Picayune*, the Montgomery *Advertiser*, and the Birmingham *Age-Herald*—carried stories placing the "loss of life as high as 22 persons and estimated damage at $8,000,000, causing *The Register's* indignant editorial comment: "Certainly, more was expected of *The Times-Picayune* than that it should consent to be represented by a correspondent so careless of the fact as

to assert that 'twenty-two lives were lost,' when, in truth, not a life was lost in Mobile and the loss of life in the waters bordering the Gulf was only nine."

Within the memory of many present-day Mobilians, however, is the terrifying northeast gale which broke over the city about 5 o'clock in the morning of July 5th. As the day wore on, the wind increased in intensity until it averaged from 80 to 85 miles an hour—sometimes as strong as 105 miles an hour, according to statements by Weatherman Albert Ashenberger. In the late afternoon, the wind veered to the south, blowing the water out of the bay up into the city. At 7 o'clock the water was running two feet deep across Royal Street. A few minutes later it was a foot deep across St. Joseph Street and business houses on both sides of Royal and in the district between Royal and the river, were flooded. Meanwhile, a heavy rainfall added to the water damage, as scores of structures were unroofed.

Highlights of the storm, as reported in Mobile newspaper accounts, ran as follows:

"The Municipal Dock was unroofed and Pier No. 1 of the M. & O. Railroad Co. was partially destroyed . . . The smoke-stack of the Battle House and its two wireless towers were blown away; some of the roof was torn off and thrown to the street below . . . Cotton, sisal, staves and cross-ties were washed out of the municipal wharf up St. Michael and St. Francis Streets . . . Street car service stopped about 1:45 o'clock in the afternoon. Hundreds of people were marooned downtown, and had to spend the night at hotels . . . Scores of persons, including a number of prominent Mobilians, county workers and court attaches fled from the courthouse into the jail. There, they remained until about midnight, as guests of the sheriff . . . In the height of the storm, *The Register* was informed that Mr. and Mrs. D. P. Bestor and Mr. and Mrs. LeBaron Lyons were missing aboard Mr. Lyons' yacht *Princess*. However, it was later reported that the four made it safely to Magnolia Springs, from Dauphin Island where they were cruising at the time the high winds struck . . . The engineers' docks at Fort Morgan were destroyed . . . A big plate glass window was blown out at Hammel's . . . Roofs of both wings at City Hospital were removed by the wind, forcing inmates to move to other quarters . . . The county courthouse was severely damaged, and faces of the clock on all four sides were blown off . . . The courthouse tower was wrecked and rain poured into the court rooms . . . The roof of the Cawthon was ripped into shreds, hundreds of windows smashed and the furnishings of many rooms were water-soaked . . . The Mobile Yacht Club's building was wrecked . . . Many buildings at

Monroe Park were badly battered . . . The grandstand and fence at the baseball park were blown down . . . Train passengers were marooned at the L. & N. station, but were finally rescued after an appeal for police aid brought a fire wagon to haul them out of the flooded area . . . Live wires were a constant menace to life, and power company executives issued warnings against coming in contact with them. One such wire killed a horse at Conception and St. Michael Streets . . . Every house on the bay front from Bay Avenue and Shell Road was demolished. Old St. Matthew's Church was destroyed. At least a dozen houses were blown down in the Oakdale area . . . The Bay boat *Pleasure Bay* sank at the mouth of One-Mile Creek and the *Carney* went to pieces and to the bottom at the foot of Dauphin Street . . . The river steamer *City of Mobile* rested on the wharf in front of the municipal wharves; nearby was the three-masted schooner *Joseph T. Cooper*, a portion of her stern torn away . . . The new mail boat *Harry Lee* was damaged, and a sister ship was reported to have sunk in the harbor . . . The bay steamer *Beaver* sank . . . The mail boat *Uncle Sam* went down opposite Monroe Park, her crew saving their lives by swimming ashore."

Sensational accounts of the storm appearing in other newspapers throughout the nation, aroused a deep feeling of resentment in Mobile, as expressed in an editorial in *The Register* on July 10th, five days after the storm:

"People outside are always alarmed when they read that the hurricane has come, that the wires are down and Mobile is shut off from the world. Newspapers have been known to print in red ink and largest letters 'Mobile Is Wiped off The Map!' but it has never happened, and if we judge by what has been experienced in the past, it will never happen. Mobile is the most comfortable place we know of in which to have an attack of hurricane."

¶*E. W. Meredith, Jr., was made trust officer of the bank in January, 1916, and held that position until September, 1918.*

Typical Liberty Loan parade in Mobile during World War I.
(From a newspaper photograph).

1917—MOBILE JOINS NATION IN ENTERING WORLD WAR

ON the morning of April 7, 1917, Mobilians were greeted with this epochal dispatch from Washington:

"WASHINGTON, April 6—The United States today accepted Germany's challenge to war and formally abandoned its place as the greatest neutral of a world in arms.

"President Wilson at 1:18 o'clock this afternoon signed the resolution of Congress declaring the existence of a state of war and authorizing and directing the chief executive to supply all the resources of the nation to prosecute hostilities against the German government to a successful termination."

Naturally, the declaration of war brought mixed reactions from Mobilians, ranging from strong expressions of approval by those who had come to resent deeply the reported atrocities committed by the German military forces, to objections from

more conservative individuals who felt that the nation had taken an unwarranted step.

But the ink had hardly dried on the declaration of war before Mobile citizens launched vigorous war activities. Members of the Red Cross Service School and the Mobile Equal Suffrage Association adopted definite work programs, and business men of the city over enlistment age and not included in the first call to the colors, called an early conference for the purpose of finding ways of rendering service to the country.

Official inauguration of the war against Germany spurred registration of volunteers at Mobile's recruiting stations. Ten men joined the navy and three the army on the day following formal declaration, and volunteers continued to come in from the city and surrounding counties up until the first draft day, June 5th. Among the most interesting volunteers was a group of 100 Choctaw Indians from Baldwin, Escambia and Monroe Counties who applied for enlistment to J. W. Roberts, at Raburn, Ala. Mr. Roberts came to Mobile and arranged to have them mustered in.

But Mobile leaders as well as those of other cities in the nation were soon to learn that it was impossible to raise a large army through the volunteer system. Faced with discouraging reluctance on the part of younger men to tender their services, numerous patriotic organizations sprang up almost overnight. Principal among these was the *Patriotic Preparedness League,* of which J. Curtis Bush was named president.

The war spirit permeated Easter Sunday services to such an extent as to cause *The Register* to say the following day: "Mobile, as a whole, on Easter Sunday, was bright with the fire of national patriotism . . . reflected in the special Easter programs of the many churches of all denominations throughout the city. In numerous instances *America* and the *Star Spangled Banner* were sung and several of the churches were decorated with 'Old Glory.' Characteristic of patriotic utterances from Mobile pulpits were the words of Dr. John W. Phillips, then pastor of the First Baptist Church: 'If I could put the strength of youth into my body I would gladly go forth and take part in the momentous movement . . . If I can do service by handling a musket or a firecracker I will be there, and when I am not ready to give up all for this great land, then I am no longer worthy of enjoying the privileges which I could not get in my native land.' " (Dr. Phillips was born in England.)

In addition to civilian activities, Mobile bustled with uniformed soldiery. The First Alabama Infantry, comprising many Mobilians, was encamped at the Fair Grounds, and soldiers were assigned to guard strategic points, such as bridges, docks, etc., which might be the object of persons having designs against the country. A unit of Home Guards was organized by Col. A. G. Quina. A military unit was formed by

the Young Men's Christian Association, and the School Board approved a proposal to offer military training in the public schools.

Patriotic rallies were held periodically in Bienville Square in an effort to swell the enlistments during the days prior to conscription. At these rallies, a band from the First Alabama Infantry played martial music and spokesmen plead with young men to enlist.

But despite all the speech-making, flag-waving and parading, it became necessary for the government to draft men to the colors, and on June 5th, the headlines read: *"Eight Thousand In Mobile County Must Register For Service."* It had become compulsory for all men between the ages of 21 and 30 to register. On that day, in registration stations throughout the city and county 7,063 men were enlisted—63 men having volunteered on the previous day.

Ninety days after the declaration of war, the first contingent of troops left Mobile. To the strains of *Dixie,* the First Alabama Infantry marched away on July 5, starting on their way to mobilization camp at Montgomery. Crowds lining the streets and filling Bienville Square witnessed a stirring scene as approximately 1,300 men marched through Royal Street en route to the wharf where they were to begin their long journey. There the last goodbyes were said and the troop ships—bay boats pressed into service for the occasion—pulled clear from the docks and headed up the river.

¶*Like all patriotic Mobile citizens and institutions, the First National Bank cooperated fully in preparedness activities during World War I. In the minutes of the meeting of the bank's board of directors on July 13, 1917, appears the following significant entry: "The chairman reported that the bank had received 310 subscriptions for 'Liberty Bonds' totalling $196,000. The board then ordered that the bank's subscription be increased to $250,000." The First National Bank eventually subscribed many times that amount, as subsequent issues of bonds were offered.*

1917—HEAVY DRYDOCK EQUIPMENT INSTALLED AT MOBILE

SPURRED by construction activities occasioned by World War I, Mobile skyrocketed into a leading position as a shipbuilding and repair center in 1917. In that year, heavy drydock equipment was installed by the Alabama Drydock & Shipbuilding Co., and several similar concerns—the first such equipment to be installed at Mobile since 1904, when Ollinger & Bruce Co., launched at Mobile the largest commercial drydock south of Newport News, Va.

All along the river, shipbuilding plants were taxed to capacity during 1917 and most of 1918. Fully a score of vessels, representing an investment of more than $17,-000,000 were under construction. Among the prominent plants at that time were the Alabama Drydock & Shipbuilding Co., the Henderson Shipbuilding Corp., the Kelly-Atkinson Construction Co., and the Murnan Shipbuilding Corp.

Likewise during the shipbuilding boom times of 1917, the U. S. Steel Corp. constructed its giant shipyard at Chickasaw, but the plant ceased operation shortly after close of the World War.

1918—MOBILE CELEBRATES WORLD WAR ARMISTICE

AS THE CLOCK neared 2:00 a. m. on November 11, 1918, all was quiet in the offices of *The Register*. For nearly 72 hours, news that a World War armistice had been signed, had been momentarily expected but had not arrived. Night employees of the newspaper, wearied by their long vigil, were listening to the telegraph ticker and copying unimportant dispatches when suddenly the instrument clacked the electrifying words, *Flash! Flash! Flash!* ...

ARMISTICE SIGNED!

Shouting at the top of his voice, the telegraph operator roused the entire newspaper staff to action. One member sprang to the telephone and gave Mobile's central telephone office the glad news. From there it was relayed to the city's industrial plants, railroad shops, shipyards, etc., and within a few moments after the ticker had brought the news to Mobile, whistles and bells throughout the city were in full blast.

Awakened from their early slumbers, Mobilians did not need to be told the meaning of the din. They knew it was the message for which they had been waiting:— *Peace!*

Within 10 minutes after the news broke, Mobilians began pouring into the streets with torchlights, flags, banners and every conceivable kind of noise-making device. An extra edition of *The Register* promptly appeared and before long the whole city was wild. As if by instinct, the entire populace turned out to celebrate.

The first gray streaks of dawn found thousands gathered at *The Register* office, where there formed a gigantic parade—the largest in Mobile's history. Employees of the Fred T. Ley Co. (better known as the Concrete Shipbuilding Co.) claimed to have been the first on the streets with a parade formation. P. T. Tuttle quickly got his men together and Robert Ingalls, as grand marshall on a white horse, led the marching column downtown. According to another newspaper account, the peace parade was formed by Grand Marshall L. G. Adams, who with his aides, Harry T. Hartwell and Frank Boykin, headed a procession estimated to have contained fully 10,000 persons.

The parade formed on St. Michael Street, marched to Conception to Dauphin to St. Joseph, then to St. Michael and to Royal to Government, west on Government to Broad ... and then countermarched. All day long the crowds surged through the streets, on foot, in automobiles and trucks ... any kind of conveyance. Men, women and children joined in a happy frenzy of joy that the war at last had ended.

The Cathedral at Mobile.

Some business houses opened, only to close at once. Shipbuilding and industrial plants directed workers to check in and join the celebration. Schools were dismissed. By noon, every shop and store in Mobile was closed.

With the coming of darkness, the exhausted populace joined in one great wind-up demonstration and parade, which included all patriotic and war work organizations. The Student Officers' Training Corps from Spring Hill College, a detachment of the U. S. Guards headed by Major Higdon, and workers from the industrial plants, were among the first to fall in line. The War Work campaigners, headed by Dr. Julius T. Wright, county chairman L. D. Dix and Mayor G. E Crawford, appeared on the streets and did a snake dance to the tune of *Hang Kaiser Bill to a Sour Apple Tree.* Numerous bands interspersed the parade and enlivened the occasion with martial airs.

The mammoth celebration continued far into the night, until the merrymakers were forced by sheer exhaustion to cease their rounds of mad delight. Thus ended the greatest jubilee in Mobile's history, officially decreed by the following proclamation which had been issued from the City Hall early that morning:

"Praise be to God and to the glorious cause of the Allies!

"The days of kaisers, kings, thrones and uncontrollable ambitions in high places are no more.

"It is very fitting at this time that we give expression to our feelings over victory and to our hope of the early return of our beloved soldier boys to their homes and friends.

"Therefore, I, George E. Crawford, as mayor of Mobile, proclaim this Monday, November 11, 1918, as a holiday for the city and call upon each and every citizen to join in all wholesome and lawful demonstrations or celebrations that may be conducted during the day and to this end all businesses that can do so are requested to cease for the day, so that the officials and employees thereof may have a part in celebrating the death knell of autocracy, Hindenburg and the Hohenzollerns.

"Signed: Mayor George E. Crawford."

———————

Mayor Crawford's proclamation that "uncontrollable ambitions in high places are no more" has proved to be ironic indeed. Forty-seven years later, as this volume is being published, the world is again convulsed by uncontrollable ambitions, and world wide unrest.

¶ *Hunter O'Rourke was made trust officer of the bank on August 29, 1918, and served until March, 1924.*

1919—FIRE DESTROYS 40 CITY BLOCKS

IN THE YARD of Howard Cunningham's meat market-grocery, located on the northeast corner of Madison and Hamilton Streets, fire broke out at 3:25 o'clock on the afternoon of May 21, 1919. It was just an ordinary small blaze, but in those days the water pressure in Mobile's southern section was not very high. Soon the fire spread beyond control of the Fire Department (which was later accused of lack of organization and efficiency in that particular emergency) and leaped from structure to structure and block to block until four hours later it had laid waste 40 city blocks containing 200 houses.

After gaining their start in the Cunningham store building, the flames swept rapidly southeastward. It soon became apparent that the fire was beyond control; in a short time a house at Conception and Canal Streets, two blocks away, was on fire.

The fire paused at Franklin Street, between Madison and Eslava, but burned fiercely south of Madison. Houses on both sides of Franklin, between Madison and Canal, were burned, and four houses on Canal between Franklin and Hamilton. It then jumped across the street to the southeast corner of Canal and Franklin, and in the meantime was also burning the square east of Franklin, between Madison and Canal.

When the all-devouring flames reached the east side of Claiborne, between Franklin and Madison, they seemed to be checked momentarily, but flying embers set fire to a dwelling east of Claiborne, between Madison and Canal, and in less than an hour they had swept across Conception, between Madison and Canal, at such speed that many people saved nothing. By 6 o'clock the fire had leaped across Conception to St. Emanuel and had headed directly southeast, taking in the dwellings and the Settlement Home at Conception and Canal.

At this point in the demon's march, a force of several thousand volunteers was on the fire-fighting line. Despite their heroic efforts, the fire reached the block on Canal and Royal Streets, when the Alabama Dry Dock & Shipbuilding Co. sent a force numbering more than 1,000 men to the scene, and they kept the fire from their plant and the riverfront. At 6:30 o'clock it seemed as though the L. & N. repair shops at Royal and Charleston would catch fire, but the company's employees strenuously wet all structures with several streams of water and saved them.

Then, with the setting sun, the wind died down and the fire was finally halted when it reached an open space at St. Emanuel and Charleston Streets and had virtually burned itself out.

As soon as it appeared that the fire was under control, measures to relieve distress were quickly organized. The fire demon had eaten away one of the most thickly populated sections of the city, leaving nothing but a forest of gaunt chimneys. Hundreds of families had lost their homes and everything in them, but relief agencies speedily responded to their urgent needs. Officials of the Red Cross arranged to have Mobile Relief Hall thrown open and equipped to house the homeless. Other organizations promptly followed suit, including the Knights of Columbus, City Hospital, other fraternal organizations, as well as scores of private homes. A Central Relief

Committee, headed by D. P. Bestor, Jr., chairman, was organized and raised a considerable fund to assist the fire sufferers.

Dawn of the following day revealed an area of several square miles gutted by the flames. Between 1,000 and 1,500 people had been rendered homeless. Insurance men estimated that fully $500,000 in damage had been done—$300,000 to residences, and $200,000 to furnishings and personal effects therein.

¶*At the annual meeting of the stockholders in January, 1919, W. B. Paterson was elected to a directorship, and served until February 14, 1933.*

¶*In line with its desire to press on to greater service and to widen always its fields of activity, the First National Bank was fully authorized by the Federal Reserve Board, on February 8, 1919, "to act as Trustee, Executor, Administrator, Registrar of Stocks and Bonds, Guardian of Estates, Assignee, Receiver, and Committee of Estates of Lunatics." Since that date a complete Trust Department has been in operation, increasing from day to day in usefulness and opportunity until today it enjoys the patronage of thousands of Mobile men and women who recognize the value and economy of experienced corporate management of estates and trusts.*

¶*In 1919, C. E. Boyd was made auditor of the bank and served until the end of 1920.*

1920—MOBILE WOMEN CAST THEIR FIRST BALLOTS

NOVEMBER 2, 1920, was a red letter day in the lives of Mobile women. On that day, approximately 3,200 of them went to the polls and cast their first ballots.

Prior to election day there had been much apprehension among the politicians and civic leaders concerning the new situation created by having such a large number of "unknown" voters added to the registration lists. Politicians feared strong opposition from the "unpledged" women voters, and civic leaders felt that presence of females at the polls might precipitate great confusion.

Some feeling was worked up over reports that the Mobile County League of Women Voters allegedly received warnings that members of their sex might be molested at the polls. A resolution from the league, addressed to the Chief of Police and Sheriff, asked protection. Sheriff William H. Holcombe and Police Chief P. J. O'Shaughnessy responded quickly with the pledge that any person interfering with any voter would be promptly arrested. All fears, however, proved unfounded. *The Register* reported on the morning following election day: "Election officers expected much confusion with women voting for the first time, but they state that the majority of the newly

Mobile women casting their first ballot in the election of 1920, (from a newspaper photograph).

enfranchised voters were evidently well schooled on how to vote and in the majority of cases cast their ballots with intelligence and dispatch." Further editorial comment pointed out that: "The women appeared to have needed no urging to vote. They were the first at the polls and were coming all day in droves."

But everything was not harmonious on that first day on which women became electors. The females, conscientious in the exercise of self-government through the medium of the ballot, thought they detected irregularities at the voting places. As a result of their observations, the Mobile County League of Women Voters, through its chairman, Mrs. James R. Hagan, voiced a vigorous protest. She complained about the presence of candidates around the election boxes, about taking ballots away from the polls to be marked, and about the practices of "many" who gave instructions as to marking ballots.

Subsequently, the League was advised by Probate Judge Price Williams that such charges could be investigated in the court in the form of an election contest. While there was much agitation among the women for such court action, the matter was eventually dropped.

Biggest surprise of the election came when returns showed that Republicans had received one-third of traditionally Democratic Mobile County's vote. Cox received 6,171 votes to the victorious Harding's 2,681 in the county. The Republican nominee chalked up majorities in Ward 7 and in Irvington precinct.

¶*As Mobile entered "The Roaring Twenties" the city's business and financial structure was still feeling the effects of World War I. Deposits in The First National Bank, however, had practically doubled during the five-year period, 1915-1920. The bank's Report of Condition as of December 31, 1920, showed deposits totaling $13,414,705.83.*

Old Medical School of the University of Alabama. The School was moved from Mobile to Tuscaloosa, in 1920.

Scottish Rite Cathedral, located on the southwest corner of Claiborne
and St. Francis Streets.

1921—CORNERSTONE OF SCOTTISH RITE CATHEDRAL LAID

WHILE A THRONG estimated at 4,000 persons looked on, the cornerstone of the Scottish Rite Cathedral at St. Francis and Claiborne Streets was laid on November 30, 1921, with ceremonies under the auspices of the Grand Lodge of Alabama, A. F. & A. M.

At 2:30 o'clock the grand parade left the Masonic Temple on St. Joseph Street and after traversing the principal streets of the city, ended at the Cathedral site. Heading the procession was A. Reese Winter, bearing an American flag. Immediately behind him

was a platoon of policemen. Next came George Stone, the tyler, with two stewards, and then the Abba Temple band, followed by members of the different Masonic lodges wearing white aprons. Behind these was the Abba Temple drum corps, and finally the Grand Lodge officers.

After following the formal course of the Scottish Rite ritual, one grand officer communicating to another, the grand secretary read the contents of the casket* to be deposited in the cornerstone and the invocation laid down in the ritual was delivered

---

*The casket contained the following articles: A Holy Bible; an American flag; proceedings of the Grand Lodge of Alabama; proceedings of Grand Chapter, R. A. M. of Alabama; proceedings of General Commandery, K. T. of Alabama; transactions of the Supreme Council, 33, South Jurisdiction, U. S. A.; allocation of the Grand Commandery of the Supreme Council, Southern district, U. S. A.; transactions of the Imperial Council A. A. O. N. M. S.; constitution and by-laws of Imperial Council A. A. O. N. M. S.; statutes of the Supreme Council, 33, A. A. S. R., for southern jurisdiction, U. S. A.; Masonic Manual, Grand Lodge, A. F. & A. M., of Alabama; Manual of Royal Arch Chapter of Alabama; program of the Thirty-seventh Reunion of coordinate bodies, A. A. S. R., of Mobile; program of the Twenty-sixth Reunion coordinate bodies, A. A. S. R., of Mobile, containing a picture of the old Scottish Rite Cathedral; copy of *New Age;* copy of *Fellowship Forum;* copy of *The Mobile Register,* November 30, 1921; copy of *News-Item,* November 30, 1921; copy of the list of Grand Lodge officers performing the ceremony of laying the cornerstone; copy of the list of Scottish Rite Cathedral Corporation; copy of the list of Building Committee, Scottish Rite Cathedral; copy of the list of Committee on Arrangements for laying of the cornerstone.

D. P. BESTOR, Jr.

President of The First National Bank from 1921 to 1938,
and chairman of the bank's board of directors from 1938 to 1940.

by the Grand Master, which was followed by sounding of the Grand Honors.

The stone was then laid by Most Worshipful Master Percy B. Dixon. On one side, at the top right hand corner, it bore the inscription *A. D. 1921*, and at the other top corner the inscription *A. L. 5921* (the date reckoned from the Masonic "Anno Lux"—meaning "Year of Light"). Other inscriptions on the faces of the stone were: *Scottish Rite Catherdal, erected to God and to the service of Humanity*, and the name of the Grand Master.

Feature of the program was an address by Lawrence H. Lee, of Montgomery, Past Grand Master of the Grand Lodge of Alabama. Introduced by the Grand Secretary, Dr. J. H. McCormick of Mobile, Mr. Lee explained the principles of Masonry in detail. Appealing for tolerance, he touched upon the beauty, gentleness and picturesqueness of Masonry and predicted that the Arms Limitation Conference, then in progress at Washington, would result in realizing the ideals of Masonry throughout the world.

¶In 1921, Thomas R. Bartee was made auditor of the bank, and served in that position until the latter part of 1926.

¶On March 30, 1921, J. J. Pettus was made assistant cashier of the bank and held that office until November 15, 1934.

¶In 1922 the Congress of the United States authorized the extension of the charters of national banks for a period of 99 years, and the First National Bank now holds a charter under which it is authorized by the United States Government to operate until July 22, 2021.

¶On August 16, 1922, J. L. Bedsole was elected to the bank's board of directors and is still a member of the present board.

1923—BUILDING OF ALABAMA STATE DOCKS AUTHORIZED

ALTHOUGH STATE AID for improving the Port of Mobile had been aggressively sought for many years by prominent Mobile citizens, that aid did not come until 1923. On September 18th of that year, legislation providing for construction of the Alabama State Docks was signed into law by Gov. William Brandon. The enabling act authorized $10,000,000 in bonds, to be issued as needed for construction of new terminals. It likewise abolished the then existing State Harbor Commission and created a State Docks Commission of three members whose duty was to supervise construction of port facilities with funds obtained from the bond issues. Appointed by Gov. Brandon as original members of that commission were Maj. Gen. William L. Sibert, U. S. A. retired, chairman; former Gov. Charles Henderson, of Troy, and Frank C. Blair, of Tuscaloosa. (Gen. Sibert was also chief engineer and general manager of the Docks for many years).

Enactment of the legislation marked the end of a campaign for Port improvements begun in 1908 when a committee representing three Mobile commercial organizations investigated the Port's situation and reported that adequate service could not be expected until wharves, warehouses, loading facilities and sufficient trackage were provided to insure prompt and equal deliveries of cargoes to all wharves and terminal facilities on the harbor front. In 1915, a vain appeal for aid from the state legislature was made. Again, in 1920, proposed legislation for Port improvements was defeated at the polls in the general election of that year. Thus for 15 years there was waged a constant conflict between the friends and opponents of the Port of Mobile throughout the state.

Finally the project was authorized through an amendment to the state constitution which was approved by Alabama voters in 1922, followed by an enabling act passed by the legislature in 1923. Sentiment of Mobile people and of the majority of Alabamians concerning authorization of the Port improvements was reflected in the comment by Harry T. Hartwell, then Mayor of Mobile, who said: "Alabama's seaport will now

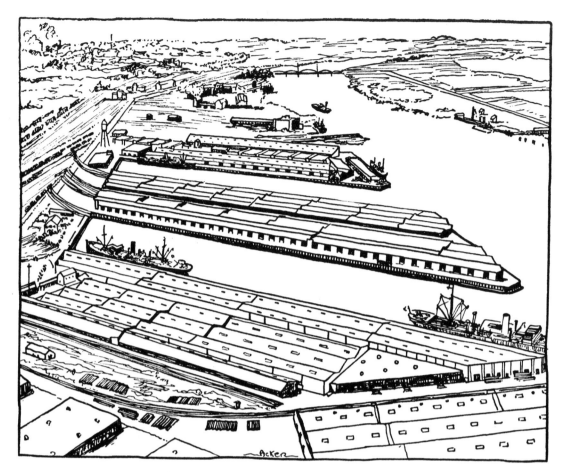

Alabama State Docks as they appeared in 1940.

take its place among the leading ports in this nation and will become one of the state's greatest assets."

Late in September, 1926, the first project, which included a cotton warehouse, was completed. Construction of Piers A, B and C, with concrete-and-steel warehouses, a Terminal Railway, and a coal and bulk materials handling plant, followed. When those new facilities were opened in 1928, they more than doubled the former capacity of the Port for handling Gulf commerce.

From 1928, a continuous program of improvement and expansion of facilities was carried on, until in 1940 the State Docks offered these attractive features:

Four steel-and-concrete piers, accommodating 21 large ocean-going vessels and affording 42 acres of covered, fire-protected warehouses at shipside.

A bulk material handling plant with space for three large ocean-going vessels and a cargo capacity of 600 tons an hour, including a 50,000-ton capacity bulk material storage warehouse.

An up-to-the-minute cold storage plant with modern quick-freezing unit and fruit shed at shipside.

A Terminal Railway with four locomotives and 41 miles of track, linking five important railroad systems at the Docks and providing three marginal tracks at shipside. All ship berths are conveniently accessible to trucks and barges.

A bonded cotton warehouse with high-density compress at shipside.

A U. S. Customs bonded manipulating warehouse at shipside.

Complete equipment, including an electric derrick of 75 tons capacity.

An industrial canal giving access to attractive industrial sites.

When Gov. Frank Dixon took office in 1939, he pressed through legislation which abandoned the State Docks Commission and substituted therefor a three-member advisory board. The governor took this step, he said, because he believed that the body should not have administrative power, as was the case with the commission, but should serve only in an advisory capacity.

[1]C. E. Sauls, who had been connected with the Docks since the days in which they were first under construction, was named director of the Docks and served until 1942. He had served the terminals in various capacities, and at the time he was appointed director, he was serving as assistant manager.

Note: Further development after 1940, of the Alabama State Docks is reported in a later chapter of this book.

¶At the annual meeting of the stockholders in January, 1923, Mark Lyons was elected a director and served until 1960. E. J. McAuley was made assistant cashier in 1923—in 1931 the board of directors gave him the title of vice-president, and in 1938 he was elected a director and executive vice-president.

¶In 1924, H. A. Pharr was elected assistant cashier and trust officer of the bank —in 1926 the board of directors conferred on him the title of vice-president and trust officer, and in 1938 he was made a director of the bank.

1925—MOBILE OBSERVES CENTENNIAL OF LAFAYETTE'S VISIT

IN APRIL, 1825, Marquis de Lafayette— French general who helped fight for America's independence—visited Mobile. On April 5th and 6th, 1925, Mobilians staged an elaborate two-day program in commemoration of his visit 100 years before.

On the evening of April 5th, a capacity audience witnessed a program at the Lyric Theater which included addresses, a musical program, the showing of stereoptican slides depicting numerous scenes of historical interest, and the presentation of medals to student winners of the Lafayette Essay Contest in Mobile schools. Lillian Westbrook, Henry Ogden, and Marguerite McDonald received medals, and John Bell received honorable mention.

Principal speaker of the evening was Rev. Fr. Edward Cummings, who traced Lafayette's career, described the great sacrifices he made to aid the American colonists during the Revolution, and cited George Washington's great esteem and affection for him. Another interesting highlight of the program was an exhibition of Lafayette's signature as it appeared on the register of Mobile Lodge No. 10 (now No. 40) A. F. & A. M. Lafayette was a Mason, and on arriving in Mobile he visited Mobile Lodge

No. 10. The lodge's register contains his signature, which, so far as known, is the only Lafayette autograph now extant.

Facsimile of signature of Marquis de Lafayette as it appears on the register of Mobile Lodge No. 40, A. F. & A. M.

On the following day, the Centennial festivities were continued with one of the most spectacular pageants ever held in Mobile. With Capt. E. Roy Albright serving as parade marshal, assisted by Maiben Cammack, more than 30 floats—beautifully decorated with flags, flowers, wreaths and portrayals of Lafayette, Washington and other Revolutionary characters—threaded their way through streets which were lined by thousands of spectators.

A handsome silver cup, offered as a prize for the best float, was won by the Convent

---

[1]Mr. Sauls' son, Edward T. Sauls, is trust officer of the bank.

Lafayette Hotel, on the southwest corner of St. Michael and Royal Streets.

of Mercy entry. "And a beautiful thing it was, too," reported *The Register*. "There was *Liberty* portrayed by Miss Mary Johanna Hatcher, holding the reins attached to the eagle that perched regally on the radiator of a car. On each side of the float were two American flags woven with 1,112 roses each.

"*Lafayette*, portrayed by Miss Rella Glennon, sat back in a beautiful coach and a very handsome *Lafayette* she was as she viewed the throngs that lined the sidewalks. Sitting behind her was *George Washington* (Miss Louise Norris) while *Martha Washington* (Miss Ethel Miller) rode with the *American Beauty* (Miss Madeline Lutz)."

One feature of the celebration had to be postponed. A bronze tablet dedicated to Lafayette had been ordered and it was planned to place the tablet on the old *Register* building, which was the location of a tavern which Lafayette visited when he was in Mobile. L. C. Irvine, general chairman of the celebration, announced that the tablet had not been delivered in time for the program. It was subsequently placed on the building at the southwest corner of Royal and St. Michael Streets.

¶*By 1925, Mobile was enjoying the unparalled prosperity which accompanied the nationwide boom-times of that period. D. P. Bestor had been president of The First National Bank for approximately four years, and under his splendid leadership the bank continued to forge forward. The bank's deposits, as reported on December 31, 1925, totaled $17,120,872.33—a gain of approximately $4,000,000 during the preceding five-year period.*

1926—OPENING OF MOBILE'S NEW HIGH SCHOOL

ON MONDAY MORNING, April 12, 1926, slightly less than 1,800 Mobile students who had previously been housed in historic old Barton Academy, trooped into Mobile's new high school building on Carlin Street and immediately took up their studies where they had left off the previous Friday when they said goodbye to old Barton. Formal dedicatory exercises were held in abeyance, pending completion of the school auditorium, which was still under construction at that time.

The new high school buildings represented the very latest design for such structures, including ample provision for class rooms, study halls, science work and other student activities. It was the realization of a joint effort by the City and County of Mobile, each of which voted bonds for the project. Originally the City and County voted $350,000 each of bonds for the project; in June, 1925, however, it became apparent that more funds were needed and the City voted an additonal $200,000—thus increasing the total authorization to $900,000.

When finally completed in the Summer of 1926, the new high school plant comprised seven major units, with the subdivisions arranged so as to permit future addition of more buildings for classrooms or other departments made necessary by increased enrollments.

The buildings include the Academic Building, the Shop Building, the Biology Building, the Domestic Arts Building, the Cafeteria Building and the Auditorium and Gymnasium Building, all supplied with the most modern equipment.

Originally named *Mobile High School;* the institution now bears the name *Murphy,* in commemoration of Samuel S. Murphy, former superintendent of Mobile County schools. Its original enrollment of 1,800 has since increased to almost 3,000, and facilities which appeared too extensive in 1926 are "comfortable" after building many new high schools.

Air view of Murphy High School.

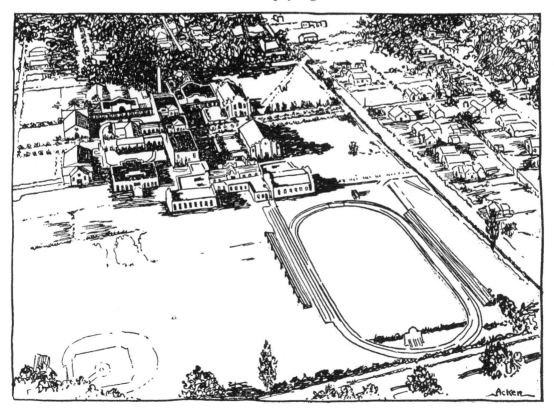

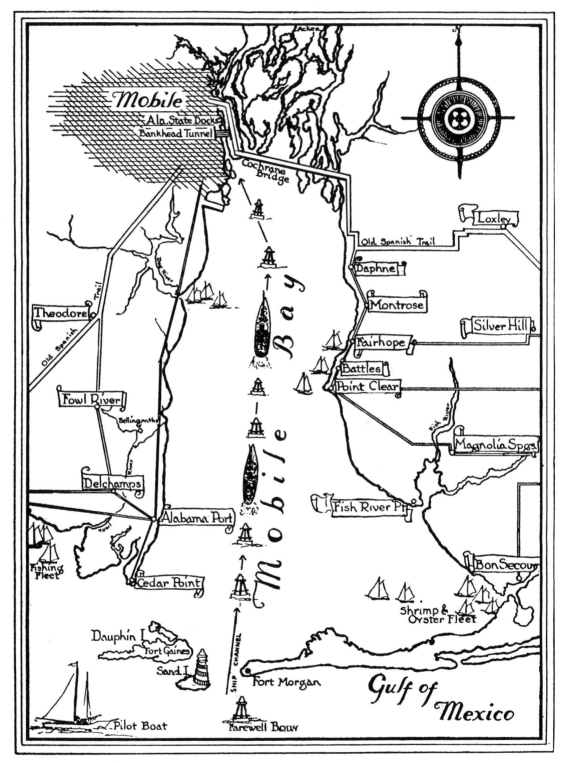

Map sketch of Mobile Bay and vicinity.

¶*At the annual meeting of the stock-holders in 1926 two new directors were elected: Aaron A. Lowenstein who served until 1941 and Thomas R. Murray who served until May 17, 1936.*

Mr. Murray's brothers, Edward,

Richard (now a director of the bank) and James of Mobile have continued the family's association with the shipping interests of the city. His nephew Richard, Jr. is assistant Cashier of the bank.

1927—OPENING OF COCHRANE BRIDGE ACROSS MOBILE BAY

A DREAM which many generations of Mobilians long had cherished, came true on June 4, 1927, when Cochrane Bridge across Mobile Bay was first opened for traffic.

Prior to completion of the bridge the only way to reach Mobile from Baldwin County by automobile was via the old Bay boats which had served as ferries since the early days of the city. Those boats charged a minimum of $3.10 per automobile, plus 40 cents for each occupant of vehicles, and in most cases the ferry charge was even higher than the above figure.

In 13 hours on that initial day of the bridge's operation, 550 motor vehicles representing 11 states crossed the 10½-mile structure, spanning five rivers and described as one of the longest bridges in the world. Toll receipts (at a rate of $1 for each vehicle, plus 10 cents for each occupant other than the driver) approximated $700.

Ten days later, on June 14, 1927, the bridge was formally dedicated and the ceremonies were attended by thousands of representatives from 10 states. Scores of persons high in public life—including Gov. Bibb Graves, U. S. Senator Pat Harrison of Mississippi, Fons A. Hathaway, chairman of the Florida State Highway Commission, many Alabama state legislators and others prominent in public life—saw Mrs. Graves christen the bridge by smashing a bottle of satsuma juice against the rail of the Tensaw River unit. Addressing the cheering multitude, Gov. Graves said: "As I stand here on this last link in the mighty chain* binding the South and the greatest union on the earth together, I feel that I am speaking for more than one commonwealth. It is with pride that I accept this bridge in the name of Alabama!"

Although Gov. Graves accepted the bridge in the name of the State of Alabama, and although the State later took over the financial and management responsibility for the structure, it was not a state-financed project at that time. Cochrane Bridge originally was a private undertaking, conceived by Mobile citizens and realized through their efforts. The project actually got under way on July 1, 1925, at a mass meeting of citizens called by Mayor Harry T. Hartwell, and the late A. S. Towle, Sr., chairman of the Mobile County Board of Commissioners. At that meeting a committee was organized for the purpose of investigating the possibility of a bridge across the Bay. The late John T. Cochrane, Sr.[22], president of the A. T. & N. Railroad, was elected committee chairman and shortly thereafter he presented a unique and feasible plan to the Mobile Chamber of Commerce, banks, and certain private citizens.

Briefly, the plan provided for organization of the Mobile Bay Bridge Co., empowered to issue bonds for financing the proposed bridge. The company organization called for seven directors—two to represent the bondholders, and five Mobilians, serving without compensation, completing the directorate. The plan further provided that when all the bonds had been redeemed, the bridge was to become the property of Mobile County.

---

*Gov. Graves was referring to the fact that Cochrane Bridge was a part of U. S. Highway 90, transcontinental highway linking the east and west coasts of the United States.

[22]John T. Cochrane, Sr., has a son living in Mobile — John T. Cochrane, Jr.

Financing of the project was completed in November, 1925, with the sale of $2,500,000 of bridge bonds. First mortgage bonds were sold away from Mobile and second mortgage bonds were all taken by civic minded Mobilians. Bids were advertised and contracts let in 1926. It took 16 months to complete the building of the 10½ miles of steel spans, concrete trestles and causeways linking Mobile and Baldwin Counties.

Because of his aggressive and unceasing efforts in behalf of the undertaking, the bridge was named after Mr. Cochrane, who displayed characteristic modesty when, at the formal dedication ceremonies, he stated simply: "We started out to build a bridge, and we kept at it until we finished. There have been a few kickers, but nevertheless the achievement is strictly a community one. The bridge is now completed and speaks for itself. We must now capitalize on it and get the full benefits of its use."

During the 38 years that the bridge has been open, traffic has yearly increased until it is estimated that fully 8,000,000 vehicles now annually pass across it. It has proved to be of inestimable value to the Mobile area, and that value has been enhanced by the opening of the Bankhead Tunnel under Mobile River, which shortens by 7½ miles the trip across the Bay.

¶In 1927, John D. Terrell was elected auditor of the bank, and in 1929 the title of assistant cashier was added thereto. The board of directors made him assistant vice-president in 1937, and vice-president in 1938. Upon the death of J. W. Woolf the directors gave him the additional title of cashier. He is now Senior Vice-President and Cashier.

1928—ESTABLISHMENT OF SOUTHERN KRAFT PAPER MILL

IN 1928 officials of the International Paper Co., one of the world's largest, announced their decision to establish the Southern Kraft paper mill in this city.

The company's engineers had previously visited several cities, including Mobile, investigating opportunities for locating a new mill. They were particularly impressed with Mobile's plentiful supply of water and wood suitable for paper manufacture, and were favorably inclined toward a Mobile location. Other cities, however, offered strong inducements.

The company finally agreed to erect its new plant in Mobile, provided the city would give the sum of $100,000, plus certain expenses incurred by the company during its investigations of the Mobile area, as evidence of good-will.

The Chamber of Commerce of Mobile, recognizing the tremendous economic benefits of the giant new industry, promptly organized a city-wide drive to meet the company's requirements. An option on land for the plant site—a tract owned by A. Meaher[23], near the State Docks—was obtained, and a campaign to raise the $100,000 fund was undertaken. When it was announced that the money had been raised, city officials and civic leaders prophesied that it would later prove to be the greatest day in Mobile's history; fire sirens were sounded and there was general celebration throughout the city.

In acknowledging receipt of the $100,000 fund and announcing that the Southern Kraft plant would be located in Mobile, an official of the International Paper Co. described plans as follows:

"This plant should increase the population of Mobile by 3,500. You can readily deduce that out of our $1,000,000 annual payroll, fully 20 per cent of this amount will be cumulative wealth that will remain in the state."

Commenting on Mobile's success in securing the new industry, G. C. Outlaw[24], who at that time was president of the Mobile Chamber of Commerce, said:

---

[23]Among the descendants of A. Meaher now living in Mobile is a son, A. Meaher, Jr., prominent businessman.

[24]Mr. Outlaw was later a director of the bank.

"The civic spirit of Mobile, ever ready to be asserted when Mobilians are called to rally to any great cause, was shown most strikingly during the last five days—days which meant much to Mobile and which will go down in history as the turning point in the economic life of the community.

"Mobile should be proud of its business heads, its industrial executives, its professional citizens, men and women in all lines of endeavor, its civic clubs and its newspapers. All have responded nobly to the cause and have served to strengthen the bonds which hold Mobilians together in one great army of patriotic boosters."

Construction started on the huge Southern Kraft plant on September 9, 1928, and actual operations began September 18, 1929. At present, Southern Kraft's mill is employing an average of 1,800 people.

1928—MOBILE'S NEW PUBLIC LIBRARY OPENED

MOBILE TOOK one of its greatest cultural strides when, on Saturday, September 15, 1928, the new $300,000 Public Library building at Government Street and Washington Avenue was opened to the public. While no formal dedicatory ceremonies were held, a committee, headed by Mayor Leon Schwarz and composed of many prominent Mobilians, were present to welcome the crowds who came to inspect the institution between the hours of 4:00 and 9:00 p. m. on that day. Actual library service was begun on the following Monday by a staff headed by Mrs. Emma C. Harris, librarian.

The beautiful building—a gem of classical Greek architecture—housing 20,000 volumes, represented the fruits of long

Mobile's old Public Library.

Mobile's Public Library.

labor on the part of Mobile's City Commission and Library Board. The building and site were financed by a city bond issue of $250,000, supplemented by contributions from the public. Among the larger contributions was $30,000 by Eli H. Bernheimer; the library's auditorium was named *Bern-heim Hall* in honor of the leading donor.

Mobile citizenry had cause to be proud of their new library. It was described as "second to none for a city the size of Mobile" and since its opening in 1929 has been a center of cultural activities in this community.

1929—ORGANIZATION OF WOMAN'S CLUB HOUSE ASSOCIATION

ALTHOUGH Mobile club women for many years had envisioned the day when the city would have a club house as a center for their activities, it was not until January, 1929, that a permanent organization—with construction of a house as its objective—was formed. Following energetic promotion by Mrs. W. S. Pugh, prominent club woman and civic worker, a mass meeting of Mobile club women was called for January 17, 1929, at the Battle House. The meeting was presided over by Mrs. Pugh and was featured by an address by Mrs. W. A. Bellingrath, of Montgomery, who advised the assemblage how a club house could be obtained . At the close of this meeting it was decided to hold another meeting on January 24th, for the purpose of organizing the Woman's Club House Association.

At the January 24th meeting, permanent organization was effected, constitution and by-laws adopted, and the following officers elected: Mrs. W. S. Pugh, president; Mrs. Harry T. Smith, 1st vice-president; Mrs. W. D. Bellingrath, 2nd vice-president; Mrs. Harry T. Inge, 3rd vice-president; Mrs. G. A. Leftwich, 4th vice-president; Mrs. B. A.

Provost, recording secretary; Mrs. H. H. Wefel, treasurer; Mrs. E. W. Faith, auditor; and Mrs. C. S. Shawhan, parliamentarian. Also elected at this meeting were the following trustee-directors: Mrs. D. P. Bestor, Jr., Mrs. M. F. Kirkbride, Mrs. B. F. Adams, Mrs. John T. Cochrane, Mrs. Ernest Ladd, Mrs. E. D. Bondurant, Mrs. Minnie H. Macartney Pearson.

The first meeting of the new organization's governing board was held on January 29th, at which time Mrs. Harry T. Smith was appointed Finance Chairman, and an aggressive campaign to secure the club house got under way. Enthusiasm was so great that the organization grew by leaps and bounds, and when the time arrived for the filing of incorporation papers the Association's charter roll contained 500 names.

Assisted by E. W. Faith as legal advisor and Austill Pharr (now President of the bank) as financial advisor, the Association filed its incorporation papers and floated a $20,000 bond issue. Site for the club house at 1200 Government Street was selected and initial payment on it was made on May 2, 1929. After five months required to convert the property (which had previously been the residence of the late Dr. and Mrs. C. P. Robinson) the Woman's Club was thrown open to members and their friends on October 22, 1929.

Roll of the Woman's Club now contains more than 1,000 names and the club house has been a center of entertainments and civic activities in Mobile for the past 11 years. It is a delightful meeting place and is considered a valuable asset to Mobile.

The People's Bank, which formerly stood where the First National Bank Building Annex now stands. The First National Bank acquired the property in 1929, razed the old People's Bank building and constructed thereon the modern Annex building which was formally opened to the public on February 18, 1930.

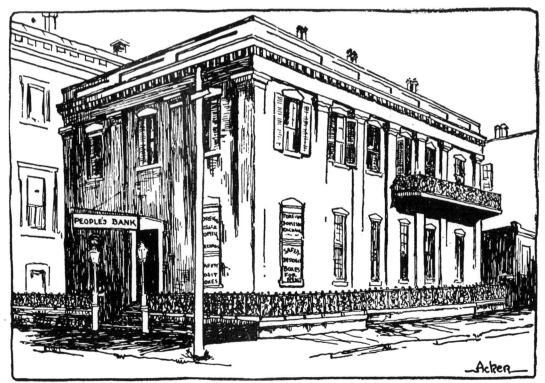

Azaleas reflected in lagoon at Bellingrath Gardens.

1929—OPENING OF MOBILE'S AZALEA TRAIL

ON SATURDAY AFTERNOON, February 22, 1929, a comparatively small group of flower-loving Mobilians formed a motorcade which left the Chamber of Commerce Building and started on a journey through 15 miles of city streets and driveways now known throughout the United States as Mobile's *Azalea Trail*. Arriving at the first sign pointing out the route of the trail, a brief dedicatory ceremony was directed by Sam H. Lackland, retired Mobile business man, who originated the *Azalea Trail* idea. From that small beginning, the Trail has become one of Mobile's greatest and most popular civic projects, with thousands of tourists attracted here annually by the magnificent floral spectacles along the *Trail* and in the nationally famous Bellingrath Gardens.

Credit for opening the *Azalea Trail* goes to Mobile's Junior Chamber of Commerce, who acted on Mr. Lackland's suggestion that azaleas could be made a tourist attraction. For a year preceding the opening of the Trail in 1929, members of the Junior Chamber were busy encouraging Mobilians to plant more azaleas. A special committee composed of Marion Draughon, chairman, with Donald Smith, S. S. Rubira, Jr., Dan Dix and Stratford White-Spunner, energetically followed up the project, with the result that large numbers of the plants set out during 1928 and early in 1929, were found to be blooming when the first tour of the Trail was made on February 22nd.

Following that first official tour, it was announced that the Junior Chamber of Commerce annually would sponsor a movement to publicize the *Azalea Trail* nationally. Publicity material for out-of-town distribution was planned. Standing committees for promotion of the Azalea Trail idea were appointed. Results of their continued efforts during the past 11 years are evident in statistics of the 1940 azalea season, which indicate that fully 100,000 persons came from outside Mobile to enjoy the flowers.

1929—STOCK MARKET CRASHES

FRIDAY, OCTOBER 24, 1929, found business in Mobile moving along at a merry clip. The new Southern Kraft paper mill—regarded as a forerunner of further industrial development for the city—had just begun operations. General business was good. Prices and wages were high. Everybody in the Mobile area seemed to have a job.

Despite repeated warnings from experienced observers that the country's boom times were unsoundly based on speculative activity many Mobilians shared the nation's blindly optimistic view of the future. "A new era of unlimited prosperity" had arrived. The tremendously inflated prices on the New York Stock Exchange "would go even higher."

Suddenly the bubble burst. On October 24, 1929, stock prices crashed in one of the worst panics ever witnessed on the New York Stock Exchange. In the following morning's *Register*, Mobilians read this vivid word picture of the disaster:

"NEW YORK, Oct. 24—(AP)—The remarkable era of avid public speculation in stocks which has swept over the country during the past five years came to a climax today in the most terrifying stampede of selling ever experienced on the New York Stock Exchange and other leading security markets.

"Not since the war panic which resulted in closing the Exchange and other leading security markets for 17 weeks in 1914 has Wall Street seen such a dark and trying day, and never in financial history have security markets been thrown into such a tumult.

"It appeared for a time that the stock market would be unable to face the situation, and that trading would have to be suspended, but the leading exchanges saw the ordeal through, although a few floor traders collapsed and had to be aided from the trading floors.

"By early afternoon, the situation became so grave that a hurried meeting of leading bankers was called at the office of J. P. Morgan & Co., and a reassuring statement issued from the conference by Thomas W. Lamont, one of the Morgan partners, finally checked the sickening drop of stock prices and saved the market from a complete *impasse*.

"Scores of important stocks tumbled from $15 to $70 a share, paper values vanishing at the rate of tens of millions of dollars a minute, until mid-afternoon when the bankers' statement prompted large operators who were reaping millions in selling the market short to cover their commitments, and prices of many issues rebounded substantially.

"Total sales on the stock exchange reached the amazing figure of 12,894,680 shares, surpassing by more than 50 per cent the previous record of 8,246,740 reached on March 26.

"The ticker quotation service fell hours behind transactions, and traders who were unable to get quotations from the floor through their brokers proceeded blindly, save at intervals when a few stock quotations were sent out through the bond market tickers.

"Standard dividend-paying stocks were thrown overboard along with the more speculative issues. Stocks were sold for what they would bring in blocks from 1,000 to 150,000 shares. Traders on the floor of the Stock Exchange shrieked and howled their offers for desperate minutes before they found takers.

"Such a roar arose from the Stock Exchange that it could be heard for blocks on Wall and Broad Streets.

" . . . The stampede of selling was generally regarded by market observers as an unavoidable climax to the headlong decline which has been gaining momentum since stocks generally reached their record high levels in last September. The situation has been aggravated by a glutting of the securities market by hundreds of millions of dollars worth of new issues of securities, a moderate reaction in business activity from record levels of recent months, and liquidation of stocks held by foreign investors, resulting from unsettlement of the London Stock Exchange.

"... Trading on the New York Curb Exchange was also spectacular and the total volume was 6,148,300 shares, a new high record."

Strangely enough, even the disastrous break of October 24th did not dim speculative faith in the future. The rally of the stock market on October 25th was reported and interpreted in Associated Press dispatches as follows:

"Wall Street came groping out of the darkness today as stalwart leaders of finance and industry swept away the black cloud of impending disaster that struck terror to the hearts of speculators and investors yesterday.

Powerful support was thrown in the stock market and hundreds of issues closed the day $2 to $21 higher, having substantially reduced the losses suffered in yesterday's stampede of selling."

"... That Wall Street was able to stand such a shock as it received yesterday was generally regarded in banking circles as convincing evidence of the fundamental soundness of the financial structure."

Despite such reassuring interpretations, "Black Friday of 1929" represented the first slip from the brink of prosperity into the mire of depression that gripped the nation for many years to come. While Mobile did not suffer so severely as most other cities, the generally poor business conditions during the early 1930's seriously retarded and postponed the city's industrial development so auspiciously begun with the establishment of the Southern Kraft paper mill.

¶*In 1929, L. B. Patrick was made assistant cashier of the bank, which position he held until June, 1935.*

1929—FIRST ALABAMA DEEP SEA FISHING RODEO

EARLY IN 1929, a movement was launched at the suggestion of State Game and Fisheries Commissioner I. T. Quinn of Montgomery, to hold a deep sea fishing rodeo in waters around Dauphin Island and Fort Morgan, at the mouth of Mobile Bay. Since that time, Mobile has become a mecca for anglers throughout the country during the annual rodeo.

Shortly after he made his suggestion, Mr. Quinn, who is now connected with the Federal Government at Washington, met with a group of Mobilians, including L. G. Adams, Pat Byrne, George Lining, R. L. Bidez, John Shaw and Sam H. Lackland for a discussion of the proposal.

Initiative in the drive was taken by Mr. Quinn and Mr. Adams, and as the plans progressed, Mr. Adams was named chairman of the first general rodeo committee. At that time, the rodeo had no name, and some of its organizers refer to it today as just a "whale-of-a-big fishing party."

On the general rodeo committee were: Dr. Sibley Holmes, of Foley; George Lining; Mayor Cecil F. Bates, Harry Crawford, Pat Byrne, R. L. Bidez, W. B. Paterson, Martin Thoss and Capt. Joe Pose.

Chairman of the various committees were: Dr. Holmes, commodore of the fleet; Mr. Byrne, housing committee; Mr. Lining, boat committee; Mr. Crawford, canteen committee, and Mr. Bidez, judges' committee.

With approximately 250 enthusiastic sportsmen present, the first rodeo got under way on August 26, 1929 and continued through August 28.

The sporting event went over with such surprising success that Mr. Quinn shortly thereafter suggested formation of the Alabama Deep Sea Fishing Rodeo Association with the view of making the affair an annual event. All details of the first rodeo had been handled under the direction of Mr. Quinn from his office in Montgomery, but the state commissioner recommended that this setup be changed and that administration of the association be vested in Mobile officers.

Mr. Adams was elected the association's first president at the organization meeting, and proved a capable and vigorous leader during the five years he held that office.

Albert Gill, printing company executive and sportsman, succeeded Mr. Adams as president in 1936 and held the office until the election of Martin Thoss in 1939.

One of the most loyal and enthusiastic of the rodeo officials is Sam H. Lackland, who has served as secretary and treasurer of the organization since it was founded. Persons who have attended the sporting event every year say, "Mr. Lackland is always so busy looking out for visitors that so far he has not wet a hook at any of the rodeos."

Each year, the rodeo attendance has grown by leaps and bounds, and numbered among those who participate are men high in public, business and professional life. It is not an uncommon sight to visit the rodeo quarters on Dauphin Island and find an average workman laughing and joking with a state governor, a senator or a millionaire business executive, for here during the short three days of each year these men have one important thing in common— fishing.

Records of the various types and sizes of salt water fish are kept at rodeo head-quarters, and at the end of the competition valuable prizes are awarded.

The invasion of sportsmen for the rodeo each year necessitates the mobilization of a large fleet of vessels to accommodate them. Each year, the event creates a demand for all small vessels from Panama City to New Orleans.

From an attendance of 250 in 1929, the event has grown to such an extent as to attract over 2,000 fishermen annually. Of these hundreds are from as many as 25 other states each year.

The First National Bank Building Annex, located on the southeast corner of St. Joseph and St. Francis Streets, which was the site of the old People's Bank. In the basement of this Annex is located the bank's Safe Deposit Department, and on the ground floor is located the bank's Trust Department.

A glimpse of the Spring Hill College campus.

1930—SPRING HILL COLLEGE CELEBRATES CENTENNIAL

WITH ALUMNI from 12 states and two foreign countries attending, Spring Hill College celebrated its 100th Anniversary with a three-day program, May 31 through June 2, 1930. Also present at the celebration were representatives from many other institutions of higher learning, who gathered to pay honor to the college founded a century before by the Rt. Rev. Michael Portier, D. D., first Bishop of Mobile.

On Saturday, the first day of the celebration, hundreds of alumni gathered on the campus to greet classmates whom they had not seen for many years. In the afternoon, they witnessed a baseball game between Spring Hill's varsity nine and a team representing the Naval Air Station at Pensacola. In the late afternoon a tea was given in their honor, followed by a stag supper.

On Sunday morning, solemn pontifical mass was held by Rt. Rev. Thomas J.

Toolen, Bishop of Mobile. Then followed the centennial baccalaureate sermon by Rev. Edward Cummings, war-time president of the college. Fr. Cummings praised Bishop Portier, declaring that although no marble shaft has been erected to commemorate his work, a monument to him nevertheless exists in the hearts of those who benefitted from his labors.

Immediately preceding the sermon, Fr. Cummings read a cablegram from Pope Pius XI, felicitating and congratulating the college on the occasion of the centennial celebration.

On Sunday afternoon, former classes held their reunions and at 3:30 came the solemn benediction and Te Deum. Then followed the laying of the cornerstone of the Thomas Byrne memorial library. The library was presented by Paul Byrne, of the class of 1911, in the name of his mother, Mrs. Nora Byrne, of Chicago, through whose generosity the modern edifice was erected to the memory of her late husband. Sunday's activities were closed with an alumni banquet at the Battle House.

On Monday, masses for deceased members of the Spring Hill faculty and alumni

were held, followed by the graduation exercises for the class of 1930—at which time several honorary degrees were likewise conferred. Principal speaker at the exercises was Bibb Graves, then governor of Alabama.

¶At their annual meeting in January, 1930, the bank's stockholders elected three new directors, namely, Milton L. Brown, who served until 1941, G. C. Outlaw, who served until 1964, and John E. Toomey, who served until 1960.

¶The directors of the bank made E. B. Peebles assistant cashier of the bank in 1930, and he was elected assistant vice-president in 1937. In 1938 the title of vice-president was given him by the board and he served until 1940.

¶Mobile, like the rest of the nation, entered the 1930's under the pall of business depression following the stock market crash of 1929. The bank's deposits, however, showed only a very slight shrinkage in comparison with deposit totals in 1925. Deposits on December 31, 1930, were reported as $17,029,914.04.

1932—DEDICATION OF BISHOP ALLEN MEMORIAL HOME

PUBLIC RECOGNITION of 20 years of service in caring for Mobile's unfortunate babies and small children was tendered the Sisters of Charity on March 20, 1932, when the new Bishop Allen Memorial Home, located on Catherine Street, opposite Lyons Park, was dedicated. The massive and architecturally beautiful new maternity home, which replaced the old Alabama Maternity Home on St. Anthony Street, was thrown open to the public immediately following the exercises. Sister Aurelia was placed in charge.

The new structure, housing the most modern accommodations for 200 children ranging from infancy to seven years of age, was made possible by contributions to the Bishop's Confraternity of the Laity, organized by Bishop Toolen in 1929, the centennial year of the Diocese of Mobile. It represented an investment of approximately

$300,000 and was recognized as one of the finest institutions of its kind in the South.

Bishop E. P. Allen, in whose memory the new home was named, was the founder of the Alabama Maternity Home—pioneer institution of its kind in Mobile and Alabama. The old Providence Infirmary on Broad and St. Anthony Streets, long unused since the erection of the modern infirmary on Springhill Avenue and Catherine Street, was secured through the cooperation of Sisters of the same organization who conduct the Providence Infirmary. In March of 1911, Bishop Allen and the Very Rev. J. J. Sullivan, C. M., superior of the Sisters of Charity, met at the City Hospital and completed final arrangements for the Alabama Maternity Home. The first child came to the old Alabama Maternity Home on Christmas Day, 1911, and was followed on the next day by a three-months-old baby.

Flower-studded flagstone path at Bellingrath Gardens.

1932—OPENING OF FAMOUS BELLINGRATH GARDENS

IT WAS on a Sunday in 1932 that Mr. and Mrs. Walter D. Bellingrath[25] first invited the public to visit their private estate on the Isle-aux-Oies (Fowl) River. The response was so overwhelming that traffic officers had to be called to help untangle the traffic snarl and control the traffic flow for miles on the roads leading to the Gardens.

Traffic to the Gardens has been continuous ever since that day. For over three decades literally millions of people have come from all over the world to visit a garden that was originally intended to be a fishing camp to provide the owners with a place to "get away from it all".

It was in late 1917, fourteen years after Walter D. Bellingrath began selling an unknown beverage called Coca-Cola to Mobilians, that he and his wife bought a few acres of land on a bluff overlooking the Isle-aux-Oies (pronounced EEL-O-WA) River. There were several frame cottages on the property. Wooden steps led from one down the bluff to a small pier. This was an ideal fishing camp and was promptly named Bellecamp.

As time passed Mr. Bellingrath became more and more active in the civic and business affairs of Mobile while fishing grew to be his main form of recreation. In the meantime Mrs. Bellingrath was able to enjoy gardening as one of her favorite hobbies. As the plants outgrew the grounds around their town house in Mobile they were transplanted to Bellecamp. Azaleas and camellias did particularly well since the climate, soil and cover provided by the trees were ideal.

As the plants grew and thrived so did their enthusiasm for Bellecamp. In 1927

---

[25] Mr. Bellingrath was later a director of the bank.

they toured Europe and visited many famous gardens which made them even more enthusiastic over the landscaping possibilities at their fishing camp.

By 1932 the Gardens were known far and wide as a beautiful private estate. Since their many friends seemed to enjoy it so much the Bellingraths decided to have the biggest party of all and invite the general public to visit Bellecamp. They were so pleased with the results that they became more determined than ever to create and maintain a beautiful garden for all to enjoy now and in perpetuity.

Mrs. Bellingrath passed away in 1943. Before Mr. Bellingrath died in 1955 he created the Bellingrath-Morse Foundation* which now owns and operates Bellingrath Gardens and has certain specified churches and church related colleges as beneficiaries.

Today the Bellingrath Gardens property consists of almost 800 acres with approximately 65 acres landscaped and open to the public. The rest of the property is used for nurseries, greenhouses and a buffer zone against possible incompatible building booms of the future.

The Gardens are best known for the radiant displays of azaleas and camellias which grow in profusion, but they are also as well known as a source of year 'round pleasure for all lovers of nature's beauty. Any visitor finds much to delight him during any month of the year. That is why the Gardens have been so often compared to a beautiful lady, the moods of both are as changeable as their seasonal dress. The natural beauty of the Gardens is attributable to the fact that they have been landscaped into the existing setting.

The camellia arboretum, one of the newer developed areas, has over nine hundred varieties of camellias. Some bloom as early as September and others as late as April. Normally, more varieties bloom in January than any other month. Called by some the Queen of all flowers they bloom in all shapes, sizes and colors. The camellia arboretum gives visitors to the Gardens an opportunity to compare the flowering and growing habits of the many differing varieties under the same growing conditions.

The Gardens has always been a haven for a large population of birds of all kinds. During the summer of 1963 the entire property was designated a bird sanctuary and a program to increase the number and species of birds was begun. The creation of new habitats and the cultivation of food plants in appropriate areas increased bird-life in the Gardens considerably. Before the program is completed visitors, ornithologists and bird watchers will even be able to watch and photograph shore and water birds in a bayou from a lookout tower.

Ideally located in the midst of the Gardens is the Bellingrath Home with its Bessie Morse Bellingrath Collection of antique furniture, priceless silver, rare porcelains, and fine china. The Home was opened to the public on January 1, 1956 after the death of Mr. Bellingrath according to his wishes as set forth in the Foundation Deed of Trust. It offers a wonderful opportunity to those who appreciate fine works of art to not only see but to learn of such things. Guests are escorted through the Home in small groups by well informed hostesses and former Bellingrath servants with a flexibility that varies according to the interests of the guests.

A new entrance facility built of old hand made jumbo brick and iron lace work houses an Art Gallery, Gift Shop and Restaurant. There is even a "Pet Motel" located at the entrance for those who travel with their pets and need a place to leave them while visiting the Gardens and Home.

Bellingrath Gardens has long been known as the "Charm Spot of the Deep South" and well it should be. Its beauty has been enjoyed by millions from all over the world.

---

*The First National Bank is corporate trustee for the Bellingrath-Morse Foundation.

1933—CONVENT OF VISITATION CELEBRATES CENTENNIAL

HOSTS OF ALUMNAE from throughout the nation gathered in Mobile on January 29, 1933, to celebrate the 100th Anniversary of the Convent of Visitation. Under the general chairmanship of Mrs. Edward Grove, president of the association, a three-day program of exercises honored the memory of individuals prominently connected with the institution and re-dedicated it to further service of sacred and humble duty.

The first day's program opened at 6:30 a. m., with a community mass offered for the living benefactors of the community and at 5:30 p. m. there was a pontifical benediction of the blessed sacrament. A community mass for the Most Rev. Michael Portier, D. D., founder of the Convent, opened the second day's program. This mass was followed at 9:30 a. m. by solemn pontifical mass. Also on the second day an allegorical drama *The Eternal Years* was presented at 3:30 p. m. by members of the student body. The third day's program opened at 6:30 a. m., with a community mass for deceased sisters of the community. At 8:30 a. m., there was a solemn mass of requiem for deceased benefactors and friends of the community.

Oldest surviving former student of the convent present at the centennial celebration was Mrs. Anna Stuardi Kenny, who at the time was looking forward to her 92nd birthday. She said she knew Bishop Portier, Mobile's first Bishop, and that she had the privilege of congratulating the succeeding bishops.

The elaborate exercises called public attention to the Convent's historical background. It was founded on January 29, 1833, by a small group of nuns from the settlement of Jamestown, who came to Mobile and opened their school under the direction of Bishop Portier. The Convent was one of the oldest educational institutions in the South when the school closed in 1952. The Visitation Monastery is under the direction of the Sisters of Visitation, a religious order founded in France in 1610 by St. Frances de Sales, bishop prince of Geneva and by St. Jane Frances Fremoit, the baroness de Chantel.

Located in a picturesque spot on Springhill Avenue, part of the original building, which was constructed soon after the arrival in Mobile of the sisters, still stands. Once, it was almost demolished by a tornado which swept the city, and in antebellum days vandalistic bands of *Know-Nothings*, an anti-Catholic political party, set fire to the institution, almost completely leveling it. However, parts of the original structure were saved and may be found in the library wing today.

1933—BANK HOLIDAY THROUGHOUT THE NATION

DURING the first few days of March, 1933, Mobile's banks joined others throughout the nation in a banking holiday.

On March 1st, Gov. B. M. Miller declared a 10-day banking holiday in Alabama, "to protect the interests of the public, bank depositors and bank stockholders." The governor's official proclamation set forth that "the banking situation has been so materially affected by state and local actions in states other than Alabama, as to threaten the public interest and the interests of the depositors and stockholders of the banks of Alabama." Many other states had already declared such banking holidays effective.

When Gov. Miller issued his proclamation the banks in Mobile, all of which were in exceptionally liquid situation, hoped that, even in spite of the growing proportions of the financial panic over the country, it would be possible for the Mobile banks to continue normal operations and consequently no bank at the time of the proclamation suspended payments or restricted withdrawals.

On March 2nd, seventeen additional states declared banking holidays and the situation became much worse. It was becoming apparent that the Federal Reserve Banks could not for long furnish, even to banks entitled to it, currency to meet growing demands. At that time currency was redeemable in gold and at various centers over the United States holders of currency were demanding gold in exchange for it. The law required that currency issued by the Federal Reserve banks should be backed, with approved collateral, including not less than 40% in gold. With the steady withdrawal of gold it could not be long before the supply of gold held by the Federal Reserve banks would be insufficient to permit issuance of additional currency. Still the First National Bank of Mobile continued to pay.

On March 3rd additional states declared banking holidays and early in the morning of that day it was apparent that all banks of the nation would shortly have to close as the demand for withdrawal of funds was increasing everywhere, and sufficient currency to meet those demands could not be obtained. It seemed that practically all holders of bank accounts wanted to convert those accounts into cash. The board of directors of the First National Bank met at ten o'clock on the morning of March 3rd and D. P. Bestor, Jr., president of the bank. issued the following statement after the meeting:

"When the governor of this State on Wednesday, March 1, declared a banking holiday, we had hoped that its observance would not be advisable for the banks of Mobile. Believing that, we decided to disregard it and try to operate our bank in an orderly way. Developments since have been disappointing, as we did not receive the full cooperation we expected. State after state has gone into the column which are observing holidays of one character or another. . . . Faced with these conditions, local, state-wide and national, for which we are manifestly not responsible, and over which we have no control, our board of directors, for the protection of and in the interest of our community and our deposi-

tors, today at 10 o'clock decided it to be the part of wisdom and of sound banking to follow the policy which has now become almost general on the part of banks which have our respect, and to restrict withdrawals substantially in accordance with the plans prescribed by the Alabama State Banking Board and as they may be modified from time to time."

On the morning of March 4th the Federal Reserve Bank of Atlanta, with its branches, did not open for business. It was then practically impossible for banks in the Sixth Federal Reserve District to continue to do business and accordingly the Mobile banks closed—the First National Bank at the time of its closing having the largest amount of cash in its vaults that it ever has had. Other Federal Reserve banks did not open for business nor did any of the banks in the important money centers of the country.

Congress convened on March 6th and immediately set to work on the banking problem. Various proposals were discussed in Washington for reopening of the banks and conversations were had among Mobile bankers looking toward reopening of the local banks should a general plan not be shortly worked out in Washington.

Congress passed the Banking Act of 1933 which was promptly approved by the President and on March 13th approved banks in Federal Reserve cities were permitted to open and on March 14th approved banks in all other cities were permitted to open. All of the banks in Mobile were approved and all of them opened on the morning of March 14th without restrictions. The First National Bank of Mobile on that day issued the following statement:

"We have received the necessary permit from the U. S. Government to resume all business on today. No permits were issued authorizing any banks to transact a general banking business before today, except in the 12 cities where Federal Reserve Banks are located, in which cities banks were reopened yesterday. Mobile is therefore among the first cities to which complete banking facilities become available. This bank will reopen without any restrictions, the United States Government having pronounced it a sound bank, and the Federal Reserve Banks will furnish all the currency needed by such banks.

" . . . Our customers have been inconvenienced—we regret it and are indeed pleased that we will be able to extend to them, beginning today, the same good service and careful attention to their banking requirements that has been accorded here for so many years past."

Thus did the First National Bank emerge from another crisis to continue its career of faithful service which this year (1940) reaches the 75-year mark.

¶The stockholders of the bank at their annual meeting in January, 1934, elected two new directors: Berney L. Strauss, who served until 1942, and S. B. Adams, who served until December, 1938. Among Mr. Adams' descendants are 2 sons, S. B. Adams, Jr., who is a member of the Board of Directors, and N. Q. Adams, Vice President and Trust Officer of the bank.

¶J. R. Crosby was made assistant cashier of the bank in 1934, and Vice-President in 1946 and he served until 1960.

¶V. L. Sibley was made auditor of the bank in 1934, and in 1937 he was made assistant cashier and later Vice-President where he served until 1956 when he retired.

1935—ORGANIZATION OF HISTORIC MOBILE PRESERVATION SOCIETY

IN THE FORENOON of March 14, 1935, a group of loyal Mobilians under the leadership of Mrs. E. S. Sledge met at the Woman's Club to discuss plans for the formation of an organization dedicated to the protection and preservation of Mobile's beautiful old homes and buildings and other things of historic interest in and around the city. Unanimously elected to head the new organization were two women who had long been active in Mobile's civic affairs: Mrs. W. S. Pugh, president, and Mrs. Ed Flynn, first vice-president. Mrs. Pugh was given the privilege of selecting the other officers and she named the following: Mrs. E. S. Sledge, second vice-president, Mrs. Lillian Trimble, recording secretary, Mrs. Tom Moore, corresponding secretary, Mrs. F. L. Tapia, treasurer, Miss Rosemary Glennon and Mrs. Ethel Creighton, historians. (Mrs. Trimble, Miss Glennon and Mrs. Creighton finding it necessary to resign shortly thereafter, Mrs. D. T. McCall and Mrs. J. W. Black were elected to the offices of recording secretary and historian, respectively.)

Meeting again in April, 1935, the new organization selected *Historic Mobile Preservation Society* as its official name, and on January 10th, 1936, the Society filed its papers of incorporation. Objectives of the Society were stated to be:

1st—The study of the history, antiquities and traditions of Mobile, and the preservation of the results of such studies. The preservation of buildings and objects of historic interest in and around Mobile, and the prevention of the destruction of such buildings and objects.

2nd—The collection and preservation of records, books, curios, etc., relating to the history of the Mobile area.

3rd—The marking of historic sites in and around Mobile.

During the 31 years that the Society has been in existence, it has steadily expanded its work and has performed valuable service in matters of historic interest in Mobile. Many markers at various points of historic interest have been placed by the Society from time to time. And for the past 27 years a "tour" of old homes has been conducted by the Society during the Azalea Season. Those "Historic Tours" have attracted great interest, especially among tourists, with approximately 1,700 visitors being registered for the tours during the Spring of each year.

Old Jonathan Kirkbride home, located at No. 104 Theatre Street, recently
acquired by the Historic Mobile Preservation Society as its
permanent headquarters.

Ever since its organization, it was the hope of the Society that some day it would be able to acquire and restore one of Mobile's historic homes, to be used as the organization's headquarters. That dream came true in 1940 when the Society purchased the old Jonathan Kirkbride home, located at No. 104 Theatre Street— one of the oldest and most historic homes in the old Fort Charlotte area. It has been completely restored and is used for many civic purposes.

Present officers of the Society are: Mrs. Sidney Van Antwerp, president; Mrs. Fred Ingate, first vice-president; Mrs. Joseph Locke, second vice-president; Mrs. Micheal Zoghby, recording secretary; Miss Anna Loding, treasurer; Mrs. John Melville, auditor; Mrs. Stewart Dowling, historian. Trustees of the Society are: Mr. Ernest Cleverdon, Mrs. Stephen Croom, Mrs. J. A. Dahl, Mrs. Leonard McCrory, Mr. Roy Smith, Mr. Mylan Engel, Mr. Dewey Crowder.

1935—LIPTON CUP REGATTA IS HELD IN MOBILE

YACHTSMEN representing the Gulf Coast from Florida to Texas gathered in Mobile on August 31, 1935, to participate in the 17th annual regatta of the Gulf Yachting Association, winner of which was to receive the Sir Thomas Lipton cup. The visitors were guests of Mobile's Buccaneer Yacht Club, which had won the cup at the regatta of the previous year. Throughout the entire Labor Day week-end of 1935, the Buccaneer's clubship *Resolute* was crowded with devotees of the sailing sport.

Scene in Mobile Bay during the sailing of the Lipton Regatta.

Feature of the regatta, so far as Mobilians were concerned, was the announcement that the Mobile Yacht Club had again become a member of the G. Y. A. after a lapse of three years. The Pensacola Naval Air Station Club also became a new member of the organization in 1935, bringing its membership up to 12.

The Buccaneers, represented by Ed Overton, who was high-point man in all of the association's regattas up until 1932, Dr. H. S. J. Walker and his son Howard Walker, Jr., made a spirited fight to retain the cup for Mobile but the Pensacola Club won the races by the narrow margin of two points—scoring 39 to Mobile's 37. Overton shoved Mobile into second place behind the Pensacolans, by winning the curtailed fourth race over a crack field of skippers. His victory set the stage for Howard Walker, Jr., to come through in the second race with another first place for Mobile.

Dr. Walker, Sr., had previously taken fifth place in the first race.

When the regatta was over, club standings were as follows: Pensacola, Fla., 39; Buccaneers of Mobile, 37; Sarasota, Fla., 33; Biloxi, Miss., 28; St. Petersburg, Fla., 27; Houston, Tex., 23; Tampa, Fla., 19; U. S. Navy, 15; St. Andrews Bay, Fla., 13; Gulfport, Miss., 13; Southern Yacht Club of New Orleans, 10.

¶*Although still suffering from the prolonged business depression of the 1930's, Mobile had already begun to make substantial strides toward business recovery by 1935. On December 31, 1935, The First National Bank's deposits were reported as $19,142,126.30—a gain of approximately $2,000,000 during the five preceding years of depression.*

1936—BUILDING OF FORT WHITING

ON THE SOUTHEAST CORNER of the fairgrounds, just opposite Arlington Park, stands Fort Whiting, the National Guard armory. Few Mobilians know how narrowly Mobile missed failing to secure the handsome structure.

Early in January, 1936, when a number of National Guard armories throughout the state were being constructed as WPA projects, a committee headed by Maj. James J. Alvarez called on Adjt. Gen. John C. Coleman, in Montgomery, seeking an armory project for Mobile. Gen. Coleman advised the committee that a WPA representative from Washington was at that very moment in Birmingham, carrying out orders to curtail WPA projects in Alabama. Gen. Coleman telephoned the WPA representative in Birmingham and was told that the proposed armory project could not be considered *unless the representative could have a personal conference with the architect and examine the plans and specifications by 2 o'clock that afternoon!*

It was already 10 o'clock in the morning, and the architect—Fred W. Clarke—was in Mobile, as were the plans and specifications.

Maj. Alvarez and Gen. Coleman hit on the idea of dispatching a National Guard plane from the Birmingham squadron to pick up Mr. Clarke in Mobile and bring him to Birmingham. The stumbling block was that Mr. Clarke was a civilian, and civilians are not permitted to ride in military aircraft. The only solution was to enlist Mr. Clarke in the National Guard!

Maj. Alvarez telephoned Mr. Clarke in Mobile and advised him that he was about to join the National Guard, and—whether he liked it or not—he was to enlist immediately and rush out to Bates Field to meet a plane which was coming from Birmingham for him. Details of giving Mr. Clarke the customary medical examination and swearing him into the guard were promptly attended to, and within two hours he was on his way to Birmingham.

Fort Whiting—National Guard Armory.

Meanwhile, Gen. Coleman and the Mobile committee left Montgomery and sped to Birmingham in an automobile, arriving there ahead of Mr. Clarke in the airplane. Given an audience by the WPA representative, they told of the effort being made to bring Mr. Clarke, with the plans and specifications, to Birmingham before the 2 o'clock deadline. So impressed was the WPA representative that he turned to Thad Holt, then WPA administrator for Alabama, and said: "If that's the way they do things down in Mobile, I'm in favor of releasing funds for this project."

By that time, the plane bearing Mr. Clarke had landed in Birmingham and just as he arrived at the WPA office he met Gen. Coleman and the Mobilians emerging from the office, all of them wearing smiles. The building of the armory was assured!

Less than a month after this exciting episode, ground was broken and shortly thereafter Mobile's national guardsmen held a big celebration on the occasion of the laying of the cornerstone. Bibb Graves, then governor of Alabama, was the principal speaker, and the stone was laid by Mobile Masonic bodies. Two years later, the building was completed.

The building was appropriately named *Fort Whiting*, after Julian Wythe Whiting, a captain in the Confederate Army and a member of a prominent Mobile family.

1937—COCHRANE BRIDGE FREED OF TOLL

ON MARCH 10, 1937, almost 10 years after Cochrane Bridge across Mobile Bay was built, the State of Alabama freed it of toll when the Alabama Bridge Authority assumed financial and operating responsibility. Removal of the toll followed a court order from Judge Claude A. Grayson, approving sale of the bridge by Mobile Bay Bridge Co. bond holders to the state for the sum of $2,146,323.56. The sale was accomplished by the exchange of $2,145,000 of 20-year state bonds, issued by the Alabama Bridge Authority, and $1,323.56 in cash.

The new bonds were dated July 1, 1937, and paid interest at 4 per cent. The court decreed that the bonds be delivered in the following manner:

"To the First National Bank of Mobile, first mortgage trustee, $1,420,000 of new bonds to be exchanged for a like amount of outstanding first mortgage Cochrane Bridge Bonds.

"To Merchants National Bank of Mobile, trustee of second mortgage bonds, $640,000 of the new state bonds to be exchanged for $1,280,000 of outstanding second mortgage Cochrane bridge bonds.

"To Horace Wilkinson (Birmingham attorney) $45,000 in new bonds in payment of his fee.

"To Register James A. Crane as master of the court, $40,000 of new bonds to be sold at not less than par, and the proceeds held for distribution under further orders of the court."

Sale of the bridge, to be operated toll-free by the state, followed a determined effort by Gov. Bibb Graves to eliminate all toll bridges in the state. Freeing of all toll bridges had been a principal plank in his platform during his campaign for the governorship. When arrangements for freeing Cochrane Bridge finally had been made, Gov. Graves commented: "The last affirmative promise in my platform of two-and-one-half years ago is now an accomplished fact. That's the last toll bridge in the state."

The late John T. Cochrane, chairman of the committee which originally worked out plans resulting in construction of the bridge by the private Mobile Bay Bridge Co., and for whom the bridge was named, remarked: "It is a glorious day for Mobile. The freeing of the bay bridge means so much to our citizens that its accomplishment carries glory enough to be divided among all who aided in bringing it about."

¶*In 1937, the board of directors elected three new officers, namely, G. O. Cooke, assistant cashier and auditor and he served until 1941, Jas. T. Overbey, assistant cashier, and Cameron Pettiss, assistant cashier.*

INDUSTRIAL NEWS of national interest originated in Mobile on July 9, 1937, when it was announced that a subsidiary of the Aluminum Company of America would establish a $4 million plant here.

The plant, which was designed to produce alumina by precipitating bauxite mixed with lime and caustic soda, required nearly a year to build. It was opened for public inspection on July 22, 1938.

Under the superintendency of Duncan C. Smith,[1] operations began immediately with a daily production of 500,000 pounds of alumina. By 1965, the plant became the largest of its kind in the world with 700 employed and a daily output of over five million pounds. Since 1937, its original investment of $4 million has grown, through repeated expansion, to more than $22,500,000.

The 1937 news that this giant industry had selected Mobile set industrial circles buzzing with interest regarding the city's vast potential. Nationwide attention was focused on the Port of Mobile's modern facilities, as well as the area's unlimited supply of low-cost electric power, its vast availability of industrial water and its railroads.

Within a short time, Mobile was selected as plant site for Hollingsworth & Whitney Co. (which later merged with Scott Paper Co.), National Gypsum Co., American Cyanamid Co. and Ideal Cement Co. Alabama Power Co. announced plans for a new steam power plant (later the Barry Steam Plant) to provide additional electricity for the growing area.

Meanwhile, work had begun on the gigantic $8.5 million Southeast Army Air Depot, which later became Brookley Air Force Base, and plans were formulated for a new million dollar Mobile Municipal Airport. Completion of the Admiral Semmes Hotel signaled only the beginning of a vast hotel improvement and motel building program which is continuing in 1965. Housing and apartment construction also has kept pace.

Waterman Steamship Corp. revealed plans for a new 16-story building and the G.M. & O. R. R. Co. (merged G. M. & N. and M. & O. railroads) designed an 8-story downtown building. Bankhead Tunnel—as the decade of the 30's ended—was taking shape underneath Mobile River. Alabama Dry Dock & Shipbuilding Co. expanded, as did the Alabama State Docks.

At the start of the new decade, Mobile's population had reached 78,720 in the city alone, with 110,805 in the metropolitan area. This continued to increase, with the 1965 estimate of 250,000 for Mobile proper while the metropolitan area neared 400,000.

As 1939 ended, Mobile was breaking from its old shell and beginning to emerge as one of the South's fastest growing cities in population and industry—as the next 25 years clearly point out.

¶*In 1938, the First National Bank installed air conditioning—the first large office building installation in Alabama.*

During the two previous decades, the bank experienced a 120% growth in deposits and in 1938 its loan customers exceeded 2,000.

Due to increasing requests for small loans, a Monthly Repayment Loan Department was opened and later broadened to include insurance premium financing.

At the beginning of 1938, checking and savings account customers totaled 1,231 more than at the same time two years earlier.

The bank celebrated its 73rd Anniversary on October 18, 1938.

Ogden Shropshire was appointed assistant cashier, which position he held until 1939.

---

[1] Mr. Smith was later a director of the bank.

L. LeBaron Lyons
President of The First National Bank from 1938 to 1945.
Chairman of the board of directors from Jan. 1, 1945 to Jan. 17, 1945

Typical of the old familiar trolley cars that ended their last runs
in Mobile on the morning of March 10, 1940.

1940—A DECADE OF TRANSITION BEGINS

THE ADVENT of 1940 brought Mobile to a period of transition—one of the most important in her long history—that was to last throughout the decade.

Europe was plunged deeper into war, and its first effects were being felt although Mobile took time out for a gay Mardi Gras with Reba Lyons as queen.[1] Marianne Hicks was elected queen of the Azalea Trial Festival.

As the European war clouds drifted closer, the federal government condemned 1,000 acres of land along the bay front; and the beginning of what would later become sprawling Brookley Field came into reality.

On Monday night, March 4, Thomas B. Bedford, manager of the Mobile Light and Railroad Co. division of National City Lines, received word that the Alabama Public Service Commission had finally approved the complete transfer to buses from the existing Mobile electric street cars.[2]

The First National Bank entered 1939 with deposits of $24,423,945—an all-time high up to that date—more than double the deposits of seven years earlier. At year's end, 28,674 customers were using regular checking and savings accounts—1,400 more than the number at the end of 1938.

In 1939 perpetual air rights were acquired over the alleyways separating the old Custom House (then owned by the City of Mobile) and the bank buildings. Air rights over the property south of the bank had been acquired several years previously.

In 1939, A. F. Delchamps was elected a member of the board and still serves in that capacity.

Robert S. Bacon was made an assistant cashier and H. E. Coale, assistant trust officer. Mr. Bacon is now executive vice president and Mr. Coale is vice president and senior trust officer.

The final street car runs were set for late the following Saturday night, with the complete change-over to a fleet of 42 new buses at 6 a.m. on Sunday, March 10. The fare was set at five cents. [3]

The day passed without incident, although a car late Saturday being ferried to the Monroe Park "graveyard" struck an automobile on Broad Street near Baltimore. Promptly at midnight Motorman Sam Williams, a 25-year-old former prize fighter of 1002 Springhill Avenue, climbed into No. 143 at Dauphin and Royal Streets for Mobile's last trolley ride. The car was on the long Whistler Route.

Sam soon found he was far from alone. A large crowd of celebrants, recognizing the histrionics of the occasion, dutifully paid their fares and prepared for the climactic journey. Within a few blocks the car had filled to more than standing room capacity.

As the car neared Prichard, the journey was being made in darkness—except for the headlight—as the happy throng removed all interior light bulbs (as well as parts of seats and window curtains) for souvenirs. The overflow, which crowded into the front and rear vestibules, alternately rang up fares on the car's mechanical totaling system, clanged the bell and kept the blatant air-horn tooting.

Sleeping Prichard residents phoned police, and three members of the force joined the car for its run to Whistler. They got off when the car came back through Prichard again and filed a report saying: "There was no great disorder, other than good-natured prankishness."

A moment later, someone pulled the trolley off the overhead wire but Ex-

Pugilist Williams had little trouble in presenting a firm opposition to such tactics.

The passengers, who by now were flushed with more than mere exhilaration, settled down for the final period of the journey and repeatedly sang "Auld Lang Syne" as they continued to rip out the woodwork. [4]

¶ *The First National Bank crossed the threshold of 1940—its 75th Anniversary year—with continued growth in deposits, showing an increase of approximately $3,000,000, (11%) over the beginning of the past year.*

In January, three new directors were elected: Francis H. Inge, who served until 1959; J. A. McGowin, until 1950; W. D. Bellingrath, until 1955.

Three new officers were also elected in January, 1940: W. E. Akridge, Jr., and L. T. Shelton, assistant cashiers; and Miss M. E. Carey, assistant trust officer . . . the first woman bank officer in Mobile, who served until 1945.

Mr. Akridge is now a vice president.

The lobby was remodeled and five additional tellers windows added. Costing approximately $35,000, the improvements included acoustical ceiling, new lighting, additional officers' quarters and a new floor.

Because of ill health, D. P. Bestor, Jr., resigned as chairman of the board of directors. He was elected to the board in 1907 and served as the bank's fifth president from 1921 to 1938.

M. O. Discher, assistant cashier since 1915, was honored for 50 years of service.

---

[1] Niece of L. LeBaron Lyons, president of the First National Bank at that time.

[2] Buses were already established on one line—the Marine Broad Route—in October, 1939.

[3] This price held until June 18, 1948, when the City Commission approved an increase to 10¢, or three tokens for 25¢. Fares have been periodically increased over the years to the current 25¢ per ride.

[4] Exhilaration came cheaper in that day than it does now. Mobile's ABC stores advertised a quality whisky, 100 proof bottled-in-bond, at $1.60 a pint or $3.10 a quart, while a more popular brand sold for 85 cents a pint or $1.65 a quart.

Promptly at 12:55 a.m., on time despite the delays caused by the merrymakers, Sam Williams turned No. 143 off Springhill Avenue and trundled the now obsolete trolley into the barns and its ultimate oblivion.

Many of the old car bodies were later sold for lunch wagons or "hot dog" stands; the steel tracks were either paved over or, if removable, sold for salvage; the overhead strands, which were pure copper, also went for salvage. As for the motormen, Dispatcher G. M. Elliott said that the majority would be absorbed in the new system; the minority (who were either too old or too disinterested to learn how to steer) turned to other fields or retirement.

The city settled with its new transportation and turned to other activities. The next day it went to the polls to select a commissioner to fill the unexpired term of the late R. V. Taylor and, after a spirited vote, Ernest M. Megginson was elected to join Mayor Cecil F. Bates and Commissioner Charles A. Baumhauer in the City Hall.

The war clouds rolled on, and the word came by mid-summer that the National Guard was on the verge of being mobilized into the Regular Army. On Nov. 25, the 337 guardsmen in Mobile and Prichard became regulars, although the infamy of Pearl Harbor was still more than a year away.[5]

Mobile's period of transition had begun in earnest . . .

On October 18, 1940, the First National Bank celebrated its 75th Anniversary with appropriate ceremonies and recognition of officers and employees. Hundreds of people attended the gala occasion and many were the letters and telegrams of congratulations received by the bank's officers and directors.

From an original staff of three officers and three employees and deposits under $100,000 in 1865, the bank had become a widely-known financial institution with some 20 officers and 150 employees.

Deposits on October 18, 1940, were $29,215,504—a gain of approximately 53% during the 5-year period from December 31, 1935.

To commemorate the noteworthy occasion of its 75th birthday, the First National Bank declared an extra "anniversary dividend" of $30,000 and published the famous "Blue Book" entitled "HIGHLIGHTS OF 75 YEARS IN MOBILE."

This volume soon was recognized as a sourcebook of Mobile's past and the demand for it resulted in three printings (1940, 1954 and 1957.)

It is reprinted herewith as the first 75 years of Mobile's history in this book, brought up-to-date as "HIGHLIGHTS OF 100 YEARS IN MOBILE."

1941—BANKHEAD TUNNEL OPENS

IT WAS a cold and showery Thursday, Feb. 20, but at noon several thousand persons had gathered at the Government Street mouth of the Bankhead Tunnel to be among the first to walk through the tube before it was turned over to vehicular traffic at 10 p.m. A large crowd also appeared at the eastern terminus across the river. Varying estimates finally put the 10-hour total between 75,000 and 100,000.

Mayor Cecil F. Bates led the first walkers through at a merry pace that put them across the 3,389-foot tunnel in just 12 minutes, including a brief midway stop to greet the group also walking westward from the Blakely Island side.

One woman pushed a baby through in a carriage and another young girl skated through, possibly laying claim to being the first "on wheels" to make the transit.

---

[5]Major George A. Haas was commander of troops, while Capt. Joseph N. Langan headed the Mobile Headquarters Company and Capt. Robert T. Ervin, Jr. headed the Prichard Military Police Company. The entire troop complement—which also included, medical, signal and ordnance detachments—moved out from Fort Whiting, Mobile, on Dec. 5 to Camp Blanding, Fla. for further training and Regular Army indocrination.

As for the first automobile to cross, several laid claim to that honor. [1]

The toll-house first official customer (traveling westward) was Howard Rayford, who had three passengers: Jim Foster, Bry Shields, and Edward Wagner. Rayford had pulled into line at 7:30 p.m. in order to have that signal honor.

The first eastward transit was made by Sherwood McBroom, who carried only one passenger, Harold Jacobson. Historians will also note that the first dog to be taken through was in the car driven eastward by Walter Cochrane. It was a Great Dane named "Poochy."

The $4 million tunnel, which cut seven and a half miles off the former Cochrane Bridge route which had been opened on June 4, 1927, was an instant success, dispelling many fears that it would become an underwater "white elephant".

Origins of the tunnel dream are somewhat obscure, but John E. Toomey, Mobile businessman and director of the First National Bank, is credited with suggesting it to the County Board in mid-1937. On Oct. 16 of that year he was appointed by Commissioner William V. McDermott to head a study committee.

Within a few months, Wayne F. Palmer of the firm of Wilberding & Palmer, Inc. (with offices in Mobile and Washington, D. C.) had formulated preliminary tunnel plans and devised a financing program. [2] Ground was formally broken on Dec. 29, 1938, and the work was completed in 26 months, a record at that time for this type of construction and engineering.

The tunnel was constructed and laid by the unique "trench system," whereby prefabricated tubes were floated into the

¶As an indication of Mobile's rapid growth in population and business during 1941, deposits of the First National Bank were $10,000,000 more at year's end than they were at the same period of 1940.

Deposits increased more in 1941 than in the four preceding years.

Lee Robinson was elected a director and currently serves in that capacity.

Albert E. Reynolds was named assistant cashier; Turner Rice, Jr., trust officer; and Robert E. Macon, manager of the Business Development Department where he served until 1942.

View of Government Street entrance to Bankhead Tunnel as construction neared completion.

river and then sunk into dredged areas. Seven gigantic steel tubes were built in the Addsco yards on Pinto Island, two being 255 feet in length and five being 298 feet.

After much consideration and no little argument, it was decided to name the tunnel in honor of Alabama's famed congressman. John Hollis Bankhead, Sr. [3] who died March 2, 1920, at 77 after 33 years in Congress.

T. Gaines St. John [4] was named tunnel superintendent. The first three tunnel policemen were Walter Burch, Gerard P. Kelly and George Howard Lambert.

Mobile's proximity to the war in Europe continued to be felt, and on Oct. 11 the Maritime Commission awarded a $97 million contract to Addsco for 36 new tankers, in addition to those already launched and under construction, bringing that yard's total to $134 million in contracts. The newly reactivated Gulf Shipbuilding Co. yards at Chickasaw held $94 million in ship contracts.

The Chickasaw yards—which had been born in the first World War—launched its first cargo vessel on Nov. 15 (a Liberty ship of 10,000 tons deadweight) for the Waterman Steamship Corp. Named the "Fairport," it was christened by Mrs. E. A. Roberts, wife of Waterman's president.

The major political activity of the year was a city election which saw Harry T. Hartwell return to the City Commission. Mr. Hartwell joined Mayor Charles A. Baumhauer and Ernest M. Megginson in City Hall on October 1.

By year's end the population of the Mobile Metropolitan Area had risen to a staggering 135,000.

¶Reflecting heavy government spending in the Mobile area for the war effort, deposits of the First National Bank increased approximately $17,000,-000 during 1942 to a new high of $58,419,866.

This represented an increase of about 40% for the bank as compared to an estimated 23% increase for banks across the nation.

In early part of 1942, the directors advanced Robert S. Bacon from assistant cashier to assistant vice president. In 1944, Mr. Bacon was made vice president and in 1949, executive vice president.

He serves in that capacity today.

Pat Hanlon was elected assistant cashier where he served until 1946 and Leslie T. Shelton, auditor.

The urgent need for war personnel resulted in many more women employees for the bank. At the beginning of 1942, 63% of the employees (other than officers) were men; at year's end, only 41%. The entire staff was on an overtime basis, and certain services were curtailed.

As a move toward better wartime service, Mobile banks early in 1942 eliminated all holidays generally known as "bank holidays." Only holidays of a traditional nature were observed. Mobile was one of the first cities in the nation to take this action.

---

[1] The basic toll for a passenger vehicle was set at 25 cents, regardless of the number of passengers. This compared with the previous toll of $1 per car via the Cochrane Bridge route, later made a free bridge. Prior to the bridge, the only way across Mobile Bay was by ferry-pleasure boat which had a $3.10 minimum for vehicles plus 40 cents for each occupant of the car.

[2] Palmer's figure of $4,000,000 was ridiculed by many who said the tunnel, if it could be built at all, could not be done for that figure. It eventually was, and the figure was raised through a Public Works Administration grant of $1.5 million, while the remaining $2.5 million came from a Reconstruction Finance Corporation loan secured by 4% revenue bonds of 30 years, to be paid for from tunnel tolls. Financially successful, refinancing of the tunnel bonds has materially aided the City and County of Mobile in providing many other projects. Furthermore, its construction was originally accomplished at no cost to the city. Palmer's top assistant engineer on the tunnel project was a young man named Robert Baker, who later became associated in the new firm of Palmer & Baker.

[3] Granddaughter Tullulah, while appearing in Mobile in the play "Private Lives," rode through the tunnel on Dec. 22, 1949, for the first time.

[4] Mr. St. John was succeeded by John W. Little in 1962, who still holds the post. Tom G. St. John, Jr., is a trust officer of the First National Bank.

City Commissioner Harry T. Hartwell speaks from City Hall balcony to group of Addsco workers protesting ferry fares.

1942—WARTIME FERRYBOAT DISPUTE

IT ALL started because of a nickel or, at the most, a dime a day.

Before it had ended, a few days later, several thousand Addsco workers had staged a march on City Hall, some were jailed, and the war shipbuilding effort—of which Mobile was very much a part—had ground to a temporary halt.

At the instance of the U. S. Maritime Commission, the City of Mobile instituted a two-boat ferry system to carry employees across Mobile River from the foot of Canal Street to the Addsco yards on Pinto Island.

¶At the end of 1942, 29 employees were in the Armed Forces. Besides regular correspondence, each received a Christmas check equivalent to his last month's salary at the bank. This practice was continued during the war.

A list of employees who served during World War II on leave from the bank appears on page 130.

¶In 1942 and the following war years, officers and employees of the First National Bank engaged in many phases of the war effort. Typical were:

H. Austill Pharr, vice president (now president) who served as executive chairman of the War Savings Committee for Mobile County; and Robert S. Bacon, assistant vice president (now executive vice president) who served as chairman of the Victory Fund Committee for the Mobile district.

During 1942 the bank contributed much publicity to the sale of War Bonds through its advertising. Air raid precautions were taken and each employee assigned specific emergency duties.

The Addsco work force had grown to more than 20,000 persons (including a large number of women welders called into the war effort), and it was hoped that the new service—at a cost of only five cents per trip—would ease the mounting transportation problem.

The two ferries, bought by the City and brought here from New Orleans, were scheduled to begin service on a 24-hour basis on the morning of Friday, Sept. 17. But workmen showing up for the morning shift found their passage barred at the ferry landing by a small group of protestors who shouted: "Take the one-armed bandits off the river!"

Although officials of Local 18, Industrial Union of Marine and Shipbuilders Workers (CIO), disclaimed that a strike had been called and continually urged the men to report for work in the interest of the war effort, a hard but small core of dissenters refused and began the march on City Hall. By 8 a.m., as the crowd gained in numbers and momentum, several thousand congregated on Royal Street in front of City Hall where a spokesman demanded that the city commissioners hear them.

Commissioner Harry Hartwell finally appeared on the City Hall balcony and spoke briefly to the crowd urging them to return to work. The crowd shouted back that they "would go back to work and build ships somewhere else, but not in Mobile."

As a precautionary measure, Police Chief Dudley McFadyen brought his entire 118-man force into action while Sheriff William H. Holcombe called in his available staff and then deputized 35 additional Mobilians. There was sporadic violence, but no serious injuries, as the men argued among themselves.

Police eventually dispersed the crowd which broke up into various meeting groups that gathered throughout the day, mainly in Bienville Square.

Addsco officials also urged a return-to-work, assuring the men that the City was "not profiteering" off the five-cent ferry fares. The appeals went unheeded at first,

but the men finally agreed to return the next day although a ban on the ferries was still in effect. Many reported at the lower yards on the Mobile side of the river, but attendance at Pinto Island was still slim.

The following day, Sunday, more workers punched their time cards at both yards as the week-end brought cooler heads into play. After another series of meetings that night, the rank and file of the union reluctantly accepted the five-cent ferry toll.

On Monday morning, after a bitter three days, work resumed normal proportions. Aside from the few leaders of the walkout, not many could remember just what the whole argument was about.

————————————

¶During the difficult years of World War II, the First National Bank cooperated wholeheartedly with industries engaged in the war effort and merchants with rationing problems, and actively supported patriotic campaigns.

By the end of 1943, thirty-seven men had been given leaves of absence to serve in the Armed Forces. Millions of dollars were invested in U. S. bonds by Mobile area citizens.

The bank continued to grow and on December 31, 1943, deposits totaled $63,508,123—an increase of 103% in three years.

At the request of the Treasury Department, the First National Bank opened its Brookley Field facility on November 15, 1943.

The bank quietly observed its 78th Anniversary on October 18.

In 1943, Wythe L. Whiting, Jr. and L. T. Shelton were elected assistant cashiers; and J. H. Williams, comptroller. Mr. Whiting is now a vice president; Mr. Shelton served until 1947 and Mr. Williams until 1953.

THE FULL story of Brookley Field, eventual home of the Mobile Air Materiel Area, is too complex and too vast to cover in a single year's highlight but, by 1943—the second anniversary of the giant installation—the civilian work rolls had reached an all-time high of 17,600 persons.

From the beginning in February, 1939, when a special board of officers surveyed the Mobile area for the specific purpose of selecting a site for a southeastern air depot, to the climactic announcement by Defense Secretary Robert McNamara in late 1964 that the facility would be gradually "phased out" as an economy measure, Brookley Field has played a major role in both the life and history of Mobile.

Actual construction first began in June, 1940, on the selected site along the Mobile Bay front and the old Cedar Point Road area of Mobile's original commercial airport, Bates Field. In November, 1940, the War Department announced that the new facility would be named in honor of an air officer, Capt. Wendell H. Brookley, who was killed in an airplane accident at Bolling Field, Washington, D. C. in 1934.

Brookley's prime purpose by this time was airplane modification, and this continued to grow as the war progressed until the 1943 peak. An ocean terminal was added, making Brookley the only air force installation with deep water port facilities.

By the time the war ended in 1945, some 11,500 were on the civilian rolls and went back on a 40-hour week.

Brookley's work was far from finished, however, and in August, 1947, personnel of the 1103rd Air Force Base Unit, Air Transport Command (later known as MATS), moved into Brookley from Morrison Field, West Palm Beach, Fla. The name was changed from Brookley Field to Brookley Air Force Base on June 24, 1948, and on July 1, BAFB began major participation in Project Vittles—the airlift of food, coal and other essentials

needed by Berlin citizens and others cut off by Russia's infamous Berlin blockade.

When North Korean troops crossed the 38th Parallel on June 25, 1950, beginning the invasion of South Korea and America's "police action role" in that vital operation, Brookley activity took on a new spurt.

New construction—including the Wherry Housing Project—was placed into effect and, as events around the globe took on new sinister signs, the civilian work force by January 1, 1953, had risen to 14,161. By October, MOAMA's new Directorate of Procurement and Production became operational and another 2,000 were added to the civilian rolls. MOAMA became responsible, or "prime," for the worldwide logistics support of several weapons systems.

On September 22, 1954, the U. S. Government acquired 5.36 acres of land on Dauphin Island from the Mobile Chamber of Commerce for one dollar and 67 acres from the State of Alabama for the same amount. Total value of this land was established at $108,540. The area was acquired for location of a radar station, air-sea rescue base and recreational facility.

In January, 1955, MOAMA assumed area support for states of West Virginia, Ohio, Indiana, and the southern peninsula of Michigan and, in May, acquired command jurisdiction of the Baton Rouge Air Force Station. In May some 30,000 visitors attended "open house" commemorating Armed Forces Day. The importance of this great Air Force Base was recognized by the fact that the principal speaker for the ceremony was Donald A. Quarles, assistant secretary of defense for research and development.

The start of 1956 saw Brookley's civilian force at more than 15,000 and Congress voted $1,541,000 for the acquisition of more land and construction of additional housing and community facilities. Brookley's civilian payroll for the fiscal year ending June 30 was in excess of $69,923,000. The secretary of defense next delegated to the Air Force the sole operational responsibility for the use of land-based intermediate range ballistic missiles (IRBMs) of over 200-mile range. This was a prelude to MOAMA's entry into the ballistic missile program, since the Mobile headquaters was slated to become the logistics support manager for the Jupiter IRBM on February 27, 1958.

As the years progressed Brookley continued its worldwide logistics support of the U. S. Air Force.

At the time of McNamara's decision to "phase out" this huge base, its resources included some 2,000 acres of land at Brookley proper and 94 on Dauphin Island,[1] with an over-all replacement value estimated at $253,700,000. Also 29 miles of roads with eight miles of railroad track; two major runways—one of them 9,600 feet long and the other one 8,852 feet; more than a million and a half square feet of covered maintenance space and covered warehouse space of 2,600,000 square feet.

The employees at Brookley have long been recognized for their generosity to their fellow man, consistently being a leader in United Fund and other local charity drives.

¶*In 1944, six more employees of the First National Bank were given leaves of absence for the Armed Forces, making a total of 43.*

The bank took an active part in the three war loan drives and, among other patriotic activities, provided facilities for the purchase and cashing of war bonds.

¶*On January 11, 1944, the bank's directors promoted James T. Overbey and Robert S. Bacon to vice presidents, and J. R. Crosby to assistant vice president.*

On April 14 of that year, Turner Rice, Jr. became assistant vice president and trust officer.

1945—HISTORIC TRINITY EPISCOPAL CHURCH HOLDS FINAL DOWNTOWN SERVICE

"IN THE name of God, amen . . . "

These words, pronounced by Dr. Herbert F. Schroeter, the rector, as he stood before the altar of historic Trinity Episcopal Church on Sunday, Sept. 9, solemnized the end of the consecration of the 92-year-old edifice at St. Anthony and Jackson Streets.

Miss Abbie Hudson led the choir for its last hymn downtown.

The next day workmen began dismantling the old house of worship to move many parts of it to the new site of Trinity Chapel on Dauphin at Rickarby Streets, which had been obtained in 1932 in anticipation of just such a move.

At the final 11 a.m. service, Dr. Schroeter (who had been rector since 1925) read the letter revoking the consecration of the building and grounds. Under authority of the Rt. Rev. C. C. J. Carpenter, bishop of Alabama, the white-robed rector closed the Holy Book on the altar, extinguished the flame of the Eucharistic candle and carried from the sanctuary the Instrument of Consecration that had been placed there 67 years previous by Bishop Richard Hooker Wilmer.

During its 92 years, Trinity had had only one interruption in its services when, in 1865 during a time when Federal troops occupied Mobile, this same Bishop Wilmer

---

[1]The facility on Dauphin Island will not be affected by any eventual "phase-out" of Brookley Air Force Base, since it is a radar unit of the Air Defense Command, while Brookley is under the Air Force Logistics Command.

**Trinity Episcopal Church as it appeared in 1878 at St. Anthony
and Jackson Streets, before steeple was added in 1884.**

directed his clergy not to pray for the
President of the United States (an integral
part of the Episcopal liturgy) and the
church was closed and the bishop arrested.
He later appealed to President Lincoln,
who agreed with the bishop that the military had exceeded its authority. Bishop
Wilmer was freed, but history does not

record whether or not the Presidential
prayer was immediately renewed.

Trinity Parish was originally founded in
1845, but a church was not built until
1853. Dr. J. A. Massey directed its building and remained as rector until 1878 when
the building debt was paid off and the

E. J. McAuley
President of The First National Bank from 1945 to 1947.
Chairman of the board of directors from July 7, 1947 to May 15, 1948.

consecration took place. The church remained in its original state except for the erection of a tall spire in 1884.

Reporter John Will[1] wrote in the Monday Mobile Register that before the final ceremonies, "scores of Trinity parishioners knelt at the altar rail to receive the last Holy Communion in the time-mellowed church. They bowed, many with white and aging heads, to hear for the last time the strains of the 'Sanctus' in the vaulted interior as the priest prepared to bless the elements."

Relocation of the church was completed in 1946 and it was re-consecrated in 1950.

¶*On January 9, 1945, Ernest J. McAuley, executive vice president, became the seventh president of the First National Bank, succeeding L. LeBaron Lyons, who was elected chairman of the board.*

The board also elected H. Austill Pharr executive vice president of the bank.

Mr. Lyons' death occurred shortly thereafter.

Mr. McAuley was named assistant cashier in 1923 and vice president in 1931. In 1938 he was elected a director and made executive vice president.

¶*In 1945, A. S. Brueggemann was elected vice president in charge of the Foreign Department and served until 1951; and Henri S. Aldridge, assistant vice president in charge of the newly-created Dealers' Installment Loan Department.*

Mr. Aldridge had served for several years as building manager.

Turner Rice, Jr. was elected vice president and trust officer; a position he held until 1950.

¶*Interesting advertisements quoting experiences of bank employees in the Armed Forces were published in 1944-45.*

These included letters and photographs from Wythe L. Whiting, Jr., A. D. Smith, John P. Sweeney, Thomas B. Rhodes, Jr., Miss Dorsey H. Ford, F. W. Drey, Robert F. Casey, William H. Sadler, Marion G. Kearley and Danner Frazer.

The names of all employees who served in the Armed Forces—and when inducted—appear on page 130.

Deposits on the bank's 80th Anniversary (October 18, 1945) totaled $73,654,526—a gain of 21% in two years.

1945—VANGUARD OF POST-WAR GHOST FLEET ANCHORED IN MOBILE RIVER

MAINLY THROUGH the efforts of Mobile's Congressman Frank W. Boykin, Mobile was selected by the War Shipping Administration and the U. S. Maritime Commission as one of the sites for storing battle-scarred merchant ships.

The local site was four miles up the Mobile River along a five-mile stretch running from Chickasawbogue to Bayou Sara. Other early locations were in Norfolk, Va., and on the West Coast.

Mr. Boykin told U. S. officials that there was space for 500 ships in the Mobile area and pointed out that some 75 had been stored here following the conclusion of World War I.

The first ship towed to the area was a merchantman, the SS Elwood, which arrived by Aug. 20. In short order, more and more came. John O. Sieber, port captain for the WSA, said the Mobile location

---

[1]On April 3, 1965, Mr. Will was stricken on a downtown street after covering a newspaper assignment. He died a few moments later in Mobile Infirmary. A native of Michigan, Mr. Will had spent more than 25 of his 60 years working on Mobile newspapers.

**Battle-scarred ships come to rest in vanguard of ghost "mothball" fleet
four miles up Mobile River.**

was "ideal as there is practically no tide and the water is fresh (thus minimizing rust)."

By Sept. 9, the total reached 12 tankers and 17 cargo vessels as well as other smaller ships.[1]

When the war ended, many merchantmen and T-2 tankers—as well as Liberty ships—were retired from service, some permanently and some on stand by basis. A new site was added another 10 miles up the Mobile River, and when this did not prove sufficient, a two-mile-long channel was cut to connect Mobile and Tensaw Rivers. In

the Tensaw River a new anchorage was created.

At its peak late in 1946, the Tensaw fleet consisted of 286 ships riding quietly at anchor. Early in 1947, more than 100 vessels were removed to haul wheat and coal to a hungry, cold Europe.

But the crisis of cold and famine passed, as Europe regained its own stability, and many of the ships returned to Tensaw.

In mid-1965, Capt. George S. Britt, fleet superintendent, said there were 232 ships in storage at the site and they have a replacement value in excess of $2 billion.[2]

---

[1]Meanwhile, Alabama Dry Dock & Shipbuilding Co. was completing its long and honorable service as a wartime contract-builder and repairer of ships. On Nov. 20, it delivered its last T-2 oil carrier, the 22,400-ton SS Black River. In all, 102 of the T-2 carriers were built at Addsco as well as 20 Liberty ships. Countless others were repaired and converted in Addsco's "lower yards" on the west side of Mobile River.

[2]The SS Jean Lafitte, which joined the "Ghost Fleet" in the summer of 1965, was the first Mobile-built ship to drop anchor in the Tensaw group.

FIRST NATIONAL EMPLOYEES WHO SERVED IN THE ARMED FORCES DURING WORLD WAR II

NAME	INDUCTED
Elbert M. Steiner	November 24, 1940
John P. Sweeney, Jr.	November 24, 1940
Thomas Rhodes	February 24, 1941
Walter Smith	March 31, 1941
*Jack Taylor	April 15, 1941
R. Walter Ogburn, Jr.	April 30, 1941
William Rowell, Jr.	May 15, 1941
Clyde Hunter, Jr.	June 15, 1941
Thomas G. St. John	June 30, 1941
W. E. Akridge, Jr.	June 30, 1941
James E. Ballweg	August 15, 1941
Marion G. Kearley	August 15, 1941
Frank W. Drey	December 15, 1941
E. S. Sledge, II	February 7, 1942
C. A. Helmer	February 7, 1942
Lee R. Seifert	March 15, 1942
R. B. Dunlap	March 15, 1942
William B. Inge	March 15, 1942
W. T. Moseley	March 28, 1942
A. D. (Pete) Smith	June 8, 1942
L. Conway Edhegard	July 10, 1942
A. Danner Frazer	July 23, 1942
James A. Casteel, Jr.	August 5, 1942
James C. Andress	September 10, 1942
John W. Stephenson	November 2, 1942
James C. Cook	December 16, 1942
T. Redmond Foster	December 29, 1942
Allan H. Blacklidge, Jr.	December 30, 1942
I. L. Davis, Jr.	January 22, 1943
Joe C. Oxley	February 1, 1943
Travis McKenzie, Jr.	February 2, 1943
Wm. H. Sadler, Jr.	February 13, 1943
Robert F. Casey	March 16, 1943
Roy H. Anderson	March 26, 1943
J. Wyatt Pettiss	June 4, 1943
Louis B. Swingle	June 17, 1943
Clarence E. Davis	August 14, 1943
W. L. Whiting, Jr.	December 14, 1943
V. L. Sibley	January 15, 1944
Charles E. VanDevender	March 24, 1944
Dillon A. Toomer	August 18, 1944
Miss Dorsey H. Ford	August 31, 1944
Owen Layman	November 28, 1944

*Died in line of duty May 20, 1942.

First National will always be proud of its 43 employees (42 men and one woman) who entered the Armed Forces during World War II.

1946—MARDI GRAS RETURNS AFTER 5-YEAR ABSENCE

MOBILE emerged from the war years with a fervent desire to get back to normalcy as soon as possible, and one of the main things on the list was resumption of the Mardi Gras celebration which had been suspended since 1941.

On Jan. 19, a meeting was called by Carnival Association President Alfred L. Staples,[1] and the four parading mystic societies (The Krewe of Columbus, Infant Mystics, Knights of Revelry and Order of Myths) voted to resume parades if at all possible. However, due to the shortage of eligible males and no plans for a debutante season, it was not determined whether there would be a court with king and queen.

As time went on, however, the prospects brightened and 18-year-old Aletta Lyons[2] became queen and James Roy Albright, 32, was named king. The first lady-in-waiting was Barbara Sherard Powell; others were Jeanne Thompson Alverez and Mabel Moore Bedsole.[3]

Things did look normal once more when the Krewe of Columbus staged its 7-float parade on Friday night, March 1, to bring Mardi Gras back to Mobile. On Saturday, the 14-float Floral Parade, under the chairmanship of Sidney Simon, was presented.

The coronation of Queen Aletta was held in glittering splendor at Fort Whiting, marking a change of locale from the Mobile Municipal Wharf where previous coronations had been held for many years.

Two U. S. Destroyers—the Gearing and the Gyatt—tied up at the L. & N. wharf. On Monday, King Felix paraded in the afternoon, and the Infant Mystics resumed at night, using mules from the Atmore Prison Farm to pull its 8-float spectacle of "Jack and the Beanstalk."

The city gave way to full joy on Mardi Gras Day, and another "first" was scored when the queen rode with the king on his float for the initial time.

The Knights of Revelry, also using mules, presented the "Legend of Rapa-Nui," a fantasy of Easter Island, and the Comic Cowboys poked fun at Mobile's plan to impose a $1,000 license fee on fortune tellers and spoofed the red tape of obtaining "GI Loans" by showing ex-servicemen standing around in barrels.

The Order of Myths, in traditional style, brought the fun and frolic to an end Tuesday night with a gala parade depicting the "Mystic of the Red Man" in seven mule-drawn floats followed by a final ball at Ft. Whiting.

Mardi Gras had indeed returned to Mobile—the original Mother of Mystics—and the following day, Ash Wednesday, Lester H. Myers, city street superintendent, estimated that his crews cleaned up a total of 25 tons of serpentine and confetti.

¶*During 1946, the First National Bank made 13,468 new loans, exclusive of renewal loans and loans made by the Trust Department.*

Loans and discounts on Dec. 31, 1946 totaled $16,400,000, an increase of $6,600,000 (65%) over the close of 1945.

The bank had 3,823 more borrowing customers than the year before.

¶*In 1946, the Trust Department was enlarged by the addition of a modern mezzanine, affording customers more comfortable and attractive surroundings.*

Because of the rapidly increasing volume of business, the staff of the Monthly Repayment Loan Department was enlarged. J. P. Hanlon, assistant cashier, was transferred to it.

---

[1]Mr. Staples is the grandfather of Staples Shearer, assistant cashier of the bank.
[2]Miss Lyons is the granddaughter of L. La Baron Lyons, former chairman of the board.
[3]Miss Bedsole is the niece of J. L. Bedsole, director of the bank.

H. Austill Pharr
President of The First National Bank since July 7, 1947.

1948—MOBILE "TOUCHDOWN CLUB" IS FORMED

THE MOBILE Touchdown Club, Inc., a non-profit organization which now consists of some 450 business and civic leaders, was organized in 1948 for the purpose of promoting community betterment through the encouragement of athletics and recreational activities of youths.

E. A. Roberts, chairman of the board of Waterman Steamship Corp., called the first meeting on Jan. 19. Pat Moulton was named chairman and a nominating committee was appointed which elected the first officers after incorporation on Jan. 23.

The incorporators were J. H. Burton, R. B. Chandler, George H. Denniston, H. M. Hempstead, J. H. Little, John F. Lyle, Mark Lyons, Jr., Melvin Metzger, Pat Moulton, W. O. Pape, H. S. Rawlings, Albert E. Reynolds, John E. Toomey and B. R. Wilson, Jr.

Mr. Moulton was elected president, Mr. Wilson first vice president, Mr. Reynolds second vice president, Mr. Lyle secretary and Mr. Denniston, treasurer.

In addition to the officers, the first board of directors was composed of J. H. Friend, Frank Leatherbury, J. Finley McRae, E. A. Roberts, Gordon Smith, Jr., Riley Smith, Noel Turner, Marion R. Vickers and Messrs. Burton, Chandler, Hempstead, Little, Lyons, Metzger and Toomey.

Unlike many other Touchdown Clubs or Quarterback Clubs throughout the country, Mobile's Touchdown Club is not a

---

¶On June 4, 1946, J. Raymond Crosby was promoted to vice president and served until 1960; Mrs. Blanche M. Dempsey, to assistant trust officer and served until 1956.

On March 20 of that year, death claimed D. P. Bestor, Jr., former president and chairman of the board. Mr. Bestor was elected a director on January 2, 1907. He became president in February, 1921, and served in that capacity until he was made board chairman in 1938. He retired in 1940.

¶In July of 1947, directors of the First National Bank elected Ernest J. McAuley chairman of the board and H. Austill Pharr, president—the title that Mr. Pharr now holds.

¶In the early part of 1947, William E. Akridge, Jr., Albert E. Reynolds, Vernon L. Sibley and Wythe L. Whiting, Jr. were named assistant vice presidents.

G. E. Weiss and William H. Sadler, Jr. were made assistant cashiers.

¶During the year, many enlargements and modernizations in the working quarters of the First National Bank—contracts for which were let before war's end —were practically completed.

These included installation of new elevators in the main building and annex, an elevator for bank personnel and new floors. Some $280,000 was spent for these purposes with another $75,000 to be expended later.

On March 20, the bank announced an interesting innovation—left-handed checkbooks for "Southpaws."

At the close of 1947 the bank had 181 officers and employees, of whom 92 were men and 89 women.

Shareholders numbered 554, among which were 274 men and 222 women. Twenty-two states and one foreign country were represented.

men's luncheon or dinner group designed mainly for its own enjoyment. It is a genuinely civic-minded organization which actively sponsors and finances a year-around recreational program for the youngsters of the Mobile County area.

Beginning with the initial summer baseball program for boys in June, 1948 (which was followed by a highly organized and well-supervised fall football program) the Mobile Touchdown Club has developed an athletic program that is considered outstanding and unique throughout the country. It is the purpose of the Mobile Touchdown Club to give every boy the opportunity to play as a member of an organized team, under experienced coaches, in a carefully regulated and supervised program.

It has been with pride that the members of the Mobile Touchdown Club have never found it necessary to refuse any boy the opportunity to participate in its programs if he wishes to do so and meets the program requirements.

Current officers, whose terms expire in February, 1966, are Ervin S. Cooper, president; Dr. E. L. McCafferty, vice president; E. B. Peebles, Jr., vice president; Mark Lyons, III, treasurer, Plumer B. Tonsmeire, secretary, and Warren H. Carpenter, executive secretary.

¶On May 15, 1948, death claimed Ernest J. McAuley, chairman of the board of the First National Bank—a position he had held since July of 1947.

The bank opened Mobile's first drive-up teller's window in May, 1948, which was used by as many as 99 cars in one day at that time.

The Christmas Savings Club was re-opened after a lapse during the war years and 16,171 such checks were mailed to depositors.

A new lunch room exclusively for bank employees was opened in September.

¶In January of 1948, John M. Griser was elected to the board of directors, a position he held until Oct. 15, 1957. In July, Robert S. Bacon, vice president, was elected a director.

In January, A. Danner Frazer was promoted to assistant cashier.

At the end of the year, the bank had 14,722 borrowing customers—an increase of 3,353 (23%) over 1947. There were 559 shareholders, 91% living within a 200-mile radius of Mobile.

¶In 1949, the Royal Street entrance of the First National Bank was modernized with a new marquee. Renovation of the air conditioning system, structural changes on the second floor and new lighting equipment in the main lobby were also completed during the year.

$500,000 was transferred from undivided profits to the bank's surplus account. Capital remained at $1,000,000 with surplus at $2,500,000.

The drive-up teller's window was used for more than 20,000 customer transactions during its first full year of operation. A new and larger night depository was built and a modern telephone system was installed.

The bank also introduced a new form of check for customer convenience, called the "Postcard Check."

The following promotions were made in January of 1949:

Robert S. Bacon to executive vice president; W. E. Akridge, Jr. and Albert E. Reynolds to vice president—positions which they hold today.

V. L. Sibley was also elected a vice president, and served in this capacity until 1957.

Frank Drey, D. O. Prichard, L. R. Seifert and C. E. Van Devender were elected assistant cashier; T. R. Foster and G. S. Strong to assistant comptroller; and J. S. Crow, Jr., to manager of the Bond Department.

¶On Jan. 11, 1949, J. R. Mighell, Jr. became a member of the bank's board of directors—a title which he holds today.

1950—MOBILE GIRL ALABAMA'S FIRST "MISS AMERICA"

WHEN Yolande "Bebe" Betbeze, 21-year-old Mobile native, left for Atlantic City early in September to compete in the 1951 Miss America Pageant, the reaction here could best be described as apathetic. To many it was "just another beauty contest that few Southerners, and no Alabamian, had ever won."

When the beauteous "Bebe" failed to place in the talent division despite an Associated Press report that she was a "crowd pleaser," enthusiasm was even less. When she took first place in a division of the bathing suit judging one night later, a few conceded she "might have an outside chance of getting into the semi-finals."

But, as more reports about "Bebe" began drifting in from Atlantic City, local interest quickened. There was no nationwide television in 1950, but a Mobile radio station scheduled the Atlantic City finals for Saturday night, Sept. 9, and virtually all of Mobile was tuned in to hear the grand announcement: " . . . and the winner is . . . Miss Alabama . . . Yolande Betbeze of Mobile!"

Her widowed mother, Mrs. William P. Betbeze, (who had not made the trip to Atlantic City) heard the news with a group of friends at her home. Her voice teacher, Mme. Rose Palmai-Tenser, one of the few who had had faith in "Bebe's" ability as well as beauty, also heard the news. So did Mayor Charles A. Baumhauer who claimed credit for nominating her in the state contest which led to participation in Miss America competition.

Honors and world-wide recognition came fast for "Bebe," as well as for Mobile.

Personal appearances, pageant commitments and other duties prevented her from returning to Mobile until Friday, Oct. 6, almost a full month after winning the title, but when she did—a royal, Mobile welcome awaited her.

Following a downtown parade from the airport, "Bebe" was feted at a gala homecoming in Ladd Stadium where more than 30,000 persons turned out to pay dutiful homage and hear her declare:

"I'll remember this night as long as I live. Since the night I won the Miss America contest at Atlantic City, I have wanted to come home. You have made my arrival here a greater pleasure than I have ever known. Thanks to each and every one of you who came out tonight. I'll never forget any of you!"

Nor did she. Despite a full schedule, she remained to attend the Alabama-Vanderbilt football game the next day and take part in a coast-to-coast broadcast by Bill Stern. She returned on Feb. 25, 1951, to reign as queen of Mobile's Azalea Trail and cut the symbolic ribbon before 15,000 persons in Bienville Square.

In the meantime, during all her reign as Miss America of 1951, she brought more glory, honors and fame to herself, to Alabama, and to Mobile.[1]

¶On Jan. 10, 1950, Harwell E. Coale was promoted to assistant vice president and trust officer of the First National Bank; A. Danner Frazer, trust officer; James C. Andress and Thomas G. St. John, Jr., assistant trust officers; and E. S. Sledge, II, assistant cashier.

In two years, 41,108 customers had been served by the bank's drive-up teller's window, for a total of 70,231 transactions. Some customers said it reduced their banking time by half.

¶On Sept. 28, 1950, the bank announced a 100% increase in Federal Deposit Insurance Corporation insurance on individual accounts — from $5,000 to $10,000.

---

[1]Miss Betbeze was married on July 4, 1954, in Van Nuys, Calif., to Matthew M. Fox, 43-year-old television and film producer. Mr. Fox died in 1964, and she has continued to make her home in New York City.

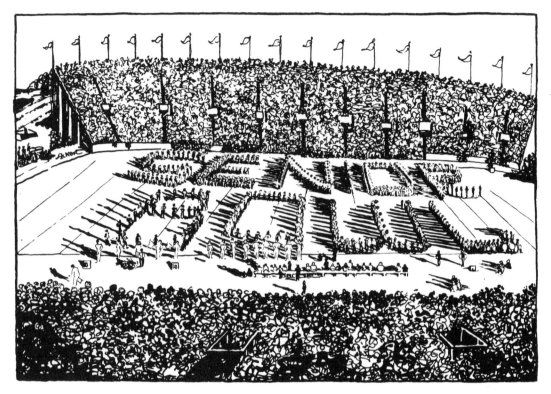

College and high school bands spell out "Senior Bowl" in Ladd Stadium
before start of annual gridiron classic.

1951-52—MOBILE BECOMES HOME OF "SENIOR BOWL"

ALTHOUGH the Senior Bowl was first played in Mobile in 1951—one year after a shaky start in Jacksonville, Fla.—it was not until the Jan. 5, 1952, game that the event came here definitely to stay.

A rare map of Mobile from the 1802-1813 period was included in the bank's 85th Anniversary advertisement in Oct. 1950. So many were the requests for it that the bank reproduced it for free distribution.

¶In his 1950 "Report to Share-holders", President Pharr noted that during the decade 1940-50, Mobile County experienced a 61% growth in population, a 50% increase in employment and an 81% expansion in dwelling units; and that deposits of the First National Bank increased 140% in the same period.

In succeeding years it has become recognized as one of the nation's major post-season games.

Conceived one rainy afternoon by a genial Nashville contractor, Jimmie Pearre, while watching a Vanderbilt-Tennessee football game, the idea was first tested on a group of coaches, sports writers and friends. The plan was to promote a "college senior bowl game" and actually pay the participants.

Neither the first game in Jacksonville, nor the second in Mobile, was a financial success; but a group of prominent Mobile civic and professional leaders saw its future potential.

This group, composed of 27 charter members, was organized in August, 1951, as the Mobile Arts and Sports Association, with the following:

— 136 —

E. Roy Albright, J. Howard Burton, Ralph B. Chandler, R. A. Christian, John T. Cochrane, Jr., Harry Crawford, Gilbert F. Dukes, H. M. Hempstead, F. M. Hicks, T. K. Jackson, Jr., Gilbert F. Ladd, Jr., Frank L. Leatherbury, Dr. Joe H. Little, H. Manning McPhillips, James McPhillips, J. Finley McRae, Melvin A. Metzger, Pat Moulton, Richard Murray, Norman Nicolson, E. B. Peebles, E. A. Roberts, H. C. Slaton, Gordon Smith, Jr., Wright Smith, Jr., Marion P. Vickers and Beverly R. Wilson, Jr.

The M.A.S.A. is a non-profit sharing corporation dedicated wholly to the public benefit for the purpose of promoting and advancing the civic, social, cultural, recreational and artistic life of the Mobile community and its area.

One of its first undertakings was to assume financial control of the fledgling Senior Bowl and place $22,500 in an escrow fund to guarantee payment of $500 to each member of the winning team and $400 to each losing member, as well as all expenses, for the 1952 game. [1]

Mobile was also fortunate in having a stadium virtually made to order for the future of the Senior Bowl. Ladd Memorial Stadium is unique in its origination, operation and purpose.

A memorial to the late Ernest F. Ladd, business and civic leader who served as president of the Merchants National Bank from 1915 until his death in 1941, the stadium was built without any public solicitation of funds and without the use of public tax money although the site was provided by the City of Mobile. [2] Its original capacity of 35,486 has been increased to 40,605 and the 16th annual Senior Bowl in 1965 was a complete standing room sellout.

The Senior Bowl is only one of the varied activities of the Mobile Arts and Sports Association. Another of its most important undertakings is its assistance to the Mobile

Touchdown Club in its widespread and nationally recognized youth program. It also provides financial assistance to the Mobile Boys' Club and the Allied Arts Council.

But the Senior Bowl, conceived by a man with a dream who remains as one of the officers of the Senior Bowl Association, is now truly the "starriest" of the all-star games. To-day nearly 200 former Senior Bowl players remain active in professional football.

¶On Jan. 9, 1951, Harwell E. Coale was elected vice president and trust officer of the First National Bank; James S. Crow, assistant cashier in charge of the Bond Department, and Miss Celia Webb, assistant manager.

On May 30, 1951, P. G. Barnes completed 50 years of service.

In September, A. Danner Frazer was promoted to assistant vice president and N. Q. Adams to trust officer.

During the year, a new directors' room was completed, lobby tellers' enclosures were redesigned and a second driveup teller's window was installed.

In 1951 the Board of Directors increased the surplus to $3,000,000 by transferring $500,000 from undivided profits.

¶More than 200,000 savings accounts had been opened by the First National Bank as of Jan. 1, 1952.

During the year, the capacity of the bank's 24-hour Depository was doubled and the Trust Department handled the largest volume of business in its 39 years of existence.

The Personal Loan Department (established in 1945) held more than 7,000 loans, totaling $3,636,000; and the Dealer Installment Loan Department (with 6,000 customers) increased its volume by 30% as compared to 1951.

---

[1]Today members of the winning team receive $900.00 and losing members receive $700.00.
[2]The First National Bank was proud to join with others in this noteworthy Civic project.

1952—THE HOSPITAL STORY ... MOBILE INFIRMARY
AND PROVIDENCE HOSPITAL DEDICATED

THE YEAR 1952 marked a giant step forward in Mobile's care of the sick as two major hospitals were dedicated and opened to the public.

Neither was a new institution, as Mobile Infirmary had been in existence since 1910[1] and Providence Hospital since 1855 —but each was a completely new, gleaming building and one, Mobile Infirmary, was on a new site.

The new Mobile Infirmary was dedicated on Jan. 19, and the new Providence Hospital followed on Oct. 30.

Excavating for Mobile Infirmary—on its new site overlooking the former Oak Hills Golf Course on Louiselle Street off Spring Hill Avenue—began on Jan. 9, 1950, after funds had been assured in a drive led by J. L. Bedsole and other interested persons and business leaders. One-half was also provided by Federal funds through the famed Hill-Burton Act, and the toal cost was estimated at $4,400,000 for the 6-story, 284-bed facility.

Mrs. St. John Wilson was president of the 21-person hospital board, with Joseph A. Mighell, first vice president; Francis H. Inge, second vice president; Mrs. Morris A. Hamilton, third vice president; Thomas A. Horst, treasurer and Miss Virginia Thomas, secretary. Miss Katherine White-Spunner retained her position as administrator, a post she assumed at the old Mobile Infirmary near Five Points in 1933, and E. C. Bramlett was business manager.

Senator Hill, Dr. D. G. Gill of the State Health Department, Rev. A. Carl Adkins, Rabbi Solomon E. Cherniak, Rev. Harold W. Seever, J. L. Bedsole (chairman of the

View of Mobile General Hospital on Stanton Road scheduled for completion in late 1965.

building committee), and Dr. A. M. Cowden (president of the Mobile Infirmary medical staff) all took part in the dedication program. Miss White-Spunner opened the infirmary doors with a dedicatory set of keys, and more than 1,000 people streamed through for a first-day inspection.

Of the $11,340,000 now invested in Mobile Infirmary, after other improvements and additions, all but three-eighths of the total has been supplied through donations by individual friends of the hospital and civic minded business leaders.

Providence Hospital (then called Providence Infirmary) was first opened in a building at Broad and St. Anthony Streets on May 1, 1855, where care was provided for 60 patients. It was moved to the Spring Hill Avenue and Catherine Street site in 1901, and two years later a school of nursing was started—this being the second oldest school of nursing in the state.

Operated by the Daughters of Charity of St. Vincent de Paul, the building was razed in 1950 for the start of the new Providence. A limited number of patients were accepted temporarily in Allen Memorial Home, on the Catherine Street side, which previously had been used for children and maternity cases only.

Dedication of the new 8-story, 250-bed facility fronting on Spring Hill Avenue was held Oct. 30, 1952, as the climax to a gala three-day celebration of the silver jubilee of Bishop Thomas J. Toolen (now Archbishop of the Mobile-Birmingham Diocese). Patients, however, had been in the facility since Aug. 1, and some maternity cases were moved in several days previous. The first baby born in the new hospital building arrived on July 30 and was named Theresa by the proud parents, Mr. and Mrs. John H. St. Laurent of Chickasaw.

Cost of the hospital was put at $4 million, with half coming from Federal funds and the remainder through personal subscriptions. Sister Marguerite of the Daughters of Charity was administrator of the new hospital, a post she had held since 1947.

Meanwhile, in Feb., 1949, construction was begun on a $585,000 hospital for Negroes at Washington Avenue and Virginia Streets, to be called Blessed Martin de Porres. It received nationwide attention and support, notably from Monseigneur Fulton J. Sheen (later a bishop) and Mrs. Claire Boothe Luce.

The City of Mobile donated $25,000 and the site—formerly Choctaw Park. About one-third came from the Hill-Burton Hospital Act, and the remainder was made up of contributions and a loan.

The hospital, designed in the form of a cross, had original accomodations for 35 patients with later expansion planned at 100 beds. Operated by the Sisters of Mercy, it was first opened to public inspection and patients on Easter Sunday, April 9, 1950. Formal dedication was held on May 14 with Msgr. Sheen participating.[2]

¶In 1953, the First National Bank offered another new service for the convenience of Mobilians — a day and night drive-up depository.

A higher interest rate (2½%) for 24 Months Savings Certificates was announced in October, and on the bank's 88th Anniversary (Oct. 18, 1953) its resources exceeded $85,000,000.

Illuminated "FIRST NATIONAL BANK" signs were also installed on the main building and the Annex.

Deposits at year's end totaled $82,057,709.

¶In January of 1953, John D. Terrell was elected senior vice president and cashier, and James T. Overbey, senior vice president — titles which they both hold today.

Charles E. Van Devender was promoted to vice president, the title he now holds.

A. Danner Frazer was promoted to vice president and continued in this capacity until 1957.

F. W. Drey was elected assistant trust officer; W. M. Feeney and S. S. Moore, assistant cashiers.

In 1953 the surplus was increased to $3,500,000 by transfering $500,000 from undivided profits.

While other hospitals were growing or being established in Mobile, the area's main hospital for low income groups and the indigent, originally called City Hospital, was undergoing a continuous headache.

Established in 1830 and still at the same site, City Hospital had grown and outgrown its facilities many times. Under legislation sponsored by Joseph N. Langan, the hospital was changed to a county facility in 1955 and the name changed to Mobile County Hospital. The county communities of Mobile, Prichard, Chickasaw, Saraland, Satsuma, Citronelle and Bayou la Batre—many of whose residents frequently used City Hospital—were all assessed a proportionate amount to provide for the new county facility's upkeep and maintenance.

In 1959, the Sisters of Charity, who had administered the hospital continuously since 1863, asked to be relieved. Administration of the hospital (the name was now changed to Mobile General Hospital) was vested in a hospital board of Mobile County citizens with a paid administrator.

During much of this period, the need for a "new" hospital to fill the county's needs became apparent and preliminary studies got underway on financing, selection of a site, plans and specifications. T. Cooper Van Antwerp of Mobile was engaged to draw the architectural plans for the new building, and on Jan. 1, 1959, the board approved purchase of a 28.6-acre site on Stanton Road at Fillingim Street in the Toulminville sector.

A 12-story structure, costing in excess of $8 million, was unfolded in the designs of Architect Van Antwerp on July 16, 1960. The original plan was to occupy nine floors, with a toal of 370 beds, and eventually expand to 565 beds on all floors. Since actual construction began, the plans have been changed many times until as late as late spring, 1965, the plan was to open only seven floors with 240 beds.

Finances continued to plague both the old and the new. Some funds were made available from the State Legislature, the Hill-Burton Act, and a three-mill countywide addition to property taxes. The voters authorized a $2 million city bond issue and a $2 million county bond issue.

The present board of Mobile General Hospital is headed by Ralph G. Holberg, chairman, with George A. Haas, vice chairman and Charles L. Waller, Jr., secretary-treasurer.

The board, along with Administrator Winston C. Whitfield, hopes to see Mobile General in its new home by the end of 1965.

¶*During 1954, First National Bank loans reached a new peak of $32,913,678 —considerably higher than the preceding year.*

W. Cameron Pettiss was named an assistant vice president.

The number of shareholders had increased to 590.

---

[1] See Page 72: 1910—Cornerstone Of Mobile Infirmary Laid.

[2] Despite Mobile's increase in hospital facilities by the end of 1960, there was still further need and a private hospital—known as Doctor's Hospital—was opened on April 9, 1962, at 1700 Center Street, about midway between Providence Hospital and Mobile Infirmary.

Officers of the new hospital—which had 200 doctors on its staff and 100 employees to service the 82 beds—were Dr. William H. Tucker, president; Dr. Warren Yemm, vice president, and Dr. Guy Rutledge, secretary-treasurer.

1954—"OPERATION SCAT" EVACUATES MOBILE

DURING THE first five years of the 1950's Civil Defense was uppermost in the minds of many Americans. The Korean Conflict had presented a new insight on Russia, and the continuous development of new long-range missiles proved the main reason for this. Underground shelters were designated for many downtown locations, and the homeowner was offered a wide variety of personal shelter plans which could be erected for him, or by himself on a do-it-yourself kit basis. Even an installment buying plan of "shelter-now-pay later" was available.

In this atmosphere, Mobile's Civil Defense Administration laid its program for "Operation Scat," a mock exercise to test the city's preparedness for sudden attack from the air by evacuation of as many as 92,000 persons from a designated 480-block downtown area.

The zone was bounded by Mobile River on the east, Broad Street on the west, Baltimore Street on the south, and a line roughly along Three Mile Creek on the north. Several evacuation and dispersal routes, and regrouping areas, were designated.

Since it was well-timed and announced in advance, many began their own evacuation long before the sirens blew at 4:57 p.m. But, when the sirens did blow, thousands calmly left offices, stores and homes to enter automobiles and begin the trek to safety. Incoming motor traffic was halted at four checkpoints entering the city.

Within a few minutes after Mrs. Katherine Burnett had pushed the siren button in the Civil Defense office, in the Mobile Police Building, the steady stream of capacity filled autos was moving out of the "target zone." Those without a pre-arranged ride were told to "start walking west," and were picked up by cars, buses or trucks which had not already been filled.

Fifteen minutes after the first siren, the downtown streets were deserted except for some 300 National Guardsmen who were patrolling the area, most on foot and some in roving jeeps. Airplanes circled overhead, and a cascade of yellow pamphlets fell from one of them—the mock attack. Primary targets were listed as Brookley Field, the State Docks and the rail centers.

Each downtown corner was manned by a Civil Defense volunteer in white helmet, and William C. Sturgeon, Mobile CD director, kept in touch with the evacuation progress from a midtown command post.

By 6 p.m. the all-clear sounded, and the cavalcade of automobiles began its reverse trip back to the city from outlying dispersal and regrouping areas.

CD officials were jubilant that "Operation Scat" had been so successfully accomplished, and the widespread cooperation of all was highly commended.

1955—CITY OF MOBILE PURCHASES "OAKLEIGH"

OAKLEIGH, Mobile's official ante-bellum mansion, was purchased in 1955 by the City to be used as headquarters for the Historic Mobile Preservation Society. In exchange, the Historic Society relinquished the Fort Conde—Charlotte House at 104 Theatre Street, which it had bought in 1940 and restored.

James W. Roper began the erection of this home in 1833. He served as his own architect, employing slaves in the building of the mansion. The bricks used in the masonry of the first floor walls were made from clay dug on the grounds. The main upper portion of the house is of hand hewn lumber. Tool marks may be seen on the

OAKLEIGH —
OLD MOBILE —

The interior of "Oakleigh" conforms to the style of
home decoration used prior to 1850

door sidings and window frames. The
original silver plated door knobs remain on
the huge doors of the two parlors.

The house was practically completed
by 1838 when Mr. Roper brought his bride
to live there. However, as late as 1852
some of the interior was still unfinished.
Oakleigh has been in the hands of several
different families after it passed from
the original owners.

In 1935, the Historic American Building
Survey chose Oakleigh to be photo-
graphed, with floor plans and architectural
details, for the Library of Congress.
Original floor plans show the house was
built in the shape of a "T".

*¶On Jan. 11, 1955, directors of the
First National Bank authorized an increase of capital from $1,000,000 to
$1,500,000. Ten thousand shares were
issued as a 25% stock dividend and on
Feb. 18, an additional 10,000 shares
were sold. The bank's surplus was
increased from $3,500,000 to $4,500,000.*

*¶As soon as the 1955 Alabama Leg-
islature authorized branch banking in
Mobile County, the First National Bank
started negotiations to acquire the Citizens Bank on Broad Street and purchased a site in Toulminville for a branch
to serve that area.*

1955—CITRONELLE OIL WELL IS GUSHER

AT APPROXIMATELY 3:30 p.m. Tuesday, Aug. 16, 1955, a new way of life became apparent for a Citronelle widow, a Citronelle automotive sales manager and a Mobile carpenter. They were, respectively, Mrs. Edna Donovan and her two sons, Edward and John, co-owners of a 40-acre plot of ground in north Mobile County where oil gushed— to the surprise and delight of owners, drillers and backers alike — that warm summer afternoon.

For 31 days, the Zach Brooks Drilling Co., oil contractors, had driven a well nearly 11,000 feet below the surface of the ground in the southeast corner of the Donovan plot, only 50 feet from Highway 45 and just north of the Citronelle city limits.

It was a wildcat test, with many backers. Zach Brooks of El Dorado, Ark., held the contract, while Halliburton Oil Well

The bank introduced a new type of checking account called "ThriftiCheck," which has continued to be popular with budgetminded Mobilians. With the endorsement of Mobile dentists, the bank also introduced a special loan service called the "Dental Loan Plan."

On the bank's 90th Anniversary (Oct. 18, 1955), resources were in excess of $96,000,000. Deposits totaled $92,-031,328 as of Dec. 30—an increase of nearly 200% during the past 15 years.

¶On June 6, 1955, Richard Murray was elected to the board of directors, which office he still holds.

In January of 1955, Lee R. Seifert was promoted to vice president, G. E. Weiss was promoted to assistant vice president; C. G. Bitzer and S. S. Mattei to assistant cashiers, and T. R. Foster to comptroller.

¶Total bank resources in Mobile and suburbs amounted to $261,000,000 on Dec. 31, 1955. In 1930 it was $47,060,000, and at the turn of the century, only $6,138,000.

Cement Co. of Natchez furnished the men, one of whom—Driller A. D. Turnage— said: "The gusher came as a surprise to me; the lack of pressure earlier indicated there was nothing there."

But there was! Oil spurted 160 feet in the air, drenching nearby stragglers, spectators and oilmen as well as parked automobiles. No one minded, for Mobile County's first gusher—the second ever discovered in Alabama—indicated that a new oil field had been born. The first opened the Pollard field near Brewton in January, 1952.

Oil blew in at Citronelle from a 51-foot test which began at the 10,872 foot level. It was not only oil, it was good oil—oil with a specific gravity of 40.5, well above average which is 30.0 throughout the United States.

When the Donovan well came in, Alabama had only 112 wells, mostly in the Pollard field. Donovan Test No. 1, as it became known to history, was No. 113. It became evident, almost from the start, that the Donovan well would produce over 100 barrels a day (at that time the limit allowable by state law) and measures were immediately planned to obtain a change in the law. State Geologist Walter B. Jones led the move.

All three Donovans took the discovery in reasonably calm stride. Mrs. Donovan, who had moved to Mobile County from New York in 1911, was "just piddling around the house when the phone rang and someone said there was oil spurting all over the place." John, when notified in his Citronelle automobile sales room, did run out for a look; Edward, the carpenter on Fowl River, was awed — but he had made a date to go shrimping the following day, and he kept it.

"It's all the same to me," Mrs. Donovan said from her front porch. "I'll be the same old six and seven if I had a million. I may go down and take a look at it all tomorrow sometime." She did on Wednesday, but it was Thursday before Edward had his first look.

Oilmen, geologists, backers and just the plain curious were not so calm, however. They converged on the new well discovery in droves. Almost immediately, oil companies had title checkers working overtime at the Mobile County courthouse examining titles to properties in the Citronelle area—hoping to gain as many leases as quickly as possible.

Through an arrangement with the then Probate Judge Tennent L. Griffin,[1] oil company representatives continued their checking after the offices closed at 5 p.m. on Friday, presumably for the weekend. Checking went on until 1 a.m. Saturday and was halted until 8 a.m. when Judge Griffin permitted it to resume, even assigning a total of four extra clerks to handle the volume of work. It continued until late Saturday, recessing for Sunday, but was resumed Monday.

Commenting on the importance of the Donovan Discovery Test Well No. 1 and its vast significance on the economy of Mobile, the Mobile Press said editorially on Aug. 18:

"Citronelle once enjoyed an enviable reputation as a health resort. Now its claim to fame is oil Such an experience couldn't happen to a better town or a better people.

"It has vast significance in that it brings oil production to within 33 miles of the Port of Mobile and further strengthens the long-time claims of many observers that this city's fortunes may some day rival those of prosperous Houston, Texas.

"But the impact that came to Citronelle was immediate. It swept away a spirit of gloom that had been evident in that community during recent months. Businessmen who had been downcast over the town's failure thus far to attract any sizeable industry, were overjoyed.

"No longer, if oilmen's predictions turn out, will Citronelle's economy have to depend on timber, cattle and limited farming operations."

Donovan Test No. 1 was capped that first day within eight minutes, but not before more than 1,800 cubic feet of oil had spouted. Oilmen knew they had a winner in Citronelle.

Drilling even deeper on the Donovan well continued, and by August 30, a new layer of about 16 feet of oil-saturated sand was struck at approximately 11,400 feet.

Dr. Jones hailed this new proving of the Citronelle oil field a definite step forward for Alabama's oil future. He was right. By year's end, the field boasted of two producers and, as the First National Bank prepared to celebrate its centennial year of 1965, some 413 wells were in production.

There are still more on the way . . .

1955—DAUPHIN ISLAND BRIDGE BECOMES REALITY

MANY INDIVIDUALS and land developers, for many decades, had longingly looked across the three-mile gap between Cedar Point and Duaphin Island and envisioned a bridge that would link the two.

Plans, surveys and schemes were brought forward through the years, but

nothing concrete was ever formulated. The advent of World War II caused a further delay, but shortly after peace was restored new plans were discussed.

Financing and a suitable development program appeared to be the main drawbacks. Attempts to obtain financing through additional taxation—notably an

---

[1] Mr. Griffin is a member of the Midtown Branch Advisory Board.

Lift span section of Dauphin Island Bridge.

additional gasoline tax—were all doomed to failure. Mobilians, in the main, approved of the bridge idea—but they didn't want to be taxed for it.

Shortly after 1950 the Mobile Chamber of Commerce conceived a development

plan which, with State of Alabama assistance, would be tax-free.

On Aug. 22, 1952, Gov. Gordon Persons[1] told State Representative Sydney S. Pfleger that he had authorized the State Highway Department to prepare plans and specifications for a Dauphin Island Bridge provided certain conditions were met. Among these were the reservation of at least four miles of public beaches on the Gulf side, construction of public parks and facilities, the sale of available lots on the Island to the public at reasonable prices, and construction and maintenance of all inland island roads by Mobile County authority. The County was also to set up a park and beach board to assure that recreational facilities were maintained for the public.

Oliver H. Delchamps, president of the Mobile Chamber of Commerce, and John E. Toomey, chairman of the Chamber's bridge committee, readily assured the governor that this would be done; while A. B. Jeffries, chairman of the County Board of Revenue and Road Commissioners, said: "We'll do our share."

In brief and simple terms, the plan was devised for the Mobile Chamber of Commerce to buy the Island (those areas not held by the State or already by Island settlers) from the Gulf Properties Corp., a holding company of individuals who owned various large tracts of the Island. The Chamber would then place the separate lots on sale to the public.

Some 2,000 lots were plotted and by the first day of the sale there were 1,200 advance orders; all to be handled by licensed realtors in the area. When that first day ended—Monday, Nov. 23, 1953—some 1,500 lots had been sold, and all 2,000 were sold by Friday, Nov. 27. These were all residential sites, some on the gulf, some in wooded areas, others along the "fingers" of the Mississippi Sound-Heron Bay areas and others at Pass Drury.

On March 9, 1954, Mobile County issued $2 million in bridge bonds which were sold to the only bidder, the Chamber of Commerce. Money for this purchase was borrowed as follows: First National Bank, $450,000; Merchants National Bank,

$450,000; American National Bank, $100,000, and the National City Bank of New York City, $1 million[2]. The bonds were 4 per cent, to be redeemed at varying times over the next 20 years.

With the proceeds from lot sales, the Chamber paid Gulf Properties Corp. $1 million for the Island land, set aside $1 million for its development and later allocated $500,000 for the public (Sand Dunes Casino) beach and a similar amount for the private Isle Dauphine Club facility, to which each property owner was assured 10 years of free membership. The state agreed to finance the cost of the bridge over and above the $2 million voted in the bond issue.

Blount Brothers Construction Co. of Montgomery, and the Kansas City Bridge Co. of that city, were low bidders on the initial work of building all bridge approaches and timber bulkheads over the span's entire 3.014 mile length, and work began immediately. The County, meanwhile, repaved Cedar Point Road and began its work on the inland roads of the Island.

The bridge was officially titled "The Gordon Persons Overseas Highway" and the opening was set for 5 a.m. on Saturday, July 2, 1955—the beginning of a long Independence Day weekend continuing through Monday.

No elaborate ceremonies were planned. On opening morning, the Rev. A. Carl Adkins of Dauphin Way Methodist Church, and Rev. M. F. Ouellet, S.S.E., priest of St. Agnes Catholic Church on Dauphin Island, joined to bless the venture. In what was virtually a prayer of prophecy, Rev. Adkins said: "May all who come to this haven of rest be drawn closer to Thee and to one another."

E. C. Doody, County administrative assistant, and Fred Muths, bridge superintendent, accepted the first $1 toll from Leroy Stevens, now President of the

---

[1]Former Gov. Gordon Persons died at Montgomery, Ala., on May 29, 1965, at the age of 63.
[2]The First National Bank was designated as trustee for these funds, and the County Board placed the proceeds of the sale there for deposit.

County Commission of Mobile County. The first car also contained Mrs. Stevens, their daughter and her husband—Mr. and Mrs. Bill Gilmer. The second car was occupied by John Toomey, the Chamber's bridge chairman of long standing, and E. Roy Albright, newly named to head the Dauphin Island Park and Beach Board.

These first arrivals found about six miles of paved roads, a temporary bath house at the Sand Dunes Casino site, and Fort Gaines (the museum was not opened until later). A restaurant was available in the Fort Gaines area.

This marked the end of a dream and the beginning of a long-wanted reality . . .

1956—BARRY STEAM PLANT

SHORTLY AFTER the close of World War II, the Alabma Power Co. realized that its facilities in Mobile County would not remain sufficient for too long a period to serve the ever-increasing needs of a growing city and a constantly-enlarging industrial area. Plans were formulated to augment the amount of electrical energy available to the area.

On July 20, 1951, ground was broken at LeMoyne (Salco), 23 miles north of Mobile on the Mobile River, about a mile east of Highway 43, for a $35 million steam plant capable of generating some 250,000 kilowatts of electrical power. The ground was broken by the long-time associate of Alabama Power Co., for whom the new plant would be named: James M. Barry.

The first unit of the plant, rated at 125,000 kilowatts, went into operation on Feb. 11, 1954, and a similar unit—giving the plant a total capacity of 250,000 kilowatts—began operating on July 11 of the same year.

Even before dedicating the original plant, Alabama Power received approval of the Alabama Public Service Commission to begin plans for a third unit of 225,000 kilowatts—adding up to 475,000 kilowatts—on May 30, 1956. The original two units and plant cost more than $35 million. The third unit, scheduled for completion by July, 1959, was allocated an additional $25 million.

The Barry Steam Plant, with its two operating units, was formally dedicated in special ceremonies on Friday, Sept. 21, 1956.

Chairman Martin presided over the dedication, with the invocation offered by Dr. Harold W. Seever, pastor of the Dauphin Way Baptist Church in Mobile. Opening remarks were made by Eugene A. Yates, president of the Southern Company, and Joseph N. Langan, mayor of Mobile.

A plaque honoring Mr. Barry was unveiled by Ann Elizabeth and Christine Marie Keeler, granddaughters of Frank S. Keeler, Mobile division vice president.

Mr. Barry followed this with the main address of the day, outlining the progress and plans of Alabama Power Co. in the past, present and future. The benediction was offered by the Rev. John N. Lukens, D.D., Independent Presbyterian Church of the United States, located in Birmingham.

¶On Feb. 1, 1956, the Citizens Bank became the Broad Street Office of the First National Bank, and the Bayou la Batre Office was opened on Sept. 10.

With the downtown office, the First National Bank now had four locations.

During 1956, interest was increased on regular savings accounts to 2% and on 1-year savings certificates to 2½%.

1957—MUNICIPAL PARK AT SPRING HILL OPENED

MAINLY THROUGH the efforts of City Park Commissioner Joseph N. Langan, aided by the support of Mayor Henry R. Luscher and Commissioner Charles F. Hackmeyer, a 750-acre tract of land—owned mostly by the city—was converted into Mobile's first municipal park of any great size.

Bounded on the east by MacGregor Avenue, south of the Gulf Mobile and Ohio Railroad tracks and north of Old Shell Road, the park was unofficially opened on June 1 and formally dedicated on Labor Day, Sept. 2.

When the park was opened in June by Mayor Luscher, a swimming lake to accommodate 5,000 persons, an 18-hole golf course and various picnic areas were ready for use. Ann Stevens and Lucy Leatherbury cut the ribbon to the swimming lake, while a total of 139 golfers tested the new course on the opening day.

Complete bathhouse facilities were available for the swimmers, who paid the adult fee of 25 cents and children's fee of 10 cents, but the $144,500 golf course club house was not finished until the spring of 1958. Eight tennis courts and additional roads were also unfinished at this time. By Aug. 25, six barbecue pits were placed in operation.

Other buildings and facilities were planned, and before the end of 1957 one-third of the required $60,000 needed for a Mobile Art Gallery in the park had already been pledged.

Mobile Art Gallery located on the beautiful southern shore of the lake in Municipal Park.

Commissioner Langan officiated at the formal dedication early Labor Day morning. He said that 5,000 azaleas and more than 1,000 camellias had been planted; and Mrs. Emile Scheuermann, representing the Federated Garden Clubs of Mobile County, promised the support of the 65 clubs and their 2,500 members in making the park an integral unit of the Azalea Trail.

The "old swimming hole long known as the pumping station" had given way to a brand new recreational facility for Mobilians, conservatively valued at more than $2 million.

In years to come, it was to develop and grow even more. Today it ranks, especially during the azalea season, as one of the most beautiful natural parks in the nation.

¶In 1956, a spacious balcony was built in the main bank to accomodate its growing number of customers.

Deposits were $99,228,011 at year's end.

W. L. Whiting, Jr., was promoted to vice president; E. S. Sledge, II, and Walter J. Smith, to assistant vice presidents: (Mr. Smith held this position until 1960) and N. Q. Adams, to assistant vice president and trust officer.

New officers elected were Joseph H. Baker, Jr., assistant trust officer; George A. Hieronymus and E. D. Simms, assistant cashiers; and B. Franklin King, III, assistant comptroller.

John A. Davis was appointed manager of the Bayou la Batre Branch and E. M. Steiner, manager of the Brookley Air Force Base Facility.

Dividends paid totaled $270,000 in 1956.

¶On July 15, 1957, the First National Bank opened its Toulminville Office, the fifth location in strategic areas.

On Nov. 1, interest was increased to 3% on six months and one year savings certificates.

¶In 1957, James C. Andress and W. H. Sadler, Jr., were promoted to assistant vice presidents; Clarence E. Davis, to assistant cashier and B. Franklin King, III, to auditor.

The bank's staff had grown to 376.

1958—WEST VIRGINIA GIRL WINS FIRST JUNIOR MISS PAGEANT

LOOKING AROUND for an additional feature to bolster its already highly successful Azalea Trail Pageant each year, the Mobile Junior Chamber of Commerce in late 1957 decided—almost on the spur of a late moment—to conduct a talent and personality contest for the outstanding high school senior in the nation. It was not in the beginning, nor has it ever been, a "bathing beauty" affair.

Moving with their usual fast, but precise, action in the matter, the Junior Chamber set up an organization to promote the annual Junior Miss America Pageant (it did not become known by its later name, America's Junior Miss Pageant, until the second year). Fred W. Holder, manager of Bellingrath Gardens, became the first president. Other officers were: R. W. Ferguson, vice president; Walter M. Cook, secretary and George E. Downing, treasurer.

Stage scene of America's Junior Miss Pageant in the new Municipal Auditorium.
It was telecast in color to the nation in 1965.

Other prominent Mobile businessmen who served on the initial board of directors were Earl P. Andrews, Jr., also chairman of the 1958 Azalea Trail Pageant; William J. Hearin, Jr., Ernest F. Ladd, Jr., James K. McLean and N. Jack Stallworth. George E. McNally, was named general chairman of the first pageant.

A budget of approximately $40,000 was set for the first pageant, and since there were no national sponsors it had to be underwritten by civic-minded Mobile firms: First National Bank, Waterman Steamship Corp., American National Bank, Merchants National Bank, Hammel's, Sears-Roebuck, Gayfer's, Delchamps, Southern Industries, Coca-Cola Bottling Co., and Smith's Bakery. The sum of

$10,000 was allocated for scholarships to be awarded the top five winners, and the remainder was earmarked for contestants' travel expenses, staging and other costs. Housing was no problem, as generous Mobilians acted as hostesses under the direction of Mrs. T. O. Howell, Jr.

The pageant was scheduled for Feb. 27-28 and March 1, hopefully to coincide with the blooming azaleas. The contest was opened to high school senior girls between the ages of 16 and 18, each to be sponsored by a state Jaycee organization.

The first actual acceptance came from Wisconsin on Dec. 21, shortly afterwards followed by Alabama and Mississippi. By Jan. 4, a total of 10 Jaycee organizations had officially entered. The rolls closed in early February with girls from 18 states.

Preliminary judging in evening dress, sports attire and talent was conducted before limited audiences at the Hotel Admiral Semmes and Murphy High School, and the finals were scheduled for the Saenger Theater. Patron tickets at $25 each, and others ranging from $5.50 to $2 were sold, but only about 1,000 persons were in the theater for the historic first winner, Miss Phyllis Ann Whitenack, 17, of Bluefiled, West Virginia.

Despite its humble beginning, the Junior Miss idea caught on throughout the nation as plans were formulated for the second event a year hence. Two national sponsors, Coca-Cola Co. of Atlanta and Bobbie Brooks, Inc., a young women's clothing concern, were signed.

The 1959 pageant drew 36 entries and 43 appeared in 1960. Ever since 1961, a full 50 states have been entered and the total amount of state and national scholarships has surpassed $150,000 annually.

The same high standards have consistently been maintained, and the number of participating girls has grown each year. Only 50 throughout the nation took part in the 1958 contest, resulting in 18 entries; 2,300 competed in 139 separate eliminations for the 36 entries of 1959; 5,000 competed in 257 state and local contests for the 43 finalists of 1960; 9,600 girls in all 50 states competed in 525 local contests in 1961; 18,000 in 750 eliminations in 1962; 33,000 in 800 eliminations in 1963, and 40,000 in 900 eliminations in 1964.

The 1965 Pageant, held in Mobile's new Municipal Auditorium and telecast nationally in color for the first time, drew a phenomenal entry list of more than 52,000 girls competing in nearly one thousand prior eliminations. James Franciscus, the "Mr. Novak" of a popular television series, was master of ceremonies for the glittering final night.

1959—SPRINGDALE SHOPPING CENTER OPENS ON BELT LINE HIGHWAY

SPRINGDALE PLAZA, the ultimate in modern shopping centers, was opened on Thursday, Nov. 19, 1959, on a 50-acre site at the intersection of the Belt Line Highway and Grant Street (now Airport Boulevard).

Plans for the $10 million center were first announced on June 26, 1954, by E. E. Delaney, president of Delaney Realty Co., who had purchased the large tract of land in what was popularly referred to as "Wragg Swamp" after a survey had been made by J. H. Harte & Co. of Atlanta, architects and engineers, to determine the best location for such a vast project.

By Sept. 4, 1955, the first seven tenants were signed for locations in the new area, and an eighth major tenant was negotiating. Mr. Delaney became president of Springdale Plaza, Inc.

Work was begun in 1958 when the first of a half-million cubic yards of dirt fill was placed on the site. A year later, January of 1959, the filling was completed and the actual construction of the center started.

Jehle Brothers, Inc., of Mobile and Montgomery, were awarded the general contract. It was a mammoth job. Six thousand pilings were driven for the foundation, and over 12,000 cubic yards of concrete were used in the buildings and sidewalks. The paving of the 3,000-car parking area could have covered a highway 15 miles long; four acres of glass went into the windows; bricks totaled a half-million or more; special concrete blocks approximated 250,000; and 2,000 tons of steel went into the buildings.

Springdale was planned to have some 50 stores under one roof—a vast building curving in a graceful arc from the Belt Line Highway around the big parking lot back to Airport Boulevard. The air in the stores was to be constantly changed by 1,000 tons of air conditioning; Southern Bell installed more than 700 telephones along 358 circuit miles of wire, and the gas usage was figured at the equivalent of 220 residential customers.

When the vast center opened for business on Nov. 19, 1959, there were 35 stores in operation. The Springdale Plaza Merchants Assn. was formed in June of 1959 with Sam J. Kayser president. Other officers were: Walne W. Donald, vice president; John A. Davis,[1] treasurer; Joseph H. Baker, Sr.,[2] executive secretary and David Roberts, secretary.

Directors were Sheldon Robinson, Leslie Davis, Rufus Moore, Frank Schrohe, W. G. McGrady, Joel Swanson, and E. E. Roth.

Mr. and Mrs. Delaney opened the center by tying, rather than cutting, a ribbon to "symbolize the bringing together of many people and organizations" that made the multi-million dollar project possible. Congressman Frank Boykin, Mayor Joseph N. Langan and County Commission President Leroy Stevens also took part in the ceremonies.

When the center was formally dedicated on Feb. 18, 1960, a total of 46 stores were in full operation and more were in sight.

Meanwhile, construction was continuing on the Belt Line Highway on the western boundaries of Springdale, an eventual 6.816-mile link to connect U. S. Highways

Shoppers stroll along the vast crescent sweep of Springdale Plaza shopping center.

Aerial view of the interchange at Navco of Interstate 65 and Interstate 10.
Interstate 65 (left) forms the "belt line" around western Mobile.

90 and 45 and later 43, and then become part of the 364-mile U. S. Interstate High way 65 in Alabama, which will interchange with Interstate 10 at Navco.

Jan. 4, 1963, was a busy day for Gov. John Patterson of Alabama, who had only 10 more days in office to go, as he first participated in dedicating the completed portion of the Belt Line Highway at ceremonies conducted on the site at Springdale Plaza and then the dedication of the new Alabama Marine Resources Laboratory on Dauphin Island.

Shortly after 9:30 a.m., Gov. Patterson cut a big ribbon, held by Azalea Trail Queen Jody Prothro and Lady-in-Waiting Vicki Powers,[3] at the south-bound lane of the Belt Line Highway under the Airport Boulevard overpass.

Then, at 2:30 p.m., the governor spoke at the dedication of the new state facility on Dauphin Island, which cost approximately $400,000—to be operated by the State Conservation Department and be used by the University of Alabama for research projects[4].

It was built by the Mobile Area Public Higher Education Foundation, Inc., and leased to the state after being spearheaded by the Mobile Area Chamber of Commerce. Others on the program were Dr. Frank Rose, president of the University of Alabama; Dr. William K. Weaver, president of Mobile College; the Rev. A. William Crandell, S.J., president of Spring Hill College; M. E. Weatherby, Jr., chamber president; Leroy Stevens, Sydney Pfleger and Ernest G. Cleverdon.

[1] Mr. Davis was assistant cashier and manager of the bank's Springdale Branch.
[2] Mr. Baker is the father of Joseph H. Baker, Jr., an assistant vice president of the First National Bank.
[3] A year later, Vicki Powers won the "Miss Alabama" title and placed in the semi-finals of the Miss America Pageant at Atlantic City.
[4] In August, 1963, the Federal government completed construction of a second research laboratory on Dauphin Island, operated under the U. S. Public Health Service, to study water pollution and oyster betterment.

The origins of a belt line highway around the City of Mobile had their beginnings when the County Board directed J. B. Converse & Co. to make a survey. On Feb. 13, 1952, the board voted to ask the State Highway Department to apply for Federal adoption of the road under the Federal-aid highway system.

Eventually it developed that the 4-lane belt line would become the link not only between Highways 90 and 43, but that it would become an integral part of the new Interstate 65 and link with Interstate 10 at Navco.

Construction work started on the first phase Nov. 23, 1958, and the road had the distinction of being (1) the first urban interstate highway in Alabama and (2) the first having a cloverleaf section in South Alabama. The construction began after the board had formally voted to undertake the job on Sept. 15, 1954, and the first houses were removed from the right-of-way on Sept. 12, a year later.

Right-of-way litigation was very involved, and a total of $1.5 million was paid for this purpose. By the dedication date of Jan. 4, 1963, another $12.7 million— mostly Federal funds—were expended on the 6.816 miles connecting U.S. 90 and U.S. 45 (the final link to U.S. 43 is under construction).

Aside from I-65, other Federal highway projects now being constructed include I-10 from within the city to the Mississippi line; new twin tunnels under Mobile River and I-10 across Mobile Bay to a point south of Spanish Fort in Baldwin County are scheduled for the future.

¶*H. Austill Pharr, president of the First National Bank, received a signal honor in 1958—election as the "Mobilian of the Year," and the bank was featured in the British magazine "Motoring" for pioneering in drive-in banking.*

Electronic bookkeeping equipment was installed and a time-saving exit into Conti Street was built at the Broad Street Office.

¶*In 1958, E. S. Sledge, II, and G. E. Weiss were elected vice presidents; Frank W. Drey and Thomas G. St. John, Jr., trust officers; Edward T. Sauls, assistant trust officer.*

The following were named assistant cashiers:

John A. Davis, Robert F. Casey, James E. Pollard, R. Leslie Adams, I. L. Davis, Jr., Harry D. Henson, Archie W. Luckie and Alfred K. Seibt. (Mr. Casey held this position until 1962).

¶*C. S. Latshaw and John L. Strauss were elected to the bank's board of directors in January. Both continue to serve in that capacity.*

The First National Bank had 861 shareholders and deposits totaling $102,410,681 at the end of 1958.

¶*The First National Bank opened its Springdale Plaza Office on Nov. 19, 1959—the bank's sixth location.*

During this year, the interest rate on regular savings accounts was increased to 3%, and a "walk-up" teller's window was installed at the Brookley Air Force Base Facility.

The employees' lunch room was enlarged and modernized, and named the "Gazzam Room" in honor of the bank's first president—C. W. Gazzam (1865-1868).

Since it was organized in 1865, the First National Bank has not missed paying cash dividends each year. The total as of mid 1965 stands at $10,880,280.

Charles H. Gibbons was promoted to assistant trust officer and J. M. Hull, to assistant cashier.

Three-story administration building of Mobile College.

1960—NEED FOR MORE COLLEGES REALIZED

Throughout the years of Mobile's growth, it became apparent that the area needed more institutions of higher learning—although Spring Hill College continued to expand and enlarge its faculty and facilities.

Baptists had long thought of a college in Mobile, and serious discussion began as early as 1944. Definite planning took shape in 1959 when the Alabama State Baptist Convention gave it its blessing and agreed to establish the college in Mobile if $1,500,000 could be raised in cash and pledges within two years. T. T. Martin was chairman of the fund drive.

By 1960, more than three-fourths of this goal was assured by individuals and churches in Mobile, Baldwin, Clarke and Washington Counties, and another $600,000 was pledged by business and industry.

Also, by 1960, officials of the University of Alabama took congizance of the widespread appeal of the Mobile Center, and tentative plans were formulated for a "University of South Alabama" to be located here.

A year later, as both events moved forward, Alabama chartered its first senior college in 57 years and Alabama Baptists established their first in 120 years when Mobile College was inaugurated. On April 1, 1961, Dr. William K. Weaver of Sylacauga became the first president and construction began on a site just 10 miles from downtown Mobile—a 400-acre campus in serene woodlands bordered by Chickasaw Creek.

It was dedicated on Sept. 6, 1963, and three days later the first freshman class was enrolled—where students attended classes, did library work and attended chapel all in one three-story administration building. A year later, two dormitory buildings and a dining hall were completed. A Christian college of liberal arts and sciences, it is continually growing—and its first senior class will graduate in 1967.

Following preliminary talks in 1960 and before, the Mobile County Foundation for Public Higher Education—headed by E. G. Cleverdon as president—spearheaded development of a new university to replace the Mobile Center of the University of Alabama.

The University of South Alabama was established by the Alabama Legislature in 1963 and operating funds were appropriated. The legislation, sponsored by the entire Mobile delegation, provided for a board of trustees and for operating the new university.

Also in late 1963, the trustees named Dr. Frederick P. Whiddon, who as formerly director of the Mobile Center, as the first president and authorized him to begin forming a faculty and to make preliminary plans for the university. In the meantime, both the Mobile County Commission and the City Commission each pledged $500,000 to the foundation for construction costs, and a site was leased from the Mobile County School Board on land adjacent to the new Mobile Municipal Park in the Spring Hill area.

On June 7, 1964, the single building was dedicated in ceremonies when Mr. Cleverdon turned it over to the University of South Alabama. President Whiddon, the youngest university president in the nation at 33, accepted and 175 freshmen and sophomores, along with a faculty of 35, were ready for the summer school term. By fall of 1964, the University surpassed its capacity of more than 900 students. [1]

On October 18, 1964 formal ceremonies dedicating the University of South Alabama were highlighted by an address by Gov. George C. Wallace who presented the University charter to Pres. Whiddon.

In its first year, the University added a swimming pool, tennis courts, dressing rooms and other physical education facilities, and the spring of 1965 saw ground breaking for an additional classroom building of five floors.

Both Mobile College and the University of South Alabama are on the way to bigger things in education.

On Jan. 19, 1960, directors of the First National Bank approved a 25% stock dividend which increased the outstanding shares from 60,000 to 75,000 and the capital from $1,500,000 to $1,875,000. Surplus remained unchanged at $4,500,000 and on Dec. 30, resources totaled $117,441,916.

During 1960, the bank made plans for future expansion by purchasing the old Custom House property, which the City of Mobile acquired from the Federal Government in 1939.

¶Four new directors were elected at the stockholders' meeting in January of 1960. They were S. Boyd Adams, Mark Lyons, Jr., G. C. Outlaw, Jr. and Howard Schramm. Mr. Adams, Mr. Lyons and Mr. Outlaw are sons of former directors.

In December, William H. Armbrecht was appointed to fill a vacancy on the board.

All are still serving in this capacity.

¶The following were promoted in 1960:

R. L. Adams, Clarence E. Davis, John A. Davis, W. M. Feeney and Edward D. Simms, to assistant vice presidents; James C. Andress, to vice president; Joseph H. Baker, Jr. and E. T. Sauls, to trust officers; B. M. Simms and E. M. Steiner, to assistant cashiers.

Edward D. Simms held this position until 1964 and B. M. Simms until 1965.

In December, 1960, Dwain G. Luce was appointed a vice president.

---

[1]State and Federal funds have been assured to increase the capacity to 1800 students by late 1966.

1961—MOBILE CELEBRATES 250th ANNIVERSARY

A CITY ONLY gets one chance to celebrate its 250th anniversary, and Mobile pulled out all the stops to make her's an event to be long remembered.

A year-long fete was planned for 1961, and Mayor Joseph N. Langan, on May 12, 1960, appointed an interim committee of 40, under the temporary chairmanship of Y. D. Lott, to coordinate early preparations. Members were:

H. Austill Pharr, Leroy Stevens, Alfred Delchamps, J. F. McRae, George Denniston, Mark Lyons, Jr., W. D. McGrady, Maj.-Gen. D. F. Callahan, Rev. A. W. Crandall, Dr. Cranford Burns, James V. Irby, Jr. Caldwell Delaney, Ernest Cleverdon, State Sen. Will G. Caffey, Jr., William J. Hearin, Jr., Wadsworth B. Pape, John Strauss, Juan Blackwell, Jay Altmayer, George Fuller, Sen. Lister Hill, Sen. John Sparkman, Rep. Frank Boykin, Gov. John Patterson, Henry R. Luscher, Jr., Charles Waller, Lewis W. Hill, Mrs. Rosemary Walsh, Hyman Berger, Julian Rayford, Alfred Staples, Rev. J. Edwin Stuardi, S. A. Alsup, Thomas A. Greaves, Joseph Wilson, Sheldon Morgan, Robert Corrigan and William Deneke. The mayor was also on the committee.

At the same time, Mayor Langan resolved:

"In the year 1711, Jean Baptiste le Moyne, Sieur de Bienville, moved the then nine-year-old settlement known as Mobile from its site at Twenty-Seven Mile Bluff on the Mobile River to its present location on the western shores of Mobile Bay; and

"The year 1961 will mark the 250th anniversary of the location of the City of Mobile at its present site; and

"Few American cities can boast of a history and heritage of two-and-a-half centuries; and

"The commemoration of the 250th anniversary of the City of Mobile at its present location is of great significance, historically, socially, culturally and economically to the people of the city, the county and the South as a whole, and should be commemorated by appropriate celebration, pageantry and festivity; and

"Such commemoration can best be effected by a committee of private citizens, be it resolved that the Board of Commissioners do hereby establish the 250th Anniversary Committee of the City of Mobile."

After this, things moved at a steady pace for the beginning of the 1961 fete. It was decided to hold the major celebration during the week of June 12 to June 18, corresponding to the period when the original settlement was believed moved, although the anniversary itself would continue throughout the entire year.

Individual groups, as well as civic clubs, made their own plans to participate. The plans gained momentum shortly after the year of 1961 began, and many male citizens started growing beards to help celebrate. On April 3, Henry R. Luscher, Sr., now mayor under the city's rotation system, proclaimed the organization of "Cavalier" groups and added:

"All males of the age when shaving is feasible will refrain from shaving from now until after the end of our glorious 250th Anniversary Celebration Week in June."

¶ *Mobile's 250th Anniversary year proved to be the greatest profit year to date for the First National Bank.*

There were 947 shareholders and 328 employees.

In July of 1961, an automatic payroll check deposit plan was offered customers of the Brookley Air Force Base Facility. In August, the bank invited Mobile residents to finance "family fallout shelters" on a 5-year repayment plan.

Deposits totaled $116,977,546 at year's end, a gain of more than 12% over the same period of 1960.

It was further proclaimed that the beards should "be readily seen and recognized at eight paces."

Proper "punishment and humiliation" was also decreed for those "males who refuse to join the fun organization, the Cavaliers, by failing to sport such wiry or silky hirsute appendages as in the days of our ancestors."

A Kangaroo Court was later held weekly in Bienville Square for those who "demanded a fair trial;" others were summarily dealt with by a group of self-appointed vigilantes, the "Keystone Kops." There was much merriment.

Not to be outdone, the ladies of Mobile followed suit on April 10 and formed the "Jubilee Belles," who made and wore elaborate gowns of Mobile's various historic periods. Each Friday was set aside for dress-up day, and many strangers in this city—who happened to pass through on a Friday—were indeed treated to a sight of splendor and gaiety.

Also on Fridays, public picnics and festivities were held in Bienville Square, and the city took on the appearance of having a gay lark—which it certainly was!

Julian deOvies, had become the permanent chairman of the 250th Anniversary Celebration, and everything pointed to a grand climactic pageant of Mobile's history, known as "Heritage and Horizons," which was scheduled for Ladd Stadium on six nights, beginning Monday, June 12.

A professional producer, George Elias, recruited some 1,200 Mobilians for the cast, and rehearsals began. It was loudly acclaimed at its premiere performance and, although the city faced a full week of rain and threatened rain, attendance topped the 5,000 mark each night.

On the final night, a time capsule was buried at Ladd Stadium, to be opened when Mobile celebrates its 300th anniversary in 2011. It included records and histories of Mobile, newspaper copies and numerous letters and telegrams, including those from President John F. Kennedy, ex-President Dwight D. Eisenhower, Vice President Lyndon B. Johnson and Gov. John Patterson. Mobilians were also permitted, for a $1 fee which went into the general celebration fund, to write individual letters on special forms, and several thousand of these went into the capsule.

¶*On Jan. 16, 1962, directors of the First National Bank approved a 6⅔% stock dividend which increased the bank's shares by 5,000, and increased the capital from $1,875,000 to $2,000,000.*

There was no change in the surplus, which remained at $4,500,000.

With other banks throughout the nation, on Jan. 1, 1962, the First National Bank increased the rate of interest on regular savings accounts and certificates of deposit to 4%, when kept on deposit 12 months or longer.

¶*On Jan. 16, 1962, H. E. Coale was elected vice president and senior trust officer; Cameron Pettiss, vice president; N. Q. Adams, vice president and trust officer; John L. Sullivan, assistant comptroller; Dillon A. Toomer, assistant cashier.*

¶*The Trust Department of the First National Bank, (founded soon after trust powers were granted to national banks in 1913) in many instances is now serving the third generation.*

The bank, at year's end had $130,-424,535 in deposits—an increase of nearly 33% in the last five years.

¶*Announcement of the new 33-story First National Bank building—to be constructed on the site of the historic old Custom House on the southwest corner of Royal and St. Francis Streets—was exciting news in June of 1963.*

As Alabama's tallest building, it demonstrated the bank's continuing faith and confidence in the growth of Mobile and the entire Gulf Coast area and justified its motto: "BUILDING FOR THE FUTURE ON THE HERITAGE OF THE PAST."

1963—MOBILE RATED AS LARGEST DIVERSIFIED PAPER MAKING CENTER IN THE WORLD

ACTUALLY, MOBILE achieved this status as early as 1955 when the Mobile mill of International Paper Company, Southern Kraft Division, underwent a $43 million expansion program; and two of the largest paper machines in the entire paper industry were added to the firm's already sprawling plant which had its beginnings here in 1928.[1]

This expansion enabled the company to produce newsprint for the first time in the South and made the Mobile mill the largest diversified paper mill in the world. Production has now reached 1,150 tons of paper each day—quite a difference from the 170 tons per day predicted for the mill in 1928.

By 1930, the mill had three paper machines in operation and some 500 employed; now there are six machines with more than 3,700 employees and a total payroll of more than $23 million. This does not include the number of people who harvest and supply the mill with large quantities of pulp wood.

Today's paper machines are giants in industry, operating at high speeds. On an average day, International turns out approximately 2,000 miles of paper, ranging in width from 10 to 22 feet. Annually, this is about 730,000 miles of paper.

The payroll of the mill had grown from $571 thousand in 1930 to $23 million annually in 1962; more than $1.5 million was also paid in city, state and Federal taxes. From an early prediction of annual freight revenue at $550,000, now more than $6 million is paid in freight each year.

A major producer at the plant is the Mobile Bag Factory, a self-contained facility turning out more than 24 million grocery bags and sacks a day. Another operation is the BagPak Division, which converts kraft paper into multiwall sacks and asphalt laminated paper used by industry to ship more than 400 different commodities. There is also the Erling Riis Research Laboratory, one of the most modern and completely equipped pulp and paper research laboratories in the world.

¶*The Cloverleaf Plaza Office was opened on Aug. 18, 1963, providing the bank with seven locations conveniently situated in Mobile and the county.*

A month earlier the bank announced a new loan service for parents and guardians of children, to assist with financing higher education, called the "College Loan Plan."

The bank's shareholders now numbered more than 1,000, with 80,000 shares outstanding.

The number of loans outstanding at year's end was 16,867, an increase of more than $8,000,000 (nearly 13%) over the same period in 1962.

The bank's staff consisted of 353 persons and deposits totaled $133,-914,325. at year's end.

¶*In January of 1963, John W. McNichol and Robert E. Stevenson were elected to the bank's board of directors. In December 1963 Carr J. Smith was elected to the board.*

Mr. McNichol served in this capacity until April 8, 1964, Mr. Stevenson and Mr. Smith still hold this title.

¶*On Jan. 15, 1963, R. L. Adams and W. H. Sadler were promoted to vice presidents; W. T. Dumas and W. H. McNair, to assistant cashiers.*

On July 15, 1963, S. R. Stephenson joined the bank's staff as assistant trust officer.

John D. Terrell, senior vice president and cashier, was honored on his 50th Anniversary with the bank. Mr. Terrell still serves in these capacities.

Scott Paper Co. entered the Mobile scene when a merger with Hollingsworth & Whitney (which had built a pulp-and-paper mill here in 1940) was consummated in October, 1954. Mobile became headquarters for the company's Southern Division, and one expansion program after another was placed on the drawing boards.

The first real major expansion was plotted in 1956 and completed by Feb. 29, 1959, when a $20 million tissue mill, for the production of household products, was placed into operation. At this time, the three kraft machines and two tissue machines represented an employee list of 1,630 and an annual payroll of $9.5 million; this very shortly rose to 2,000 employees by 1963 and an annual payroll in excees of $13 million.

On July 25, 1963, Paul C. Baldwin, executive vice president of the parent company, and John McNichol,[2] general manager of the Mobile plant, announced an additional $45 million expansion and modernization program which would increase the tissue output another 60,000 tons annually and hike the pulp output 100,000 tons.

Within a few months (by Dec. 5), another $10 million was added to the $45 million project when it was revealed that two new high-speed paper machines would be installed instead of the one previously announced. The program was expected to be in full swing by late 1965, when 350 anticipated new jobs would be filled and the annual payroll hiked to nearly $16 million.

In early 1965 the Mobile facility of Scott was the largest of its 13 in the United States and larger than any of its affiliates in 11 foreign countries.

Bemis Bro. Bag Co. opened a plant at Magazine Point on May 17, 1943, with 32 employees. Manufacturer of small bags for packaging and shipping, it obtains most of its supplies from its nearby neighbor Scott Paper Company.

Bemis has continued its growth in Mobile and now has nearly 400 employees with a payroll touching $2 million annually, and still buys about 90 per cent of its products locally. It manufactures more than 100 million small bags and 65 million large shipping bag-sacks annually, and it uses 1,500 tons of paper monthly.

Looking back, Mobile can point with justifiable pride and profit to the $100,000 it invested in the first paper mill and plant in 1928. The returns have been vastly rewarding.

¶*The First National Bank's slogan, "NEARING A CENTURY OF SERVICE TO MOBILE AND THE SOUTH" became even more appropriate as the bank crossed the threshold of 1964, with its Centennial in 1965 "just around the corner." Newspaper and national publicity began to point up this noteworthy occasion.*

On Jan. 29, 1964, President Pharr turned the first spadeful of dirt on the former location of the old Custom House —symbolic of the beginning of the new 33-story downtown building.

Granite blocks from this hisotric edifice (built in 1856 on inverted arches of hand-made brick and huge virgin pine timbers) were used to frame a bronze plaque in Bienville Square commemorating the Centennial of the Battle of Mobile Bay.

On May 24, a new type of loan called the "PROPERTY IMPROVEMENT LOAN PLAN" was announced.

The bank's 99th Anniversary, On Oct. 18, 1964, was appropriately celebrated at the annual employees' party at which President Pharr was master-of-ceremonies.

---

[1]See Page 96: 1928—Establishment of Southern Kraft Paper Mill.

[2]Mr. McNichol was elected a member of the board of directors of the First National Bank on Jan. 15, 1963, and served in this capacity until April 8, 1964.

Mobile's new Municipal Theater and Auditorium in East Church Street
Historical Redevelopment Area.

1964—MUNICIPAL AUDITORIUM IS OPENED

MOBILE'S NEW Municipal Auditorium—which opened on July 9,
1964, with the presentation of an ice
show, although far from finished—virtually dazzled the 5,000 or more persons on
hand for the premiere look. Many who
were viewing it for the first time could
not believe Mobile had finally graduated
into "big time" auditorium circles.

¶ *The bank's earnings for 1964 (before
taxes) were in excess of $2,000,000—a
record figure. It had 17,721 loans outstanding as of Dec. 31, an increase of
854 over the same period in 1963.*

*Deposits at year's end were $142,-
804,322.*

¶ *On Jan. 21, Harry D. Henson was
elected assistant vice president; Robert
J. Blackwell, Fred L. Caver, Richard
Murray, III, Richard S. O'Neill, L.
P. Patrick, Jr. and Staples L. Shearer,
assistant cashiers.*

*On July 7, James E. Pollard was
promoted to assistant vice president.*

Behind all this lay some 15 years of
"auditorium talk" and at least six full
years of active planning.

On Oct. 27, 1959, architects and engineers for the new project were selected.
The Church Street area was chosen, with
the auditorium to be part of a vast urban
renewal, rehabilitation and renovation
project. In May, 1960, Mobile voters
approved a $6 million auditorium bond
issue. Some of the bonds were to be retired by a one-cent city sales tax which the
Commission had voted one year earlier as
part of the city's $21 million five-year
capital improvement program.

By mid-1960, land parcels in the auditorium area were appraised at between
$1.5 million and $2 million. Delays arose
when many property owners, dissatisfied
with individual appraisals, took the
matter into the courts. The elections of
1961 brought two newcomers to the City
Commission—Mr. Trimmier and Mr. Mc-
Nally—who had ideas of their own regarding auditorium costs and plans.

The Commission opened bids March 14, 1962, and J. A. Jones Construction Co. was low bidder with $7,750,000. A week later, the Commission awarded the contract and Mayor George McNally signed it on April 3.

In the months that followed, the auditorium complex slowly took shape. Some historic buildings were preserved to become part of the new East Church Street Historic and Redevelopment Area, and at least two—the Phoenix Fire Station and the Old Telegraph Building—were moved to new locations in the general auditorium sector.

Mario Bottesini was named to head an auditorium board with eight other members, while Walter C. (Buddy) Clewis, a native of Macon, Ga., with many years of experience in auditorium administration, was appointed general manager. Fifteen other full-time employees were placed on the auditorium staff, while the part-time roster called for between 35 and 200.

So, despite the rising costs, Mobile's Municipal Auditorium was opened on July 9 and then formally dedicated in a three-day celebration beginning Sept. 18. The adjoining 1,960-seat Municipal Theater was unveiled to a Mobile audience for the first time in October, when Van Cliburn, internationally famed pianist, was guest artist with the Mobile Symphony.

In its first year, the Auditorium-Theater has housed many events, from a circus to a concert, from an indoor track meet to midget car racing, from basketball to boogie-woogie, from small meetings in one of the 16 meeting rooms to large conventions and religious gatherings in the 10,000-seat arena, and from the Mardi Gras balls and coronation to the America's Junior Miss Pageant.

"It took a lot of talk and money," a Mobilian said, "but it's worth every word and every penny!"

1964—USS BATTLESHIP "ALABAMA" BROUGHT TO FINAL HOME AT MOBILE

ON MAY 17, 1962, the Mobile Area Chamber of Commerce initiated the first efforts to save the famed and historic USS Battleship "ALABAMA" from the scrap heap. The Navy had declared the $200 million, 35,000-ton vessel as surplus and obsolete in its mothballed status in Bremerton, Wash. It was to be dismanteled on June 1, 1962.

The Navy agreed to postpone the scrapping, and on Aug. 29, 1962, Gov. John A. Patterson appointed a 21-man battleship committee to study the feasibility of acquiring the ship. Henri Aldridge was named chairman, while other Mobilians included Stephens G. Croom, Alfred F. Delchamps, W. G. McGrady and State Sen. John Tyson.

With the turn of the year, Gov. George C. Wallace took over the governor's seat, the Legislature approved a $50,000 fund for a study, and a letter was dispatched as a formal request for the vessel to the Navy Department. Alabama was well on her way to gaining her namesake battleship.

A delegation from Mobile, as well as other areas in the state, went to the Bremerton yards and inspected the vessel, and the Mobile Planning Commission in February, 1963, called a public hearing on selection of a site. Mr. Croom suggested a site west of the Tensaw River Bridge south of the Mobile Bay Causeway, and this was ultimately accepted.

Gov. Wallace named a new, 18-man permanent USS Battleship Commission and, at its organizational meeting Nov. 6, 1963, Mr. Aldridge was again named chairman. Other Mobilians now included Mr. Croom, Mr. McGrady and State Rep. Robert S. Edington, with terms to expire Nov. 1, 1971.

A million dollar, statewide fund drive was started in early 1964, with Frank P. Samford, Birmingham insurance executive, as chairman. Dwain G. Luce,[1] and Ernest F. Ladd, were subchairmen for the Mobile area.

---

[1]Mr. Luce is a vice president of the bank.

Civic clubs, schools, industry, and individuals contributed generously. Gov. Wallace issued "admiral" commissions for all donations of $100 or more, and the response was gratifying.

Towed by two ocean tugs, the battleship left the Seattle area on July 21 and arrived in Mobile Bay on Sept. 13, 1964, after a record-breaking 5,600-mile trip marred by turbulent seas and the tragic loss of one tug (with one death) in the Pacific area off the Panama Canal. A Mobile tug, the "Margaret Walsh," was dispatched to complete the tow, which was accomplished without further mishap.

The USS Battleship "Alabama" at her temporary anchorage off Pinto Island on Sept. 14, 1964, after record-breaking 5,600-mile tow from Bremerton, Wash.

On Sept. 14, the proud vessel reached a temporary berth off Pinto Island and was given a rousing welcome from Mobile's citizenry. The ship was towed into her permanent berth on Sept 23.

Vice Admiral William V. Davis, Jr. (retired) was piped aboard Nov. 4 to become the ship's executive director, and work continued in transforming the Causeway site into a memorial park and shrine.

The formal dedication was held Saturday, Jan. 9, 1965, with two Mobile vice admirals, Page Smith and Alfred G. (Corky) Ward on hand, as well as Undersecretary of the Navy Paul B. Fay, Gov. George C. Wallace, Sen. John Sparkman, Linda Felber (1964 Junior Miss), and some 600 military and 2,500 civilians. The names of 2,000 "admirals" were made a part of the ship's official log.

The ship is now open for public inspection and work is progressing on final completion of the adjoining park area and memorial shrine. By mid-year of 1965, more than 250,000 visitors had been "logged aboard."

1965—INDUSTRIAL REVIEW AND A LOOK TOWARD A PROGRESSIVE FUTURE

AS THE First National Bank—"*Building for the Future on the Heritage of the Past*"—enters its second century of service, the vast and gratifying potential in store for the entire Mobile area is quite evident.

This emphasis on Mobile's future was dramatized on March 23, 1965, when—with impressive dedicatory rites—the cornerstone was sealed in the new 33-story First National Bank building which is expected to be completed during 1966.

H. Austill Pharr, president, told his audience of bank officials, dignitaries and other citizens "we trust this building will become an important part of the heritage we pass on to future generations."

Many phases of Mobile's industrial, cultural and religious growth have been briefly described in this book. It is impossible, in commenting upon the "highlights" of the past century, to include everything—but one must pause and consider the chemical industry which in recent years has become a major factor in the economy of the Mobile area.

More than $100 million has been expended by national companies in establishing plants or expanding existing facilities in just the past decade. Among these are Diamond Alkali, Geigy, Olin Mathieson, Stauffer, American Cyanamid and Union Carbide.

Aside from these, Courtaulds, Ltd. of England, began a $25 million venture 20 miles north of the city at Salco in 1951. The original rayon plant had tripled its output to 150 million pounds of rayon fiber annually by 1956.

Ideal Cement Co., located on the State Docks property since 1946, announced in May, 1955, an expansion program to hoist its output to 31 million barrels.

The growing city saw a new station built for the L. & N. Railroad, a new county courthouse, a new city and county jail, extensive additions to the State Docks (including a grain elevator and more cold storage warehouse space), three new country clubs and untold millions in both residential and commercial housing developments.

The city has undergone a vast urban renewal program, including the historic projects in the Church Street Area and De Tonti Square; and the opening of one of the finest auditorium-theatre complexes in the nation.

As the new Federal-state highway net begins to take shape around Mobile, work continues at a rapid pace on Interstate 10 and Interstate 65. Twin tunnels under Mobile River are scheduled as a part of this program.

Never-ending dredging of the Mobile Ship Channel is expected to shortly fix its depth at 40 to 42 feet and allow even larger vessels to enter the Port of Mobile harbor.

By 1961, various annexation programs had increased Mobile's land area to 152.9 square miles, with an additional 25 square miles of water in the city limits, making it the 11th largest in the nation.

Mobile even added an astronaut to her long list of achievements in October, 1963, when Capt. C. C. Williams, son of veteran Mobile Water Works official Cliff Williams, was named among 14 new aspirants for space training.

Mrs. Lyndon B. Johnson, wife of the President, visited Mobile on Oct. 10, 1964, and took part in dedication ceremonies for the replaced and reconstructed Phoenix Fire Station.

Although the future of Brookley Air Force Base—Mobile's largest single civilian employer and a dominant factor in the city's growth since its inception more than 25 years ago—remains at mid-1965 an undetermined decision by the military and defense chiefs of the nation, the "City of Six Flags" looks confidently ahead!

¶ *The New Year of 1965 was greeted by the raucous but welcome sound of heavy pile driving equipment, sinking the firm foundation of the new 33-story First National Bank building deep into the earth . . . prophetizing an even greater era of prosperity for Mobile.*

On March 23, impressive cornerstone dedicatory ceremonies were held on the corner of Royal and St. Francis Streets, adjacent to the steelwork of the $10,-000,000 building which even then was beginning to reach skyward.

President Pharr and other dignitaries used silver trowels, and the dedicatory address was delivered by Henri M. Aldridge.

Sealed in the cornerstone at the Northeast corner of the new building were the old Mobile newspapers of 1854, coins and artifacts found when the cornerstone of the old Custom House was opened on Feb. 21, 1964; also the names of hundreds of Mobile citizens who were given membership cards in the First National Bank "Sidewalk Superintendent's Club", mementos of the current year and a letter from President Pharr to the president of the bank in the year 2065 — one hundred years hence!

¶ *The First National Bank opened its modern Midtown Branch at 914 Government Street on Jan. 25, 1965, to take the place of its outgrown Broad Street Branch which opened in 1956.*

¶ *On Feb. 18, 1965, the bank's capital was increased from $2,000,000 to $3,000,000 by increasing the shares from 80,000 to 240,000. This resulted in a "stock dividend" for the bank's 1,069 shareholders. There was no change in the surplus, which remained at $4,500,000.*

Drury O. Prichard was promoted to assistant vice president; Chobee Slay, Odie E. Williams and William V. Bosarge, to assistant cashiers; and Rodney M. Farris, to assistant comptroller. Charles H. Gibbons and Samuel R. Stephenson were promoted to trust officers.

On Aug. 10, 1965, Joseph H. Baker, Jr. was elected assistant vice president and Thomas E. Sharpe, Jr., assistant trust officer.

¶ *As this book goes to press, plans are being made to celebrate the 100th Anniversary of the First National Bank on Oct. 18, 1965, in an appropriate manner.*

Just as the long-familiar "Blue Book" entitled "HIGHLIGHTS OF 75 YEARS IN MOBILE" was dedicated to the bank's Diamond Anniversary in 1940 (described on page 119), so is this new and greatly enlarged volume, "HIGHLIGHTS OF 100 YEARS IN MOBILE" dedicated to the bank's first century of service to Mobile and the South!

The towering new 33-story building of The First National Bank, bounded by Royal, St. Francis and St. Joseph Streets. Dramatically piercing the sky, it stands as evidence of First National's confidence in the future of Mobile and the entire Gulf Coast area.

On the one hundredth anniversary of the First National Bank of Mobile, Alabama, we list the bank family as this book is published.

DIRECTORS

S. Boyd Adams
Wm. H. Armbrecht
Robert S. Bacon
J. L. Bedsole
Herbert C. Brown
A. F. Delchamps
C. S. Latshaw
Mark, Lyons, Jr.

J. R. Mighell, Jr.
Richard Murray
George C. Outlaw, Jr.
H. A. Pharr
Lee Robinson
Howard M. Schramm
Carr J. Smith
Robert E. Stevenson
John L. Strauss

ADVISORY BOARD
Midtown Branch

E. E. Delaney

Tennent L. Griffin

Earle W. Long, Sr.

W. O. Pape

Joseph C. Sullivan

OFFICERS

H. Austill Pharr
President

Robert S. Bacon
Executive Vice President

John D. Terrell
*Senior Vice President
and Cashier*

James T. Overbey
Senior Vice President

R. Leslie Adams
Vice President

W. E. Akridge, Jr.
Vice President

James C. Andress
Vice President

Dwain G. Luce
Vice President

W. Cameron Pettiss
Vice President

Albert E. Reynolds
Vice President

William H. Sadler
Vice President

Lee R. Seifert
Vice President

Edward S. Sledge, II
Vice President

Charles E. Van Devender
Vice President

G. Evans Weiss
Vice President

Wythe L. Whiting, Jr.
Vice President

Joseph H. Baker, Jr.
Assistant Vice President

Clarence E. Davis
Assistant Vice President

John A. Davis
Assistant Vice President

William M. Feeney
Assistant Vice President

Harry D. Henson
Assistant Vice President

James E. Pollard
Assistant Vice President

Drury O. Pritchard
Assistant Vice President

Charles G. Bitzer
Assistant Cashier

R. Juan Blackwell
Assistant Cashier

W. Vincent Bosarge
Assistant Cashier

Fred L. Caver, Jr.
Assistant Cashier

Isaac L. Davis, Jr.
Assistant Cashier

Walter T. Dumas
Assistant Cashier

George A. Hieronymus
Assistant Cashier

Jewett M. Hull
Assistant Cashier

Archie W. Luckie
Assistant Cashier

Sylvester S. Mattei
Assistant Cashier

William H. McNair
Assistant Cashier

Sanford S. Moore
Assistant Cashier

Richard Murray, III
Assistant Cashier

Richard S. O'Neill
Assistant Cashier

Lloyd B. Patrick
Assistant Cashier

Alfred K. Seibt
Assistant Cashier

Staples L. Shearer
Assistant Cashier

Chobee Slay
Assistant Cashier

Elbert M. Steiner
Assistant Cashier

Dillon A. Toomer
Assistant Cashier

Odie E. Williams
Assistant Cashier

Harwell E. Coale
*Vice President and
Senior Trust Officer*

N. Q. Adams
*Vice President and
Trust Officer*

Francis W. Drey
Trust Officer

Charles H. Gibbons
Trust Officer

Thomas G. St. John, Jr.
Trust Officer

Edward T. Sauls
Trust Officer

Samuel R. Stephenson, Jr.
Trust Officer

Thomas E. Sharp, Jr.
Assistant Trust Officer

T. Redmond Foster
Comptroller

Rodney M. Farris
Assistant Comptroller

Gregory S. Strong
Assistant Comptroller

John L. Sullivan
Assistant Comptroller

B. Franklin King
Auditor

PERSONNEL

Betty J. Ade
David H. Akridge
Pauline Alexander
Clifford H. Anderson
Frank J. Andrade
Charles A. Andrews
Christine Arnold
P. Lynn Arnold
Seymore Bagby
M. Ann Baggett
Bonnie Barnett
Angela Barter
Mary C. Beauvais
Catherine Bertolino
Giacomo Bertolino, Jr.
Billie Blackwell
Penelope J. Bolerakis
Joseph M. Bolling
Joan G. Borham
Warren J. Boutreis, Jr.
Agnes Boykin
L. Russell Brandau, Jr.
Sarah D. Brandon
Linda Bratcher
Mable E. Brettel
Shirley K. Bridges
Claudius H. Broadus
Josephine M. Bronold
Barbara A. Brooks
Betty Brown
Shirley M. Browne
L. Thelton Bryant, Jr.
P. Randolph Bryars, III
Patricia H. Bullock
Barbara G. Burgess
E. Rogers Burgett
Aundrie Burroughs
Judy R. Bush
Eugenia G. Butler
Jerilyn W. Byrd
Bessie R. Camilleri
Jayne L. Capps
Cecelia A. Cassady
Martha L. Catlin
S. Anita Catlin
N. Sue Cavanaugh
Byron O. Cawthon, Jr.
Sara B. Chance
Eliza M. Churchwell
Alberta Cieutat
Carolyn Clark
Dora L. Clayton
Robert G. Cloud
Antoinette C. Coker
D. Faye Cole
M. Hugh Coleman
Cecelia B. Compston
James M. Cook
Patricia Corwin
Mary G. Coumanis
Frances Cowley
William M. Crabtree
Katie J. Crane
Sylvia Crigler
Jo Ann Crocker
Esther M. Cunill
Barbara A. Curry
Richard J. Curry
Agnes E. Daly
Thelma Daugherty
Mary L. Daves
Lucille D. Davis
Kathryn D. Deas
Judith E. Dees
Fannie Dennard
Lynn M. Dolan
Lee F. Dowdell

M. Dianne Duffy
Florence S. Dukes
Hugh R. Dukes
Frank Dunning
Muir J. Edney, Jr.
Diane B. Edwards
Barbara J. Ellis
George E. Ellis, III
John E. Ellis
Eugene L. Elmore
O. Duane Etheredge
Louise G. Evans
Harriet A. Fagan
Ruth Farrar
James P. Ferrill
Virginia T. Finnegan
M. Theresa Ford
Georgeine L. Foy
Maryneil Frederick
Shelia J. Freeland
Henry W. French, Jr.
Shirley R. French
Jasper D. Gay
Mary A. Gaydos
Mona R. Gazzier
Suellen Geary
J. Earlin Geil
William T. George
Anita McA. Gibson
Jimmy Giles
Jeanette C. Gill
Virginia W. Glover
Carolyn Godwin
Russell C. Goolsby
Emil T. Graf, III
Leonna D. Graf
M. Kathryn Gregory
Margie Greiner
Collins P. Guidry
Cary Hall
Lorna B. Hall
Mary F. Hallet
Rose M. Hallett
James R. Hancock
Florence P. Hardy
Thelma L. Harrington
Robert L. Harris
Kathleen H. Harrison
Frederic T. Harteau, Jr.
Joe B. Harwood, Jr.
T. Jean Hastings
Audrey H. Hawkshead
Willie S. Hayes
Charles A. Helmer
Barbara D. Henderson
C. Norma Hendry
George L. Hester
Patsy U. Hewitt
Harron Hines
Elizabeth W. Hinkle
Carolyn A. Hogan
Doris H. Horton
Linda K. Howard
Lynn Hudson
Dorothy L. Hughes
M. Pearl Jackson
Andres Jimenez, Jr.
Norman R. Jobe
Bobby J. Johnson
F. Jean Johnson
Malcolm A. Johnson, Jr.
S. Macey Johnson, Jr.
Alvin C. Jones
Sharon K. Jones
Waurine Keefe
Alma T. Kelly
Joseph McC. Kemp

Joy M. Kemp
Hugh F. Kennedy
Rose M. Keppler
Katherine A. King
Charlene McC. Kirkland
Eldeana Knight
Willie Mae Knight
Barbara A. Kountz
Lelia Laird
John T. Lambert
Lavelle M. Langan
Edwin L. Langus
Clement A. Laurence
Gladys C. Lavender
Marion L. Leach
M. Earl Lee
M. Kaye Legge
Ann L. Lewis
Billy R. Lewis
David Lindsey
Joel N. Lipscomb, Jr.
Shirlee A. Lloyd
Margaret L. Logan
Thelma M. Lowry
Patricia A. Ludlow
Mary K. Marshall
Linda A. Mayson
Betsy L. McAdams
Cecilia H. McAleer
Raymond H. McAllister
Ralston G. McBeath
Vivian O. McCary
Angela McCaskey
Susie B. McClain
Betty G. McConnell
W. Donald McCrory
E. Cary McDonnell
Patrick A. McGowan
Judy M. McInnis
Mervin McKinnis
Patricia E. McMahon
Jane N. McMillin
G. Angus McRae
Dessie B. Mellgren
Gertrude H. Middleton
Norma K. Mikkelsen
Elaine H. Miller
Georgia M. Minor
Annie L. Mitchell
Sharon C. Mitchell
Bobbie G. Moore
M. Louise Morgan
Carol C. Mosser
Janice P. Mulherin
Miriam M. Murray
Jon O. Naef
Hollie S. Newton
Kenneth G. Norton
Bobby D. Nowell
Helen V. Oberkirch
Joan H. Odom
Amelia A. Oliver
Roy Osborne
Margret P. Oswell
Carolyn M. Owen
Fannie L. Packard
Maria Z. Parker
Earline Parson
John G. Partridge
Deborah J. Patterson
Margaret Y. Peacock
James R. Pendleton
James J. Peterson, Jr.
J. Wyatt Pettiss
Ora L. Pettway
Lucille Phillips
Wynona S. Phillips

Carolyn E. Pollard
Pearl E. Porter
Virginia B. Potter
Julia D. Powers
Edna E. Purvis
Emily P. Quarles
Georgia L. Raby
Carolee Rain
Johnny Rainer
Mary W. Rainer
Saundra A. Ramm
Andrea J. Redmond
Paul P. Redmond, Jr.
Dorothy W. Reed
Gordon E. Robbins
Isabell G. Roberts
Sara E. Robinson
A. Lawson Rogers
Joan H. Rogers
Marie Rosen
Jean M. Rumpanos
Betty W. Rush
Elmer F. Sanders
Aleen O. Schley
Sarah A. Schmaeling
M. Carolyn Sciple
Gertrude L. Sclater
Mary M. Self
Shannon V. Shelton

Elsie E. Shouldis
R. Stephen Sibley
Margaret E. Simmons
David M. Simms
Henry W. Sims
Dorothy C. Sirmon
Beverly M. Smith
Edward C. Smith
F. Nicholas Smith, III
Henry A. Smith
E. Faye Squires
Una M. Stallworth
P. Lyn Stanard
John W. Stephenson
Joy A. Stevens
Kathryn P. Stevens
Frances Stewart
Judy A. Stricklin
Ann R. Stuardi
Marion P. Sullivan
Marjorie N. Sutherland
Louis B. Swingle
Alice P. Tapia
Joseph Taylor
Anna M. Teal
Charles S. Terrell
Gertrude D. Thompson
Nan A. Thompson
Artelia Tiggs

Elaine Tillman
John W. Todd
Margaret T. Toomey
Thomas J. Torbert
Mary Townsend
Bobby L. Trawick
Cornelia A. Turner
J. Tyler Turner, Jr.
Annie B. Walker
E. Sharon Wall
Frances Wallace
Emily D. Walters
Julia B. Watson
Lillian Webster
C. Richard Weinacker
Claire W. West
James West
Margaret P. White
Charles H. Willcox
Barbara A. Williams
John W. Williams
Donald H. Winn
Mary J. Wittmann
Joyce G. Wold
Virginia L. Woodard
Freda E. Wright
T. Potter Yeend, Jr.
Twynette Young

BUILDING PERSONNEL

Frank J. Terrell
Building Manager

Dan W. Parks
Asst. Building Manager

Mary C. Mills
Secretary

K. L. Lloyd
Superintendent

Bertha R. Alexander
Amy V. Bernhardt
Durward J. Bernhardt
Mary B. Blocker
Joanna Blunt
Ed Boykin
Lucy I. Boykin
Ruby L. Brye
Augustine Byrd
Wallace M. Cain
Rosie L. Chany
Bobbie J. Chapman
Gladys Crawford
Agnes Dinkins
Joseph Dougherty
Lela English

Patricia A. Fell
Maggie C. Fields
Virginia F. Fleming
Louise M. Gough
James E. Harris
John E. Harris
Daisy G. Hunt
Tom Jones
Odell Knight
Herman B. Lowery
C. C. Matheny
Agnes McMillan
Luberta Mickles
Emma Minor
Clarissa D. Mitchell
Lillie P. Mooney

Norman Odom
Rosetta L. Ray
Mary A. Ridings
Paul E. Ross
James Sheffield
R. Tony Skelton
Marjorie Stisher
J. F. Sutter
Bertha Taylor
Ike B. Taylor
Ethel B. Tucker
Marvin V. Turner
V. V. Varner
Wilber Williams